# CHINESE CALLIGRAPHY

## Contributing Authors

Shizuka Shirakawa
*Professor Emeritus, Ritsumeikan University*

Kenjirō Yoneda
*Professor, Bukkyō University*

Ken'ichi Nakagawa
*Curator, Osaka Municipal Museum of Fine Art*

Kenshō Hirano
*Professor, Ōtani University*

Kunihiko Sugimura
*Associate Professor, Kyoto University of Education*

Yutaka Adachi
*Lecturer, Japan Women's University*

Masaaki Chikusa
*Professor, Kyoto University*

Masakazu Fukumoto
*Professor, Tezukayamagakuin University*

Arihito Fujiwara
*Lecturer, Kyoto City University of the Arts*

Shōichi Nishibayashi
*Professor, Atomigakuen Women's University*

A HISTORY OF THE ART OF CHINA

# Chinese Calligraphy

*General Editor*

Yūjirō Nakata, Professor Emeritus
Kyoto City University of Arts

*translated and adapted by*
Jeffrey Hunter

WEATHERHILL/TANKOSHA
*New York, Tokyo, Kyoto*

*Chinese Calligraphy* is one volume in a series of six under the series title *A History of the Art of China*. Other titles are: *Chinese Ceramics, Chinese Buddhist Sculpture, Chinese Painting, Chinese Bronzes,* and *Chinese Decorative Arts.*

Originally published in Japanese by Tankosha, Kyoto, under the title *Chūgoku no bijutsu: shoseki* (The Arts of China: Calligraphy), 1982.

First English edition, 1983

Published jointly by John Weatherhill, Inc., of New York and Tokyo, with editorial offices at 7-6-13 Roppongi, Minato-ku, Tokyo 106; and Tankosha, Kyoto. Copyright © 1982, 1983, by Tankosha; all rights reserved. Printed in Japan.

LIBRARY OF CONGRESS CATALOGING IN PUBLICATION DATA: Chinese calligraphy/ (A history of the art of China/ Adapted from: Chūgoku no bijutsu./ 2. Shoseki./ Includes index./ 1. Calligraphy, Chinese./ I. Nakata, Yūjirō, 1905–/ II. Hunter, Jeffrey./ III. Chūgoku no bijutsu./ 2. Shoseki./ IV. Series./ ND1457.C5454    1983    745.6'19951/ 83-3490/ ISBN 0-8348-1526-5

# Contents

Introduction     9
*by* Yūjirō Nakata

Color Plates     19

Historical Survey     101

   The Origin of Chinese Characters     103
     *by* Shizuka Shirakawa

   Wooden Tablets and Silk Writings     107
     *by* Kenjirō Yoneda

   Qin Stone Inscriptions and Han Steles     111
     *by* Yūjirō Nakata

   The Masterpieces of Wang Xizhi and Wang Xianzhi     116
     *by* Yūjirō Nakata

   Stone Inscriptions of the Six Dynasties     119
     *by* Ken'ichi Nakagawa

   Buddhist Manuscripts     123
     *by* Kenshō Hirano

   The Sui, Tang, and Five Dynasties     127
     *by* Kunihiko Sugimura

   The Northern and Southern Song Dynasties     132
     *by* Yutaka Adachi

Chan Calligraphy of the Song and Yuan Dynasties          137
    *by* Masaaki Chikusa

Zhao Mengfu and His Followers          141
    *by* Masakazu Fukumoto

The Ming Literati          146
    *by* Arihito Fujiwara

Copybook and Stele Studies of the Qing Dynasty          150
    *by* Shōichi Nishibayashi

Commentaries on the Plates          159

Chronology of Calligraphers and Their Works          213

Index          231

# CHINESE CALLIGRAPHY

# Introduction

## The Origin and Evolution of Chinese Characters

Calligraphy is one of the most beautiful of all the arts that have been cultivated in the East. It originated in China and spread from there to all countries that use Chinese characters. Of these, Japan has been perhaps the major recipient of Chinese influence. It is difficult to say in a word just what forms the basis for the beauty of the calligraphy of the East, but the greatest factor in producing this beauty is no doubt the construction of the Chinese characters themselves.

Chinese characters began as primitive pictographs, diagrams depicting things. From these pictographs of natural objects—the sun, moon and constellations; mountains, rivers and vegetation; all sorts of birds and beasts, as well as the human body and man's dwellings and utensils—another kind of character developed: the ideograph. The early pictographs were concrete signs, while these ideographs were symbolic, showing relative position, number, or expressing other relations. The combination of the concrete and the symbolic is the base from which all other varieties of characters developed.

By combining two characters a new character with its own semantic value could be produced. One of these new types of character was a juxtaposition of two semantic units to produce a third whose meaning was a synthesis of the first two. Another type was a combination of a semantic unit with a phonetic unit, taking its meaning from the first and its sound from the second. In addition to these simple combinations, new adaptations of characters produced by the extension of meanings and pronunciations of other characters developed. All Chinese characters have been produced following these six principles: pictorial representation (pictographs), diagrammatic representation (ideographs), semantic combination, phonetic combination, borrowing, and extension. These six types of characters are known as the *liu shu* in Chinese.

Every character includes three elements: form, sound, and meaning.

Whatever type of character it is, it will possess all three. But perhaps the most arresting of these three elements is the form—the remarkable graphic-design quality of the Chinese character. The fact that Chinese characters not only developed from but retained through time their pictorial or diagrammatic forms indicates just how central the element of visual form is in the Chinese character. Various forms of written characters were bound to develop as writing implements and techniques developed throughout the long history of writing's evolution. Each era produced its own particular variations in form, and as these forms became established and were employed in writing, various *styles* of these forms were to develop. The appearance of these styles marked the first emergence of calligraphy as an art, the art of writing beautifully.

The tools and techniques of writing are also very important in Chinese calligraphy. Chinese characters are written in a particular kind of ink, known as *mo* in Chinese. It is said that in ancient times charred lacquer was used for writing, and cinnabar has been used in some cases, but ink was also employed from the earliest times and has always been the main writing substance. The character for ink (墨) provides some hints about the origins of this material. The upper component of the character 黑 means black. It is a diagram of a chimney (田) written over the sign for fire (火 or ⺣). This forms the character for soot, which was collected from the mouth of a chimney under which a fire had burned, indicating that soot was one of the ingredients for making ink from a very early period. The lower component of the character for ink means earth (土), the other raw material mixed with soot to produce ink. Though there is a theory that a mineral substance was also used in ink, the main ingredient was soot. The fact that in later times all ink was indeed made from soot offers indirect support for this conclusion.

In China black has traditionally been regarded as the color of the heavens, the night skies without the sun's illumination. Black corresponds to *yin* in the *yin-yang* dichotomy of traditional Chinese cosmology. Without shape, color or scent, black ink is the embodiment of Lao Tzu's "negative form," for it gives form to the "original mystery," and combining with color and shape, can produce many subtle effects. The attraction of ink as a medium of artistic expression for the Chinese and Japanese is partly due to this quality it possesses.

If writing in ink is one of the basic features of Chinese calligraphy, another, of course, is the writing brush. The use of the brush resulted in new writing techniques and opened up many aesthetic possibilities, playing a major part in the development of the calligraphic art. The invention of paper and its production in certain standard sizes also contributed to calligraphy's evolution, as did the inkstone, which began as a simple stone or ceramic slab and gradually developed into a special, high-quality stone selected to bring out the beauty of the ink. Thus, the tools of writing and their techniques of use are also defining features of Chinese calligraphy as an art.

## The Origin and Development of Calligraphy

Chinese calligraphy has a three-thousand-year history. This long, uninterrupted tradition during which great works of calligraphy have been created, appraised, and passed down through the ages has produced an artistic genre that is remarkable for its continuity. The number of works that have been preserved until today in the Orient is incalculable. Though we cannot hope to investigate all of them, we can divide this great body of work into certain historical categories and artistic lineages.

First, ancient calligraphy can be divided into the bone and shell inscriptions of the Shang dynasty (1523?–1122? B.C.), the cast metal writing of the Zhou dynasty (1122?–256 B.C.), the stone inscriptions of the Qin (221–206 B.C.), and the tablets or steles of the Han dynasty (206 B.C.–220 A.D.), all writings that existed before the invention of paper and were inscribed or cast in hard materials. Next come the stone inscriptions of the Six Dynasties period (222–589), in the main from the northern states, and the Tang dynasty (918–c. 907) steles. These, too, are inscriptions rather than ink writings. A Chinese proverb has it that "paper endures but five hundred years, and silk some eight hundred." Except for rare exceptions, nothing older has survived in either of these forms. Thus, one feature of the history of calligraphy is that the writings of ancient times are known to us only through stone and metal inscriptions. There is a classic beauty to these inscriptions in which a chisel takes the place of a brush, sometimes referred to as "the beauty of the steel brush." In contrast to this tradition of inscriptions are the writings with ink and brush on paper and silk. Zhang Zhi is said to have produced the first calligraphy recognized as a work of art. He lived at the end of the Han dynasty and was the first professional calligrapher, said to excel in the *cao* (literally, "grass"), or cursive, script. It was also in this period that the five-syllable *shi* form of poetry was created and individual poets can first be identified. Of course poetry had existed previously, but it was from the end of the Han through the Wei (220–64) that poetry and its composition came to be considered a literary art. The same can be said for calligraphy.

Soon after that, in the Eastern Jin (317–420), the two Wangs—Wang Xizhi and Wang Xianzhi—together created the first golden age of Chinese calligraphy. At this point the three new forms of *kai* (block), *xing* (semi-cursive) and *cao* (cursive) script emerged, and calligraphic works—mainly letters—were produced which were to become the models for later calligraphers. After this, from the Six Dynasties to the Tang, the works of the two Wangs would become more and more revered. From the middle of the Tang dynasty, a new current in calligraphy in opposition to the orthodoxy of the Wangs arose, and the literati of the Northern Song (960–1126) preferred the writing of poetry in large characters on horizontal scrolls to the traditional epistles of the Wangs. Theirs was a tendency toward large-scale, innovative works of calligraphy vibrant with emotion.

In the following Yuan dynasty (c. 1280–1386), China was ruled by the Mongols, and conservative tendencies were once again ascendant in the arts. This return to tradition was interrupted in the second half of the Ming dynasty (1368–c. 1664), when calligraphy moved again in a new direction. In the Qing dynasty (c. 1664–1912), the Manchus had usurped political power in China. Reflecting the temper of this period when the leaders of society were scholar-officials, the first half of the dynasty was dominated by the copybook school, which honored the ancient classics as preserved in that medium. In the second half of the period, the stele school gained many enthusiasts, spurred by the increase in studies of the ancient inscriptions and steles.

Chinese calligraphy of the Qing can thus be roughly divided into the copybook school and the stele school. Works of the stele tradition are mainly in the *zhuan* (seal script), *li* (scribe script), or the block style which had developed as a variation of the scribe script. The characters are inscribed in rock, and are remarkable by virtue of their ability to communicate the very spirit of the writer to later generations. Though they have been repaired and restored due to wear and chipping, they remain the means through which the living words of the past are communicated in their original form. However, to increase the availability of these inscriptions, ink rubbings were frequently made and circulated in the form of albums. It was in this form that the inscriptions were most influential in the development of calligraphy. Further, because most inscriptions were of a public nature, formal styles of characters were the rule. On the other hand, the copybooks' province is mainly examples of semi-cursive and cursive script, and since they are based on ink-written originals, they might be considered more valuable than inscriptions. But these originals, written as they were on silk and paper, were difficult to preserve for long and in most cases met destruction rather quickly. As a result, copies of these originals had to be made, and wooden blocks made from these were used in printing the copybooks. More than half of the two Wangs' works are to be found in the form of these copied and printed bound collections, or albums. Passing through the processes of tracing, carving into wooden blocks, and rubbings, the amount of human contrivance gradually increased, as did the risk of destroying the beauty and integrity of the originals. And, in the course of these processes, forgeries were likely to creep in. In fact, one of the difficulties with the copybook versions of the calligraphy of the two Wangs produced during the Ming and Qing dynasties is that many works of doubtful authenticity appear in them. As a result, one must always be on guard for false attributions.

From the second half of the Qing dynasty, most energies were devoted to the study of stele inscriptions. With the rise of the new study of metal and stone inscriptions, the copybooks were put aside as less reliable. In recent years, however, with the discovery and introduction of many new samples of calligraphy, a succession of ink writings from ancient times have also come to light, and these, together with other new evidence, continue to be introduced—making it unlikely that researchers will cling exclusively either to steles or copybooks in future studies.

## Influences on Japan

The relationship between China and Japan with regard to calligraphy must be considered. Japanese calligraphy developed from ancient times under continental influence. In general terms, it was the calligraphy of Paechke that influenced Japan in the Yamato period (300–710). The calligraphy of the Sui dynasty (c. 581–618) was influential in the Asuka period (552–645), Jin and Tang calligraphy in the Nara period (645–794), Tang calligraphy in the first half of the Heian period (794–898), Song calligraphy in the first half of the Kamakura period (1185–1249), Yuan calligraphy in the second half of the same period (1249–1382) and the Northern and Southern Courts (1336–92), and Ming calligraphy in the Muromachi period (1392–1568). "Chinese style" or *karayō* calligraphy was popular during the Edo period (1600–1868), and this category was further subdivided into Jin and Tang calligraphy, and Ming and Qing calligraphy. With the arrival of Yang Shoujing in the Meiji period (1868–1912), there was an interest in the northern stele school of calligraphy. A great number of works have been brought to Japan from the Nara period to the present, representing each period of Chinese calligraphy and including not a few masterpieces. For the most part, the kind of works that were brought to Japan in ancient times have long since ceased to exist in China, making a consideration of Chinese calligraphy incomplete without a study of works brought to Japan.

First we must look at the type of works that were transported to Japan. We might categorize them as follows. In the Nara period, we have the copybook editions of Wang Xizhi's works. A considerable number of Wang Xizhi's originals and collections of rubbings are recorded in the *Tōdai-ji Kembutsu Chō,* the catalogue compiled when Emperor Shōmu's belongings were entrusted to the Tōdai-ji. Rubbings taken directly from the works of Wang Xizhi (pls. 16, 17) were also transmitted to Japan. Of all copies of his work extant, these are perhaps the best. Unrivaled even by Chinese copies, they are indeed rare masterpieces. In the Asuka and Nara periods, Sui-dynasty sutras were brought over. A superb example dated 610 is located in the Seigo-zō. From the first half of the Heian period we have many pieces brought back by the Japanese monks Saichō and Kūkai on their visits to Tang China. In Kūkai's catalogue we find Wang Xizhi works from the Jin period, as well as autograph works by Ouyang Xun and Li Yong of the Tang listed. These have not been preserved, but we do know that original masterpieces of the Tang dynasty existed in considerable numbers. From Saichō's catalogues we can see that he, too, brought back many articles from China. In addition, related works, Tang copies, and numerous albums provide us direct contact with the calligraphy of Tang China even today.

Tang copies of sutras and Chinese classics were transmitted to Japan from the Nara period to the early Heian period. These were called in Japan *Tōshō hon,* or Tang writings. The *Commentary and Notes on the Spring and Autumn Annals (Chunqiu Jing Chuan Jijie,* pl. 40), the *Biography of Yang Xiong, Han Annals (Han Shu Yang Xiong Chuan,* pl. 42), and other works command our attention for the skill of their small block script. It is very fortunate that we are able to view these original ink-written works of the Tang Chinese, renowned as they were for their block style. Many of these works have already disappeared from China, and these very rare texts and documents are precious not only as calligraphy, but for scholarly purposes.

The founder of the Tōfuku-ji, Shōichi, brought many books of Song-dynasty rubbings with him from China. Works by Su Shi and Gaozong of the Song, Fan Chengda's "Memorial Poem for Chan Master Fo Zhao" (*Zeng Fo Zhao Chanshi Shibei,* pl. 59), and many others still exist. The original memorial steles of Fan Chengda's poetry, like other such Song works, of course no longer exist in China, but these rubbings show that they deserve our admiration as the best of this genre, with their bold and exciting beauty.

Many printed works of the Song dynasty were also brought to Japan. A considerable number of these are to be found in the Ashikaga College or the Kanazawa Library, and a few belong to the Tōfuku-ji. All of these are very rare pieces, even in China. Another rarely seen item is the Northern Song printing of the *Commentary on the Historical Records (Shiji Jijie)* in the former Konan Naitō collection. These Song printings were influenced by the block style of the Tang, and must not be overlooked as calligraphy.

Next, in considering ancient copybooks and albums, the autograph copy of Zhiyong's "Thousand-Character Essay in Block and Cursive Scripts" (*Zhen Cao Qian Zi Wen*, pl. 31) is clearly related to the "Thousand-Character Cursive Essay" that has been preserved in the Shōsō-in, attributed to Wang Xizhi. This, too, is unknown in China except in the form of a Song ink rubbing. The "*Classic of Filial Piety* in Cursive Characters" (*Caoshu Xiaojing*) by He Zhizhang (pl. 44), now in the ownership of the Japanese imperial family, is a rare find that has arrived in Japan only recently. As for the Jin-dynasty copybooks, an album of the work of Wang Xizhi was once in Japan, but is now lost. A Wang Xianzhi epistle, the "Di Huang Tang Epistle" (pl. 20), is still in Japan, but the Song-dynasty "*Cold Meal in Huangzhou* Poem Scroll" (*Huangzhou Hanshi Shijuan*, pl. 49) by Su Shi has been returned to Taipei. Su Shi's "*Hermit Li Taibo* Poem Scroll" (*Li Taibo Shijuan*, pl. 50) is also in Japan. Signature works of Cai Xiang (pl. 48), Huang Tingjian (pls. 51, 52), and the three famous works of Mi Fu— "Three Semi-cursive Albums" (*Xingshu San Tie*), "Four Cursive Albums" (*Caosi Shu Tie*, pl. 55), and "Gangxian Poem Scroll" (*Gangxian Shiji* pl. 54) all exist in Japan. We are presently unsure where other works by Mi Fu are being stored in Japan, but they are recorded as being there. Southern Song works such as Gaozong's "*Preface to the Collected Writings of Huizong*" (*Huizong Wenji Xu*, pl. 57), Wu Shou's calligraphy, Zhu Xi's "Cursive Draft of Collected Notes on the *Analects*" (*Caoshu Lunyu Jizhu Gao*, pl. 60), and a Buddhist scripture copy by Zhang Jizhi (*Jingong Banruoboluomi Jing*, pl. 61) are represented in Japan.

Yuan works in Japan include Zhao Mengfu's "Three Gates Record" (*San Men Ji*), "Thirteen Postscripts to the Orchid Pavilion" (*Lan Ting Shisan Ba*), "Biography of Han Ji'an" (*Han Ji'an Zhuan*, pl. 68), an epistle (pl. 67), and an epitaph. We also have works of Kangli Kuikui and Yang Wei (pls. 70, 71). Both of these men excelled in cursive script, and their works hold a unique place in Yuan-dynasty calligraphy. The copybooks of the Ming and Qing dynasties are to be found in considerable numbers in both public and private collections and are too numerous for individual mention. Some works were brought to Japan during the Edo period, and many works of painting and literature entered Japan from the early part of this century to the present. Most of these still exist as collectors' items.

Copybooks and albums of stele impressions stand in contrast to original calligraphy manuscripts. These bound albums, printed for distribution, exist in single volumes of one quire and collections composed of several. The practice of collecting and printing these works probably originated in the Tang or the following Five Dynasties period (907–60), but the earliest extant work known as a copybook, the "Chunhua Pavilion Copybook" (*Chunhua Ge Tie*), was printed in 992. These copybooks gained popularity from the Song dynasty on, and many were printed in the Ming and Qing dynasties. Collections of stele rubbings were first brought to Japan in the Kamakura period, when the founder of the Sennyū-ji, Shunjō, brought back the "Copybooks and Calligraphy Albums of Monument Inscriptions in Seventy-four Volumes" (*Hōjō Goshodōjō-tō Hibun Shichijū-yon Kan*). The copybook referred to in this entry was probably the "Chunhua Pavilion Copybook" or some related work. "Calligraphy albums" (*Goshodōjō*) refers to other collections. A great many copybooks and stele rubbings arrived in Japan after 1400, but at this early period these were very rare works.

Finally, in the second half of the nineteenth and early twentieth centuries, the appreciation of these materials advanced, and high-quality rubbings known as Tang and Song impressions arrived in Japan. The works now extant in Japan are almost all from this period, and in the hands of collectors. A number of great works were brought to Japan at this time, including Wang Xizhi's "Orchid Pavilion Preface" (*Lan Ting Xu*) and "Shiqi Album"(*Shiqi Tie*: the Ueno text, the Mitsui text, and the Seventeen-Missing-Lines text), as well as the *"Preface to the Great Tang Buddhist Canon"* (*Da Tang Sancang Shengjiao Xu*), and many others. The four renowned works, known as the "four jewels of Lin Chuan" and treasured by the Song collector Li Zhonghuan—Ding Daohu's work, the "Qifa Temple Stele" (*Qifa Si Bei,* pl. 32), Yu Shinan's "Tomb Tablet of Confucius" (*Kongzi Miaotang Bei*), Chu Suiliang's "Dharma Master Meng's Stele" (*Meng Fashi Bei*)*,* and Wei Xiwu's "Shancai Temple Stele" (*Shancai Si Bei*)—are all known as unparalleled rubbings. The present location of all of these except the "Qifa Temple Stele" is unknown. The well-known Song rubbing of the "Huadu Temple Pagoda Inscription" (*Huadu Si Ta Ming*) by Ouyang Xun was also once in Japan, but is presently lost. The Weng Fanggang text (pl. 37), which was the companion piece to this work, is now in the possession of Ōtani University. The "Chan Master Xin Xing Stele" (*Xin Xing Chanshi Bei*) of Xue Ji, once a precious treasure of He Shaoji of the Qing, is also a unique work which was a part of the Ōtani collection and is now also at Ōtani University. In addition to these, the Changtan text, one of the three Song impressions of the Han stele "Tomb Tablet of the Western Peaks of Mt. Hua" (*Siyue Huashan Miao Bei*),is in the Museum of Calligraphy in Tokyo, together with a considerable number of other Song impressions of stele inscriptions.

The works of monks of the Song and Yuan dynasties, almost nonexistent in China today, were also transmitted to Japan. With the rise of the Rinzai sect from the latter Kamakura through the Northern and Southern Courts period, many Japanese Zen monks traveled to China during the Song and the following Yuan dynasty to meet and study under the high-ranking Chan (Japanese, Zen) monks of China. Upon their return to Japan, they brought with them the writings of these monks in considerable quantities. These writings included "diplomas" testifying to the spiritual achievements of their possessors, documents granting new religious names, sermons, and letters. These were regarded as documents to be preserved for eternity and were carefully installed in the temple storehouses of Japan. With the rise of the tea ceremony in the Muromachi period, these writings of distinguished monks were made into scrolls and hung in the tearooms. The appreciation of these works was regarded as a means to cultivate the ways of both tea and Zen. This custom has continued up to today, and writings of Chan monks of the Song and Yuan dynasties are still very numerous in Japan. Although of course calligraphic works were appreciated in China, there was no custom of treating the works of high-ranking Chan monks as a special category. Again, the calligraphy of the Chan monks, written with a mind free from attachments and often with religious intent, fell outside the bounds of established aesthetic standards and was not to be viewed from that perspective. Thus, in China, this kind of calligraphy attracted little attention, and very few examples of it were preserved. It is very rare luck that so many of these works, shunned within the traditions of Chinese calligraphy, should have been transmitted to Japan. The calligraphy of these monks occupies its own special realm, showing a high spiritual quality that resists conventional aesthetic judgements. The uniqueness of these works in the context of orthodox Chinese calligraphy cannot be overlooked.

Ink autographs of the highest-ranking monk of the Yangqi sect of the Linji Chan school, Yuanwu Kekin, his disciple, Dahui Zongguo, Ying'an Tanhua, the disciple of Huqiu Shaolong, and his disciple Mi'an Xianjie were all brought to Japan. It is indeed unfortunate that such works were not preserved in China itself. The lineage of Mi'an Xianjie later subdivided into three branches, the Songyuan-Chongyue, the Paan-Zuxian, and the Caoyuan-Daosheng branches. From these three branches, many illustrious monks came forth, among them Wuming Huixing, Lanxi Daolong, Xutang Zhiyu, Wuzhun Shifan, Wuxue Zuyuan, Wu'an Puning and Chijue Daochong. The ink autographs of these monks exist in considerable numbers in Japan. In general, the calligraphy of the Song monks has an elegant simplicity that ably communicates the Chan spirit.

As we enter the next period, the Yuan, times change, and with the new popularity of Zhao Mengfu, Chan calligraphy in the Zhao style also appeared. In contrast to the elegant but sometimes rustic simplicity of the Song, works by monks that commanded admiration on their calligraphic merits alone appeared. Monks such as Chushi Fengqi, Yuehjiang Zhengyin, Gulin Qingmao, and Liaoan Qingyu were the authors of such works. They are in fact mentioned in Tao Zongyi's *Outline of the History of Calligraphy (Shushi Huiyao)*, a work of the late Yuan and early Ming dynasties, as "skilled in semicursive and cursive script, with fine reputations as calligraphers." This indicates that high-ranking monks who had made a name for themselves as calligraphers were to be found by the yuan. At this point, also, lower-ranking monks of the three sects and Chan monks in general were becoming proficient calligraphers. Zhongfeng Mingben, who associated with Zhao Mengfu, wrote a unique script called "bamboo-leaf script" which resembled a seal script. Still, the calligraphy of Chan monks in both Yuan and Song dynasties was naturally different from the calligraphy of the scholars and literati of the world. Though of course different people showed varying degrees of expertise, in general this calligraphy exhibits a lofty, spiritual quality. The fact that great numbers of these writings were preserved in Japan speaks for the zeal with which the Japanese guarded the lamp of the dharma and protected manuscripts and written documents.

A special category of works of calligraphy extant in Japan is the Dunhuang manuscripts. Dunhuang is located on the western border of China. At the turn of the century, expeditions led by Stein of England and Pelliot of France discovered an enormous number of artifacts, ranging from the Han dynasty, through the Wei, to the Tang and Song. At almost the same time, the Ōtani expedition from Japan unearthed a great quantity of materials from this region. These materials were introduced to the world in the collection, *Sei-iki Kōko Zufu* (Archeological Catalogue of Northwest China). Not a few ancient manuscripts from Dunhuang have been brought to Japan since that time, and a considerable number are kept in collections and public libraries in Japan. The most important of these artifacts are ancient sutra copies. A copy of the *Zhufo Yaoji Jing* (The Essentials of the Buddhas' Teachings) dated 296 was among the finds of the Ōtani expedition. This was famous as the oldest sutra copy to be found, but its present location is unknown. In addition several copies that, though undated, are recognized as being from the Western Jin have also been found. These are extremely valuable in research on calligraphy simply because they are ink-written originals. In spite of the real scarcity of artifacts from this period, most of those we do have are useful in the study of calligraphy. The majority of the sutra copies from the northern and southern dynasties are dated, and though southern copies are relatively few, those we do have are graceful and beautiful, making both categories of works precious materials in the study of calligraphy. Many of the Sui sutras are also dated, and works of outstanding calligraphic technique have come down to us far surpassing the stone inscriptions in beauty. In addition to sutra copies, the original ink works such as the *"Writings of Li Bo"* (*Li Bo Wenshu*, pl. 14) and related letters that are supposed to be from the early Eastern Jin, which would correspond to the youth of Wang Xizhi, are especially valuable materials. Of the manuscripts unearthed at Dunhuang, most are sutra copies, and a portion of these are presently located in Japan in the collection of the Museum of Calligraphy, the Ōtani University Library, the Ryūkoku University Library, the Moriya Collection of the Kyoto National Museum, and the Mitsui family's collection. These Dunhuang manuscripts are a special category of calligraphic materials that have reached Japan. As ink originals they are rare finds, and because they are also valuable as calligraphy, they are very precious.

COLOR PLATES

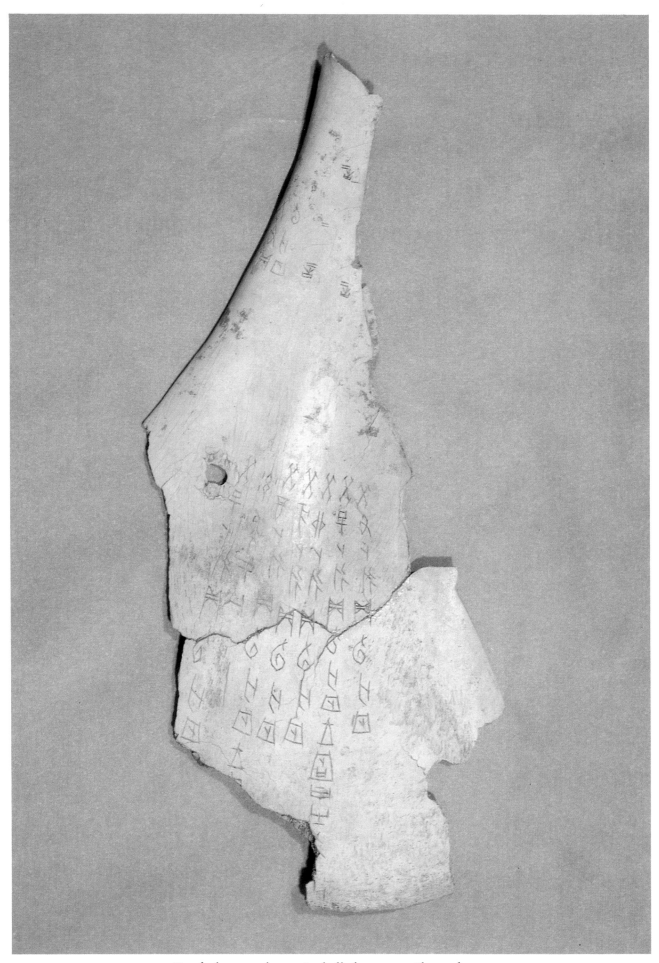

1. Oracle-bone and tortoiseshell characters. Shang dynasty.
Tokyo University Research Center for the Humanities.

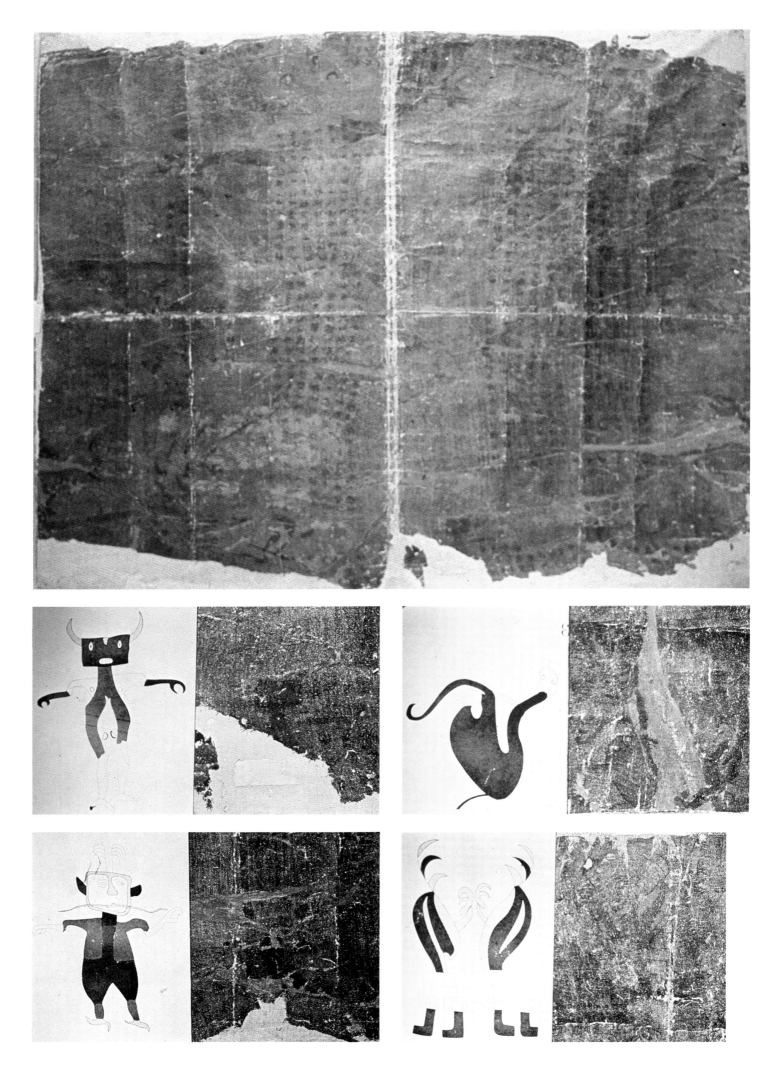

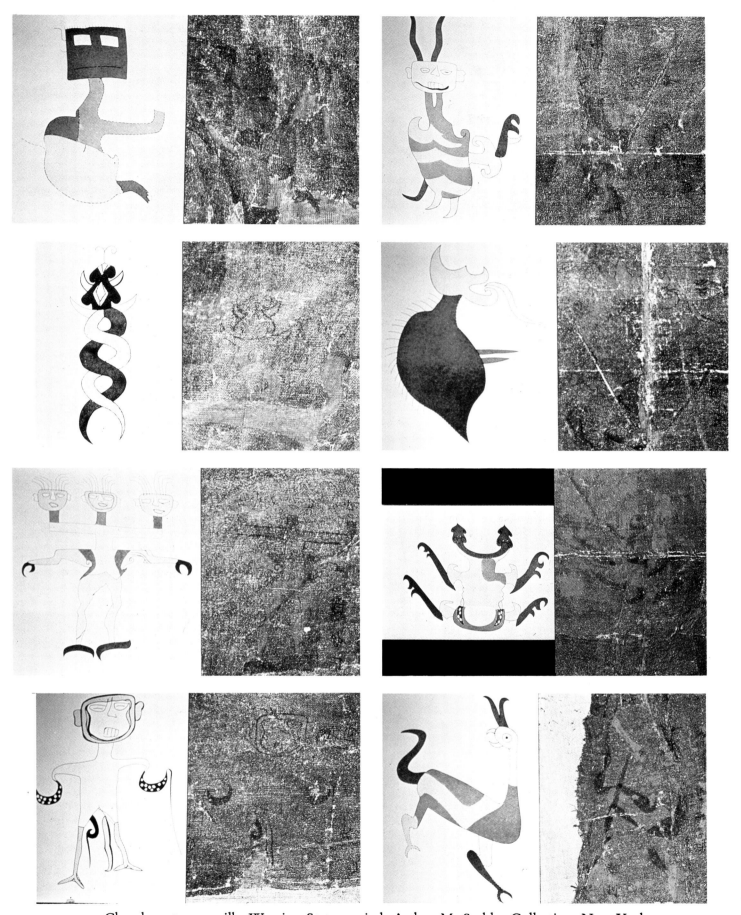

2. Chu characters on silk. Warring States period. Arthur M. Sackler Collection, New York.

3. (*above left*) "Gou Jian, Prince of Yue's sword inscription." Spring and Autumn Annals period. Ink rubbing.

4. (*above right*) Ink rubbing of large bronze tripod. Warring States Period.

5. Large bronze tripod. Warring States period.

6. *Laozi*. Han dynasty. Ink on silk.

7. Ink rubbing of Langye Terrace inscription. Qin dynasty. Museum of Calligraphy, Tokyo.

8. Wooden tablets unearthed at Juyan. Han dynasty. Gansu Provincial Museum.

9. "*Liqi* Stele at Confucius' tomb." Han dynasty. Ink Rubbing. Tokyo National Museum.

10. "Cao Quan Stele." Han dynasty. Ink rubbing. Mitsui Bunko, Tokyo.

11. "Zhang Qian Stele." Han dynasty. Ink rubbing. Mitsui Bunko, Tokyo.

12. "Divine Omen Stele." Three Kingdoms period,
Wu. Ink rubbing. Neiraku Art Museum, Nara.

13. Lu Ji: "Ping Fu Album." Western Jin dynasty.
Ink on paper. Beijing National Palace Museum.

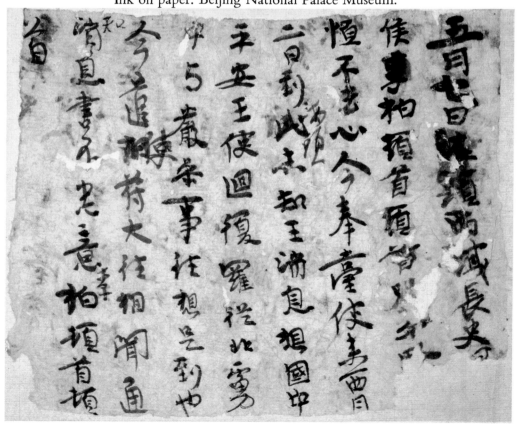

14. Li Bo: "Draft of a Letter." Eastern Jin dynasty.
Ink on paper. Ryūkoku University Library, Kyoto.

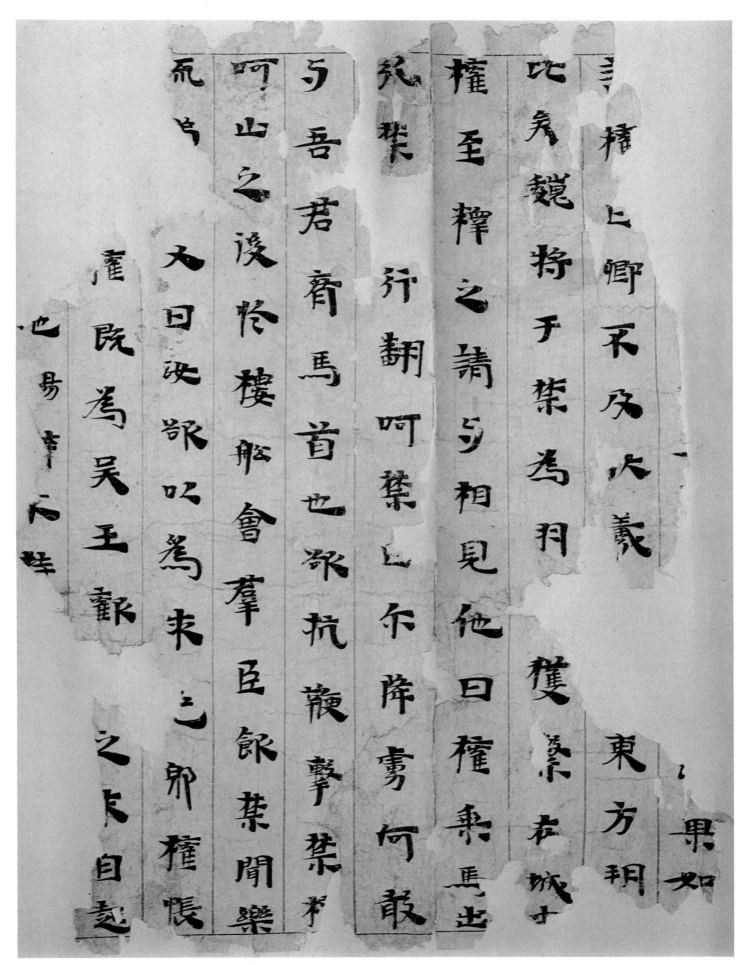

15. Anonymous: *Wu Annals,* from the *Annals of the Three Kingdoms,* fragment of the twelfth volume. Western Jin dynasty. Ink on paper. Museum of Calligraphy, Tokyo.

16. Wang Xizhi: "Sang Luan Album." Eastern Jin dynasty. Ink on paper. Collection of the Japanese Imperial Household, Tokyo.

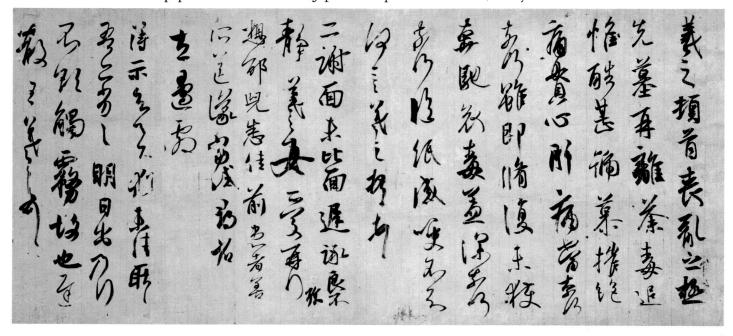

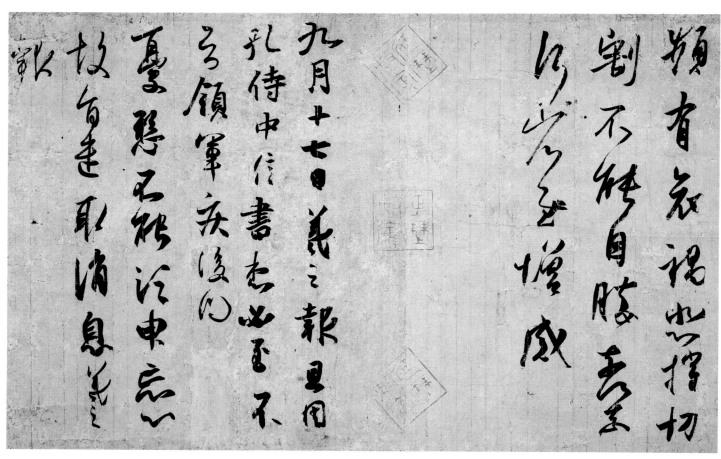

17. Wang Xizhi: "Kong Shizong Album." Eastern Jin dynasty. Ink on paper. Maeda Ikutokukai, Tokyo.

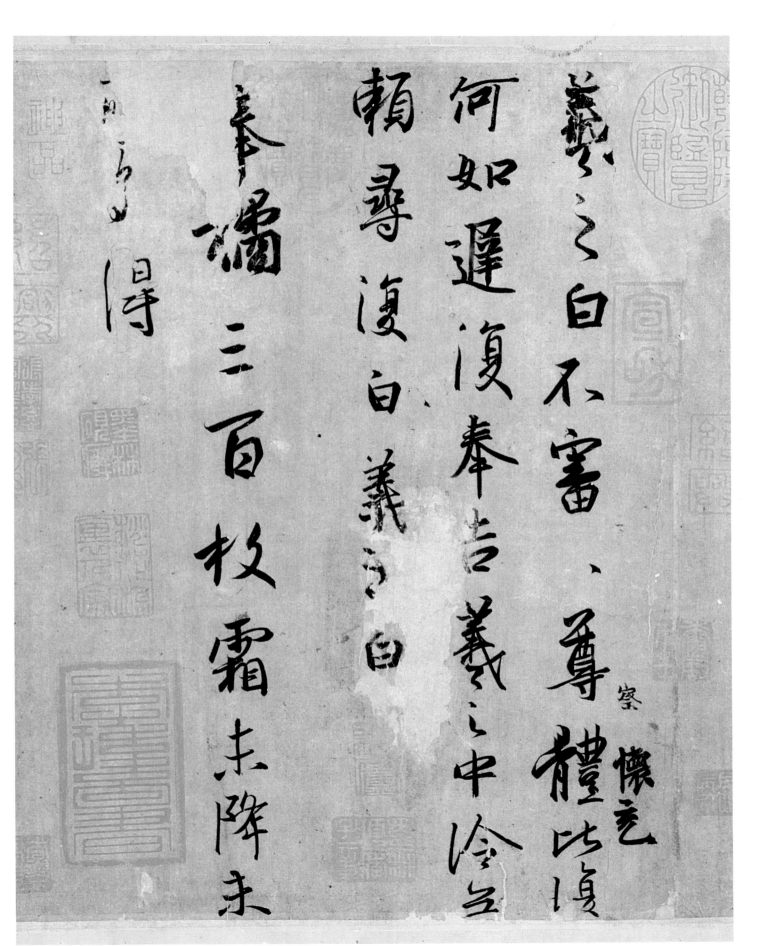

18. Wang Xizhi: "Feng Ju Album." Eastern Jin dynasty.
Ink on paper. Taipei National Palace Museum.

十七日羲之報近日不快不知
思不没好字不知弟書為達之
不知東粗足他達為逼足之惶
久羲之頓首

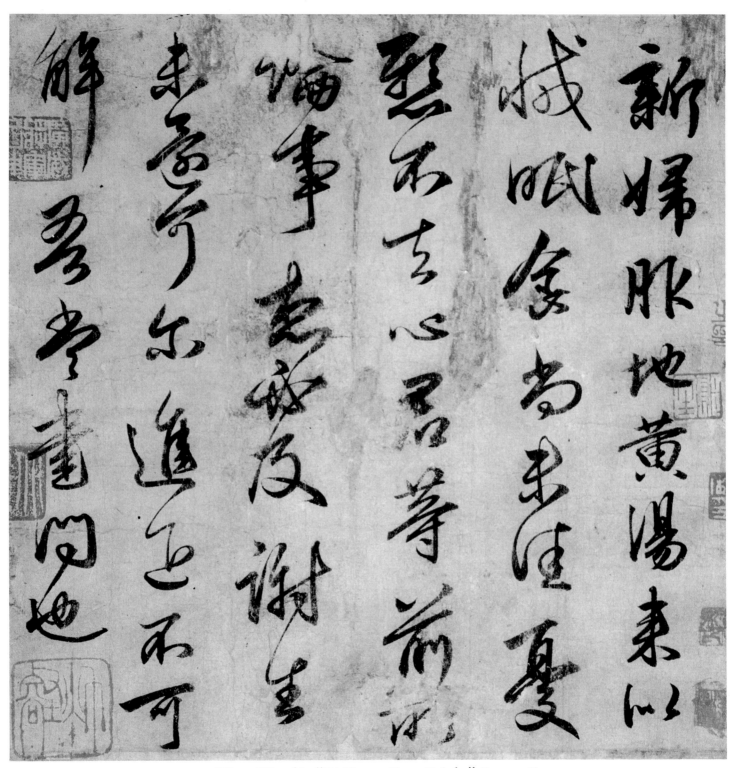

20. Wang Xianzhi: "Di Huang Tang Epistle." Eastern Jin dynasty. Ink on paper. Museum of Calligraphy, Tokyo.

◀ 19. Wang Xizhi: "Shiqi Album."
Eastern Jin dynasty. Ink rubbing.
Kyoto National Museum.

魏故驃騎將軍營州刺史高使君懿

俊輝銘

君諱貞字羽真勑

海媚人也其先蓋帝炎氏之苗裔昔

往黃君是為田叔于

爰述但入空知

21. Anonymous: "Memorial Stele for Gao Zhen." Northern
Wei dynasty. Ink rubbing. Mitsui Bunko, Tokyo.

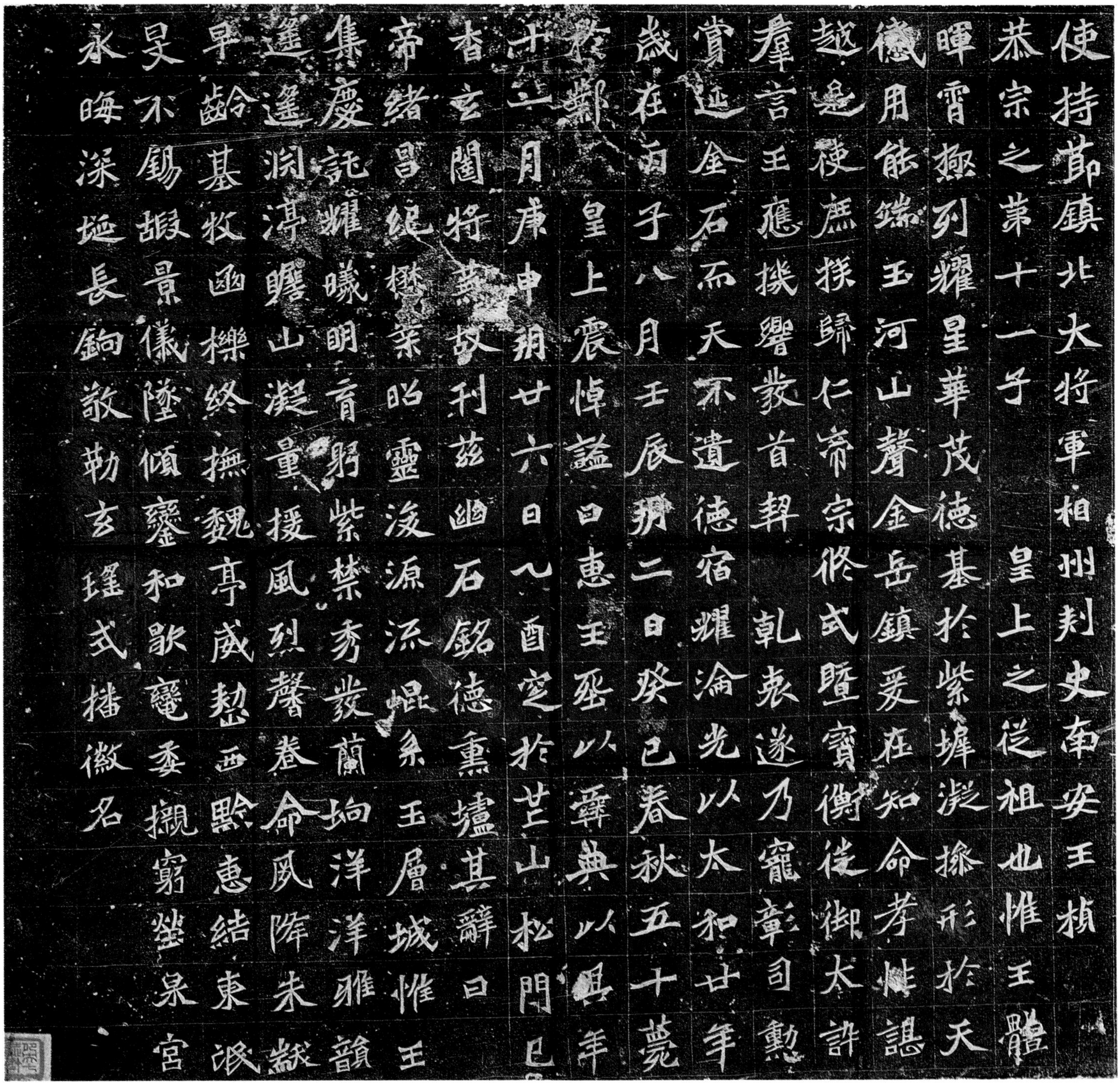

使持節鎮北大將軍相州刺史南安王楨
恭宗之第十一子皇上之從祖也惟王體
暉霄挻列耀星華茂德基於紫墀濬撫形於天
德用能庶端玉河山聲金岳鎮爰在知命孝惟
越是使庶揆歸仁帝宗佇式暨寶衡從御太許
羣言王應播響敷首軺乾袞遂以太和廿年
賞延金石而天不遺德宿耀渝光以竉章司勳
歲在甲子八月壬辰朔二日癸巳春秋五十薨
於鄴皇上震悼謚曰惠王巫以彝典以殂年
于十一月庚申朔廿六日乙酉窆於芒山松門巳
者玄闈將蓋故利茲幽浚石銘德熏玉層城惟王
帝緒昌紀耀業昭靈源流崐系德均洋洋雅韻
集慶潤詫耀瞻明音躬量援風烈聲蘩蘭均命凤陣未嶽
遙遙慶潤詫耀瞻明音躬量援風威勢西黔惠結朿退
早齡齒基牧函櫟終撫巍亭威勢西黔惠結朿退嶽
昊不錫胡景儀隆傾鑾和歌鑾委攬窮鑿泉宮
永晦深延長鉤敬勒玄瑾式播徽名

22. Anonymous: "Epitaph for Yuan Zhen." Northern Wei dynasty.
Ink rubbing. Osaka Municipal Museum of Fine Art.

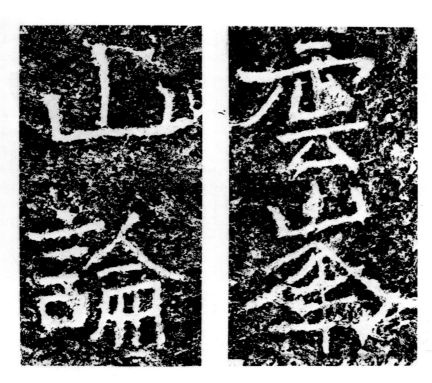

24. Zheng Daozhao: "Confucian Didactic Verses at Yunfengshan."
Northern Wei dynasty. Ink rubbing. Mitsui Bunko, Tokyo.

23. Anonymous: "Title Inscription of Buddhist Image Constructed by Duke Shiping." Northern Wei dynasty. Ink rubbing. Osaka Municipal Museum of Fine Art.

25. Anonymous: "Yi He Inscription." Liang dynasty. Ink rubbing. Fujii Museum, Kyoto.

26. Bei Yiyuan: "Liang Stele for Zhongwu Xiao Dan, Prince of Shixing." Liang dynasty. Ink rubbing. Mitsui Bunko, Tokyo.

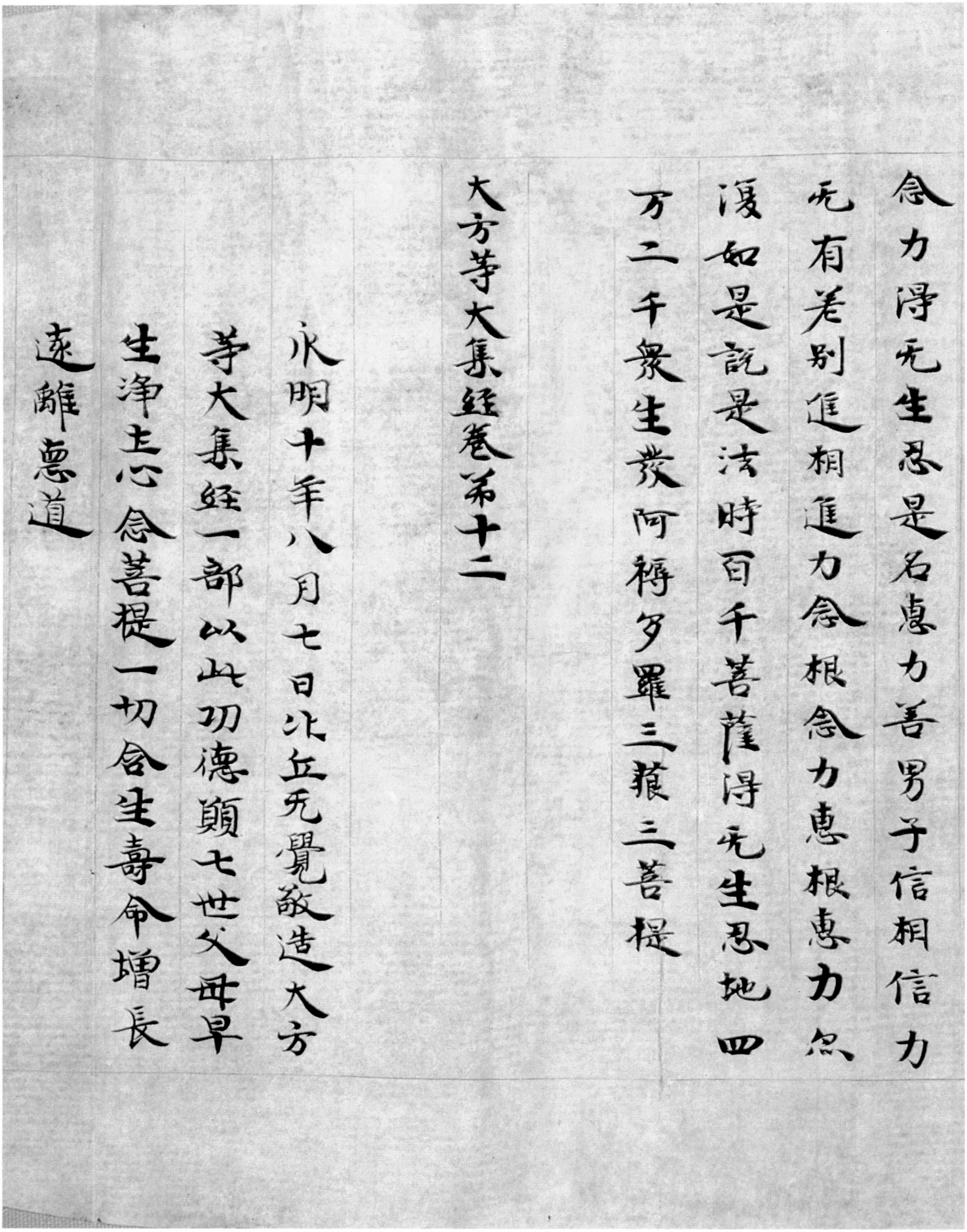

念力得无生忍是名慧力善男子信相信力

无有差別進進力念根念力惠根惠力忿

復如是說是法時百千菩薩得无生忍地四

万二千眾生發阿耨多羅三藐三菩提

大方等大集經卷第十二

永明十年八月七日比丘无覺敬造大方
等大集經一部以此功德顋七世父母早
生淨志念菩提一切合生壽命增長
遠離惡道

27. Anonymous: *"Dafangdeng Daiji Jing."* Qi dynasty. Ink on paper. Kyoto National Museum.

出住是冨閣籟弥羅出三昧説偈索閣門

婆羅私弗國　諸舊比丘中　持偉多聞人　以断諸狐疑

今従彼閣来　婆羅梨弗國　諸舊比丘中　持偉多聞人

調御六情根　今従彼閣来　在此門下立　婆羅私佛國

諸舊比丘中　持偉多聞人　級閣籟弥羅　今従彼閣来

在此門下立

律序卷第上

梁普通四年太歳　卯四月匝法元畫威寫偉流

通供養

28. Zhengfa Wujincang: "*Vinaya* Preface." Liang dynasty. Ink on paper. Private collection.

陟伏衆魔長養成就自在遊趣淨諸佛刹種

八大衆化教衆生家大光明轉淨法輪神力

變化皆迷灵持正念思惟智慧分別破諸佛

法顯現衆生知見未來弥勒佛苐一切諸佛

華嚴經卷第卅七

延昌二歲次癸巳七月十八日燉煌鎮

經生張顯昌所寫經戎記竟

用帋廿二

典經帥令狐崇哲

校經道人

29. Zhang Xianchang: *"Huayan Jing."* Northern Wei dynasty.
Ink on paper. Ōtani University Library, Kyoto.

菩薩處胎經卷第三

以慈念眾生　得通无罣閡　从人五通慧　轉退无處就

我通墮囿法　要入涅槃門

尒時世尊與妙勝菩薩說此法時有百七十

億眾生捨諾五通得六通慧

大魏十六年歲次鶉火隹在狹鍾八日丙寅仏弟子陶仵席

卅人等資光偏慈體耀乘門敬崇玄範淵敷靈教於簡

蘭寺幹遵沖業廓大魏國內一切垂藏概訪畫飾至三年功記

洪基創時福映三千鐵闕憫沉遂當万葉顛法界四生無

復六塵依尋弥鄣俱驪覺道

30. Anonymous: *"Pusa Chutai Jing."* Western Wei dynasty.
Ink on paper. Chion-in Treasure House, Kyoto.

調陽　雲騰致雨　露結爲霜

調陽　雲騰致雨　露結爲霜

金生麗水　玉出崑岡

金生麗水　玉出崑岡

劍號巨闕　珠稱夜光

果珍李柰

果珍李柰

31. Zhiyong: "Thousand-Character Essay in Block and Cursive Scripts." Sui dynasty. Ink on paper. Private Collection.

32. Ding Daohu: "Qifa Temple Stele." Sui
dynasty. Ink rubbing. Private collection.

遺具者罪亦五倍大王我今定知王之惡業
必不得免唯願大王速往佛所除佛世尊餘
无能救我今愍汝故相勸導尒時大王聞是
語巳心懷怖懼舉身戰慄五體掉動如芭蕉
樹仰而荅曰天為是誰不現色像而但有聲
大王吾是汝父頻婆娑羅汝今當隨耆婆所
說莫隨耶見六臣之言時王聞巳悶絶躃地
身瘡增劇見穢倍前雖以冷藥塗治將療瘡
蒸毒熱但增无損

大般涅槃經卷第七

仁壽三年五月皇太子廣為眾生敬造流通供養

33. Yang Guang: *"Daban Niepan Jing."* Sui dynasty.
Ink on paper. Kyoto National Museum.

銘肇其得姓卜洛啓其興王道盛中原業光
具諸史冊可略言焉六世祖遵假節侍中撫
收常山王高祖素言假六世祖假節侍中都中
相太二州王刺史侍中尚書左僕射城陽宣王大
徐州刺史宗正卿父冢使持節公侍中驃騎大
六州諸軍事青州刺史司徒公樂平慎王維
羊落落高標排於松獨擅臂亭卓峻節映綠
許史友之稱其孝友斯授聲譽流洽孟晉迫群
弟實符束指乃齎辞名士俊才不寵方降此縈
上士粤自居中之邊於內竅自非不言如子夏
月轉為掌式中士君清惰疾惡正色讜言簧

34. Anonymous: "Epitaph for Duke Yuan, Officer of the
Stables." Sui dynasty. Ink rubbing. Private collection.

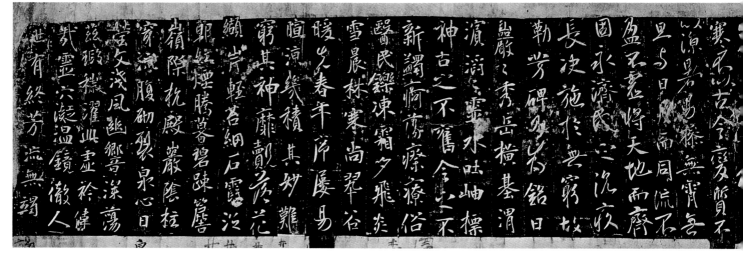

35. Taizong: "Hot Spring Inscription." Tang dynasty.
Ink rubbing. Bibliothèque Nationale, Paris.

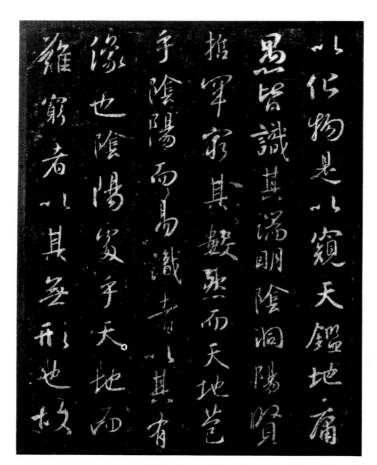 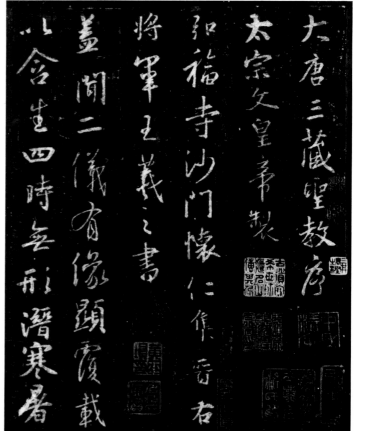

36. Huairen, after Wang Xizhi: "*Preface to the Buddhist Canon, from a Collection of Wang's Calligraphy.*" Tang dynasty. Ink rubbing. Mitsui Bunko, Tokyo.

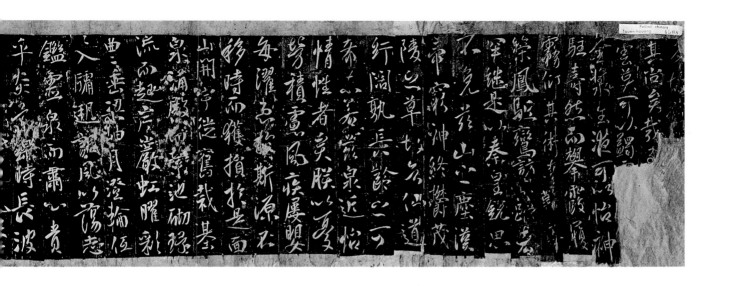

37. Ouyang Xun: "Inscription for the Memorial Pagoda of Chan Master Yong"(Huadu Temple Stele). Tang dynasty. Ink rubbing. Ōtani University Library, Kyoto.

大唐三藏聖教序

太宗文皇帝製

蓋聞二儀有象顯

覆載以含生四時

集卷第廾九

行狀

祭文

　張公行狀一首

　祭石堤山神文一首

　祭石堤女郎神文一首

　祭白鹿山神文一首

　為虞霍王諸官祭故長史一首

　為雟王祭徐王文一首

　祭高祖文一首

行狀

張公行狀一首

某郡某縣某鄉某里張公年廾

若夫孝神基於峻岳撲曾霞於靈宮奇峰非

數遵而戌崇堂豈一村而立是以蒼溪赤岸

方騰噴曰之波珠藪瑤林心疊梢雲之幹

呪乎柏天孤而錫氏驛地梗而居尊文物

光乎萬弈聲問乎千古功臣北的樓殭越

39. Anonymous: *"Collected Works of Wang Bo."* Tang dynasty. Ink on paper. Tokyo National Museum.

◀ 38. Chu Suiliang: "Yan Pagoda Prefaces to the Buddhist Canon." Tang dynasty. Ink rubbing. Tokyo National Museum.

經五年春正月甲戌巳丑陳侯鮑卒

未同盟而書名

或本如字下春
齊欲賦紀四

者未赴以名故世甲戌前年十二月廿一日巳曰此
年正月六日也陳亂故再赴乙雖日異而皆以正月
月赴文故但書正月慎
疑審事故從赴兩書也

夏齊侯鄭伯如紀外

朝聘言如紀人懼
而來告故書

天王使仍叔之子來聘

仍舊天子大夫也稱仍舊之子李於
文字幼豹辭也讒使童子出躬

葬陳桓公 傳無

城祝丘 無傳齊鄭
特龔襲紀故

秋蔡人衛人陳人從王

伐鄭 王自為伐鄭之主君臣之辭也
王師敗不書不以告也

大雩 傳例日
書不晰

冬州公如曹 奔以
不書

見之時 螽
也龍失 無傳蚳蝑之屬
也為尖故書也

---

40. Anonymous: *"Commentary and Notes on the Spring and Autumn Annals."* Tang dynasty. Ink on paper. Fujii Museum, Kyoto.

42. Anonymous: *"Biography of Yang Xiong, Han Annals."* Tang dynasty. Ink on paper. Private collection. ▶

41. Anonymous: *"New Version of the Anecdotes."* Tang dynasty. Ink on paper. Kyoto National Museum.

43. Sun Guoting: *"Treatise on Calligraphy."* Tang dynasty. Ink on paper. Taipei Palace Museum.

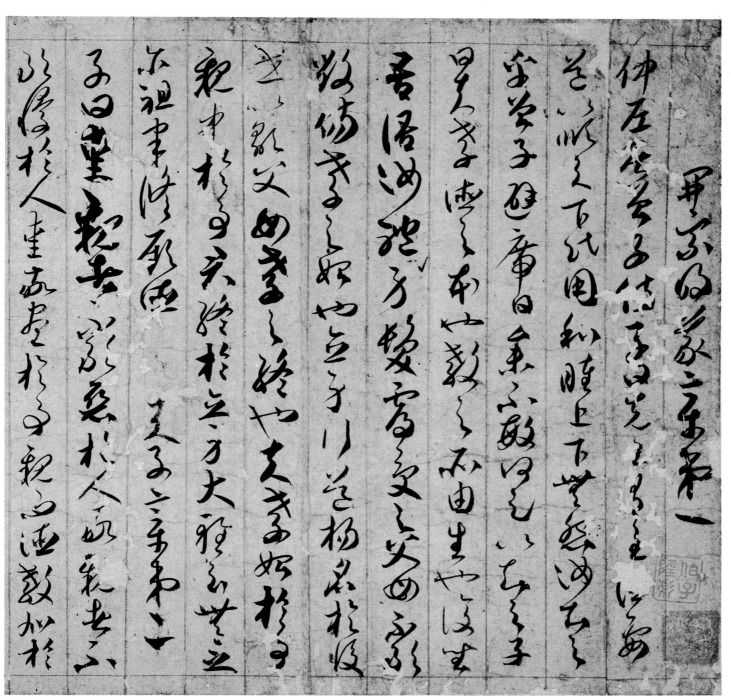

44. He Zhizhang: "*Classic of Filial Piety* in Cursive Characters." Tang dynasty.
Ink on paper. Collection of the Japanese Imperial Household, Tokyo.

45. Anonymous: "Epitaph Inscription for Princess Yongtai."
Tang dynasty. Ink rubbing. Shaanxi Provincial Museum.

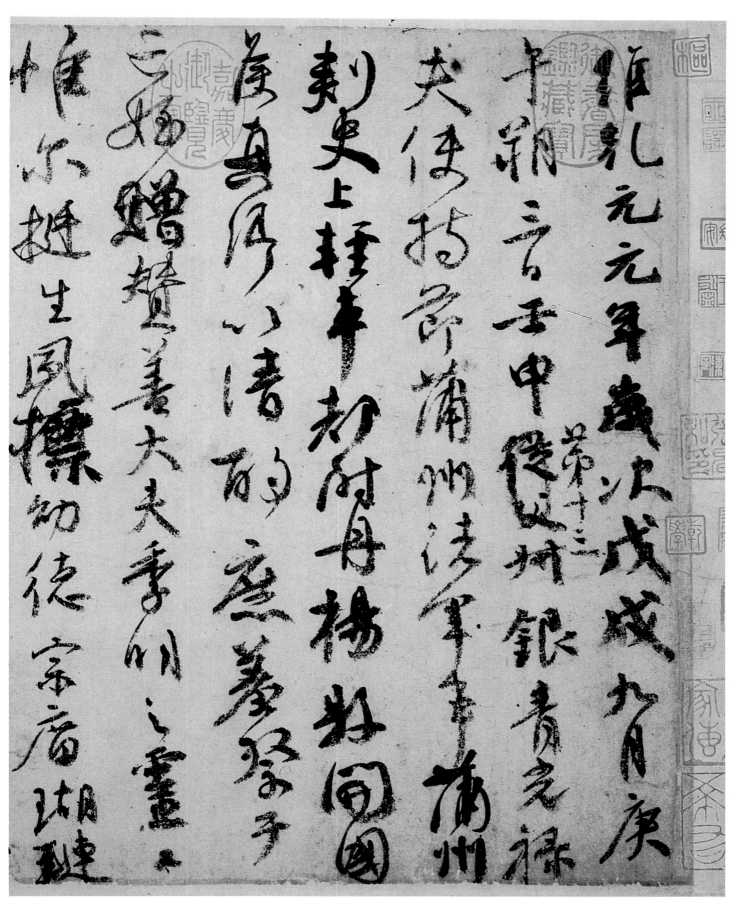

維乾元元年歲次戊戌九月庚
午朔三日壬申第十三叔銀青光祿
大夫使持節蒲州諸軍事蒲州
刺史上輕車都尉丹陽縣開國
侯真卿以清酌庶羞祭於亡姪
贈贊善大夫季明之靈曰惟
爾挺生夙德宗廟瑚璉

46. Yan Zhenqing: "Eulogy for a Nephew." Tang dynasty. Ink on paper. Taipei Palace Museum.

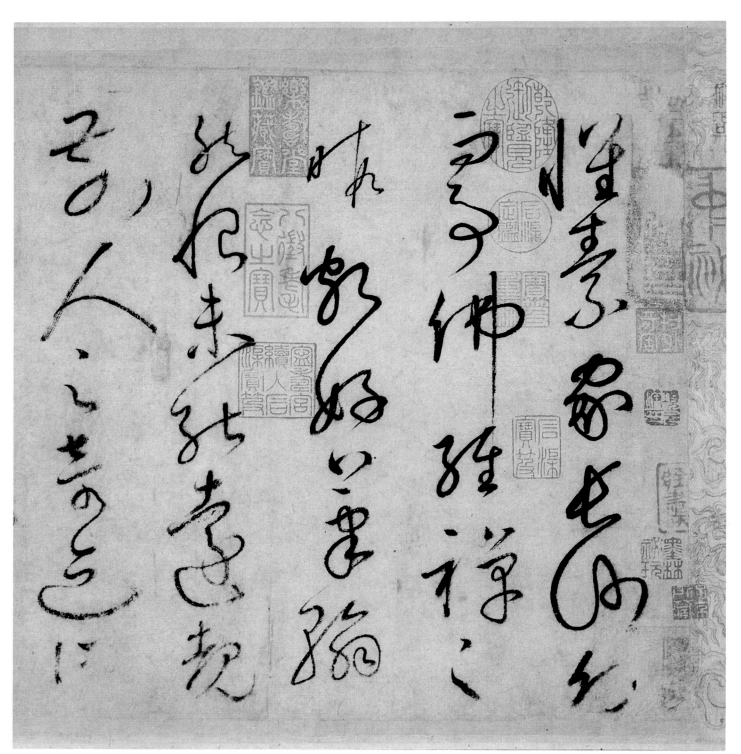

47. Huaisu: *"Autobiography."* Tang dynasty. Ink on paper. Taipei Palace Museum.

皇華使者臨清晨手開

寶軸香煤新泛名

與字敘深盲

宸毫灑落奎鉤文

精神高遠照日月

勢力雄健生風雲

48. Cai Xiang: "Poems in Thanks for an Imperial Gift." Song
dynasty. Ink on paper. Museum of Calligraphy, Tokyo.

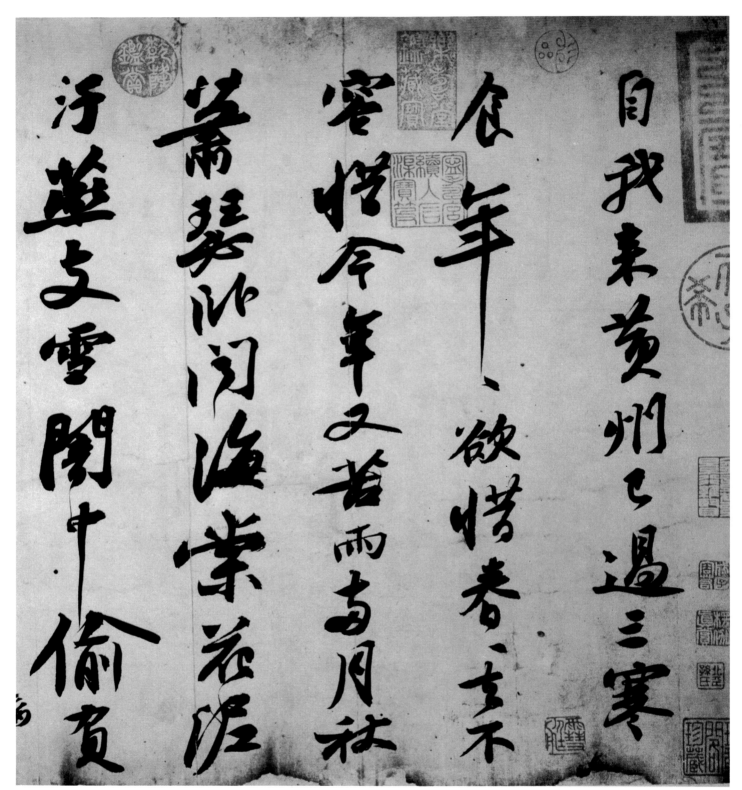

49. Su Shi: *"Cold Meal in Huangzhou Poem Scroll."*
Song dynasty. Ink on paper. Private collection.

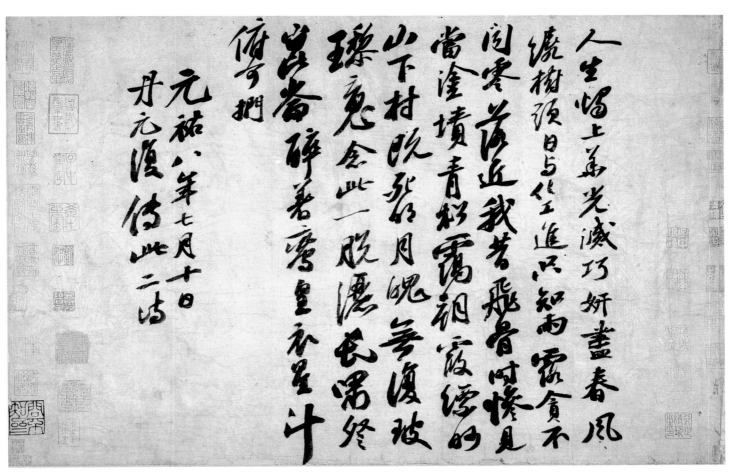

50. Su Shi: "*Hermit Li Taibo* Poem Scroll." Song dynasty.
Ink on paper. Osaka Municipal Museum of Fine Art.

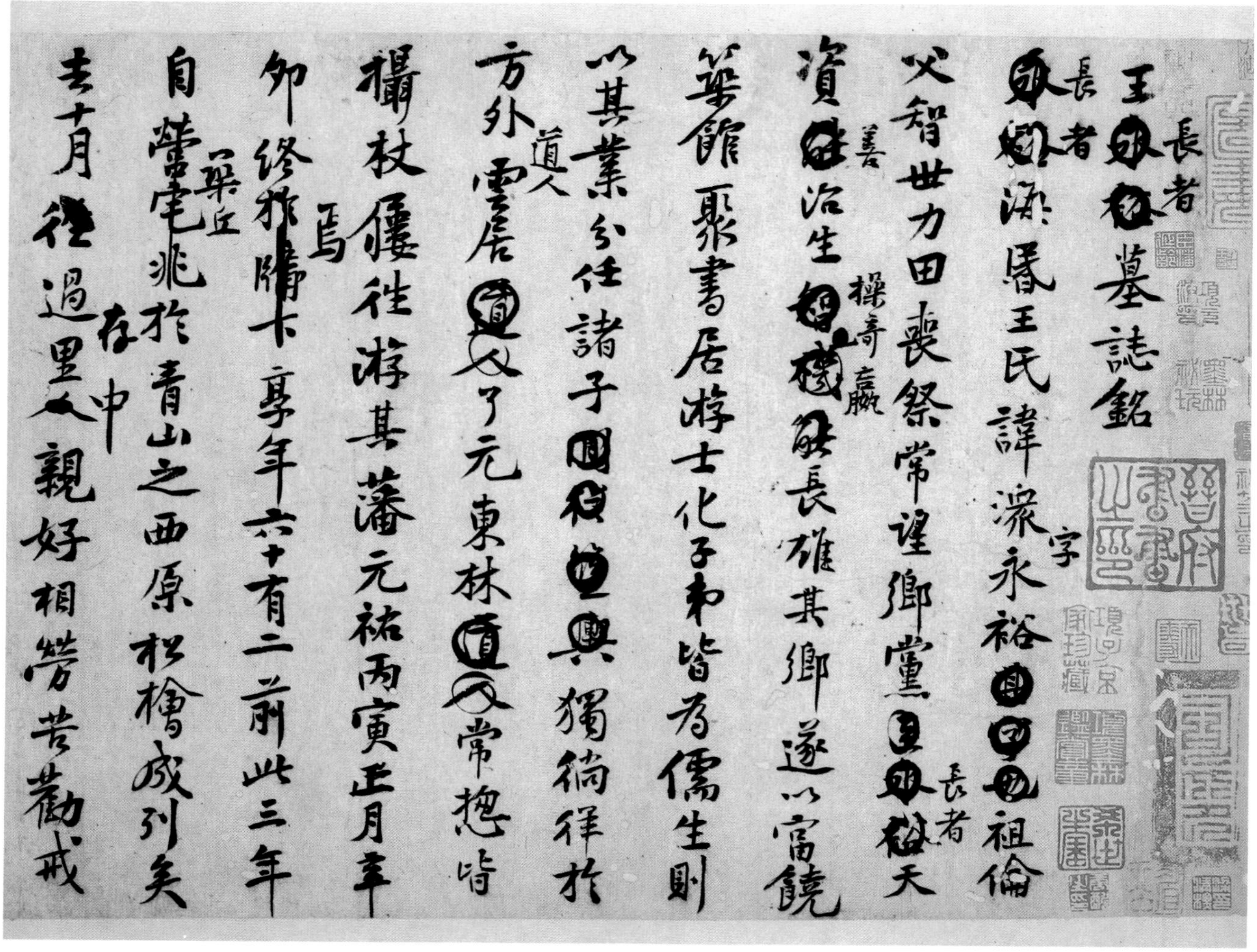

承事郎王永材墓誌銘

長者

王永材墓誌銘

承事郎族屬王氏諱滾字永裕　祖倫

父智世力田喪祭常望鄉黨　長者

資　治生　藏　長雄其鄉遂以富饒

箸館聚書居游士化子弟皆為儒生則

以其業分任諸子　與獨徜徉於

方外雲居　了元東林　常抱

攜杖屨往游其藩元祐丙寅正月率

卯修於隋卡享年六十有二前此三年

自營窀穸兆於青山之西原松檜成列矣

去十月往過里又親好相勞苦勸戒

51. Huang Tingjian: "Epitaph Drafts for Wang Zhong and Shi Fu." Song dynasty. Ink on paper. Tokyo National Museum.

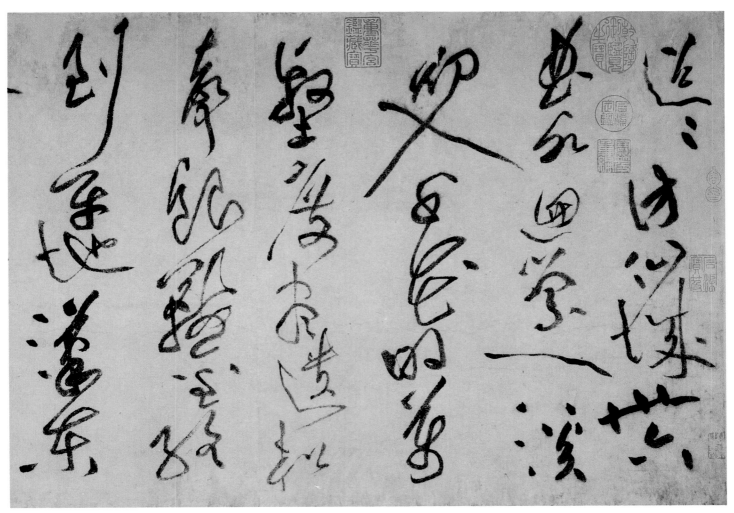

52. Huang Tingjian: "Li Taibo's *Recalling Past Wanderings* Poem Scroll." Song dynasty. Ink on paper. Fujii Museum, Tokyo.

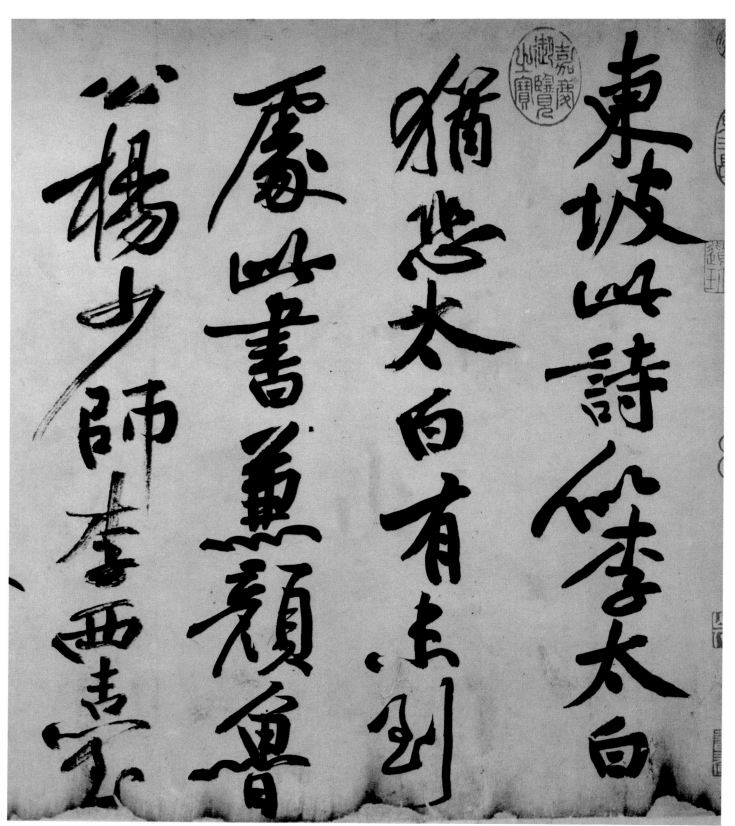

東坡此詩似李太白猶恐太白有未到屬此書兼顏魯公楊少師李西臺

53. Huang Tingjian: "*Cold Meal in Huangzhou* Poem Scroll Postscript." Song dynasty. Ink on paper. Private collection.

54. Mi Fu: "Gangxian Poem Scroll." Song dynasty. Ink on paper. Tokyo National Museum.

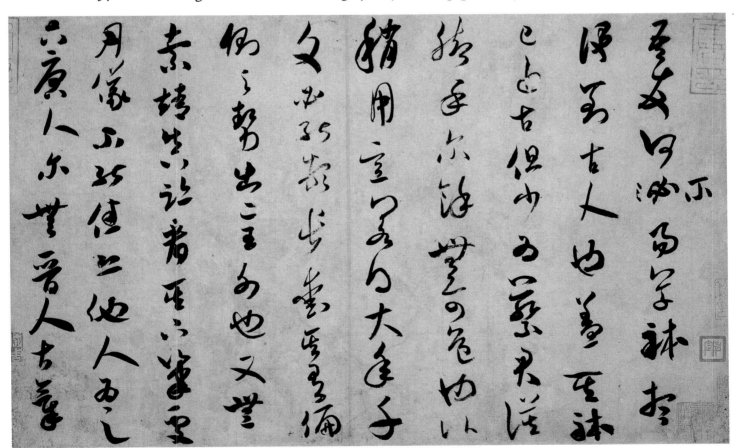

55. Mi Fu: "Four Cursive Albums." Song dynasty.
Ink on paper. Osaka Municipal Museum of Fine Art.

56. Yuanwu Keqin: "Diploma." Song dynasty. Ink on paper. Tokyo National Museum.

音容之晬清
日表之明潤追惟曩昔軍前使回迎
鑾興於應天蒙
親解玉帶以賜歲月飄忽緬懷
恩育涕泗無從復依故實謹為叙引
用眙示
成憲允伸達孝若夫
範圍天地
表章六經與三才比隆並二典同煥
詔百世至于萬世則期與子孫共祇于
明訓 臣構 謹序

57. Gaozong: *"Preface to the Collected Writings of Huizong."*
Song dynasty. Ink on paper. Private collection.

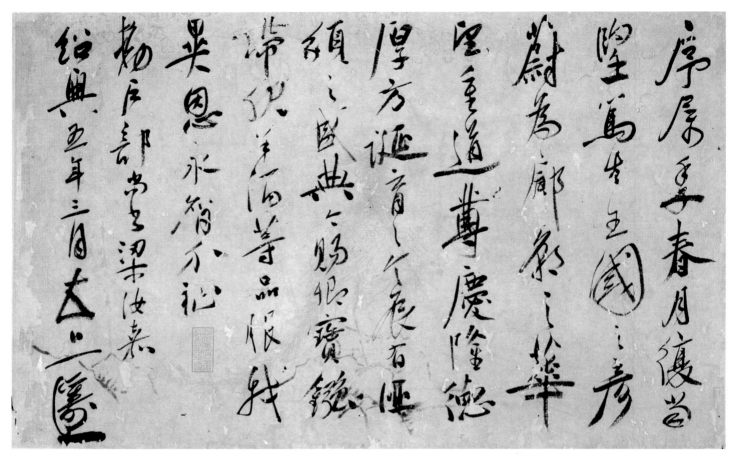

58. Gaozong: "Volume of Proclamations Granted to Liang Rujia."
Song dynasty. Ink on paper. Tokyo National Museum.

59. Fan Chengda: "Memorial Poem for Chan ▶
Master Fo Zhao." Song dynasty. Ink rubbing.
Imperial Household Agency, Archives and
Mausolea Department, Tokyo.

縹緲神通未易論兩靜逼雲夜觀龍遁不群歸

春泥滑且之秧四舊水痕

海雷雨霧籠按特光中萬象空想見

蓬茉西望眼應知我立長風

小麥深秧田水滿保浮斗今年一　蓬海事

飽金無慮寬盡歸舟去客心　青莊

竹巘窈窕入蕭森迤兩跡風冷客禮翠錦居巘　松經

三十里不知師痕白雲深

右贈　佛眼禪師詩

奉政府政院公范公辛丑季余袚鎮金陵近顏出開公開月窪
山川之壯麗碳妙觀之無窮勝跡攷寿凌今石丹齊人帳
不膝緣脩運刻旺祇以俟嘉規六欣八月

晁氏曰不憂不懼由乎德全而無疵故不疚

憂懼而除却去之耳

○司馬牛憂曰人皆有兄弟我獨亡　亡讀為無

牛有兄弟而云然者憂其為亂而將死也

子夏曰商聞之矣　○蓋聞之夫子　死生有命富貴在天

命禀於有生之初非今所能移稿　莫能變焉

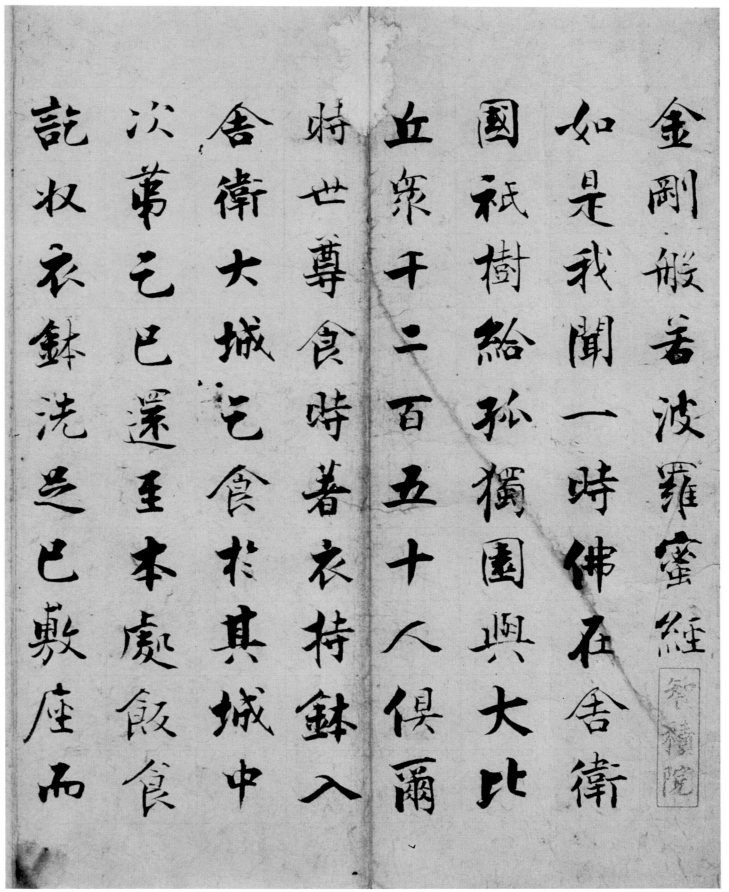

金剛般若波羅蜜經

如是我聞一時佛在舍衛
國祇樹給孤獨園與大比
丘眾千二百五十人俱爾
時世尊食時著衣持鉢入
舍衛大城乞食於其城中
次第乞已還至本處飯食
訖收衣鉢洗足已敷座而

61. Zhang Jizhi: *"Jingang Banruoboloumi Jing."* Song dynasty.
Ink on paper. Chishaku-in Storehouse, Kyoto.

◀ 60. Zhu Xi: "Cursive Draft of the Collected Notes on the *Analects.*"
Song dynasty. Ink on paper. Kyoto National Museum.

高︙︙有人於海上見之盖
太白玄維事涉荒怪殆決邪
火食肉人所能贋作嗟夫二
公未遺世時戈皆以誦仙目
之今嘗相從折閣風弱水之
上醉笑調欹靈音相荅皆
丸霞空洞中諸衆不一盖
後復有神游八表老傳誦
而来洗出萬古俗氣要
老矣当戎見之正隆四年
閏六月西山蔡松年題

竹枝搭之以
自料程
年

63. Wang Tingyun: "Postscript to Painting of Bamboo." Jin dynasty. Ink on paper. Fujii Museum, Kyoto.

62. Cai Songnian: "Postscript to Su Shi's 'Hermit Li Taibo Poem Scroll.'" Jin dynasty. Ink on paper. Osaka Municipal Museum of Fine Art.

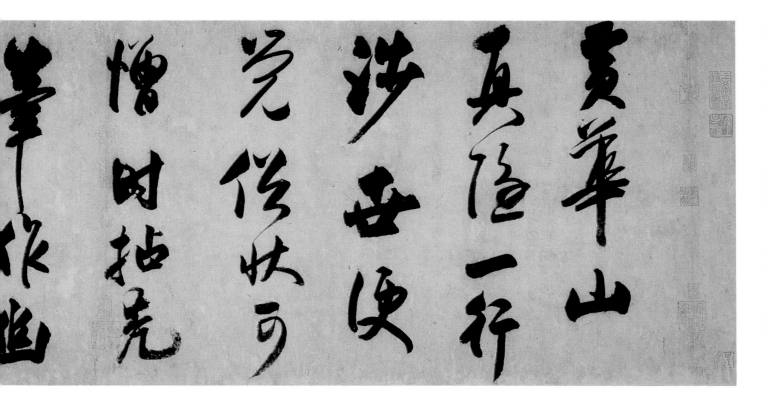

老坡平生為與異人遇此
帖云傳於丹元者道人姚安
云自號如
先生将赴雲武亥兩月5姚
相會於京师出南岳典寶
東華李真人宗及所作二

賁華山
真隂一行
涉垂便
覚脩妖可
憎时拙克
筆作幽

65. Wuzhun Shifan: "Diploma." Song dynasty. Ink on paper. Tōfuku-ji Storehouse, Kyoto.

64. Mi'an Xianjie: "Sermon." Song dynasty. Ink on figured silk. Ryūkō-in Storehouse, Kyoto.

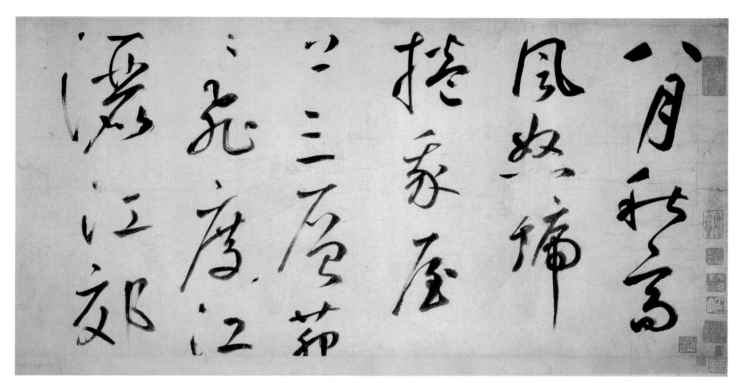

66. Xianyu Shu: "Du Fu's *Thatch Roof Destroyed by the Autumn Wind.*" Yuan dynasty. Ink on paper. Fujii Museum, Kyoto.

67. Zhao Mengfu: "Epistle ▶
to Zhongfeng Mingben."
Yuan dynasty. Ink on paper,
Seikadō Bunko, Tokyo.

孟頫

和南 跋復

中峯和上至沛侍者 孟頫手

生雖承祖父之蔭無飢寒之

窘讀書不敢謂博粗二粗解

大意其於佛法十三冊百卷之

向蒙可己迂後見人說東坡

漢汲黯傳

汲黯字長孺濮陽人也其先有寵於古之

衛君至黯七世為卿大夫黯以父任孝景時

為太子洗馬以莊見憚孝景帝崩太子即

位黯為謁者東越相攻上使黯往視之不至

吳而還報曰越人相攻固其俗然不足以辱天子

之使河內失火延燒千餘家上使黯往視之還

報曰家人失火屋比延燒不足憂也臣過河南

河南貧人傷水旱萬餘家或父子相食臣

謹以便宜持節發河南倉粟以振貧民臣請

歸節伏矯制之罪上賢而釋之遷為滎陽

令黯恥為令病歸田里上費乃召拜為中大

68. Zhao Mengfu: *"Biography of Han Ji'an."* Yuan dynasty.
Ink on paper. Eisei Bunko Foundation, Tokyo.

69. Feng Zizhen: "Words Presented to Muin Genkai."
Yuan dynasty. Ink on paper. Gotō Art Museum, Tokyo.

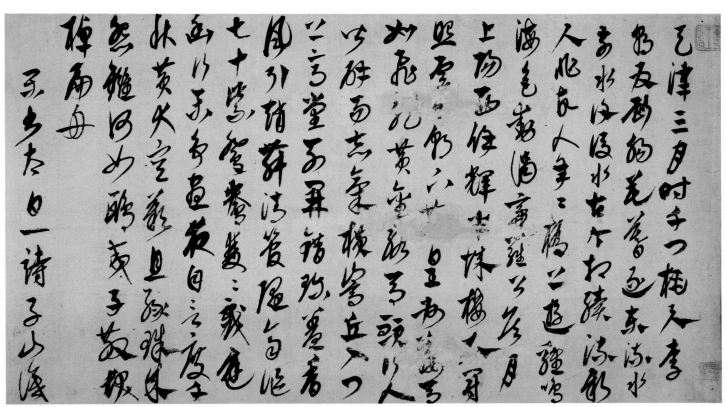

70. Kangli Kuikui: "Li Bo's *Ancient Wind* Poem." Yuan
dynasty. Ink on paper. Tokyo National Museum.

71. (*above*) Yang Weizhen: "Draft for Zhang Clan Memorial Stele." Yuan dynasty. Ink on paper. Private collection.

72. (*below*) Zhang Bi: "Postscript to Su Shi's '*Hermit Li Taibo* Poem Scroll.'" Ming dynasty. Ink on paper. Osaka Municipal Museum of Fine Art.

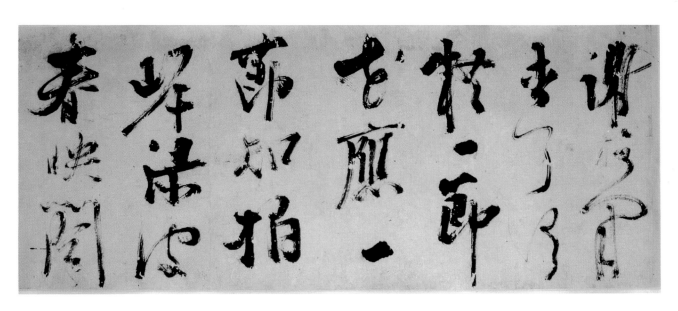

73. (*above*) Chen Xianzhang: "Poem Scroll." Ming dynasty. Ink on paper. Eisei Bunko Foundation, Tokyo.

74. (*below*) Zhu Yunming: "*Li Sao Classic* Scroll." Ming dynasty. Ink on paper. Chōkaidō Bunko, Yokkaichi.

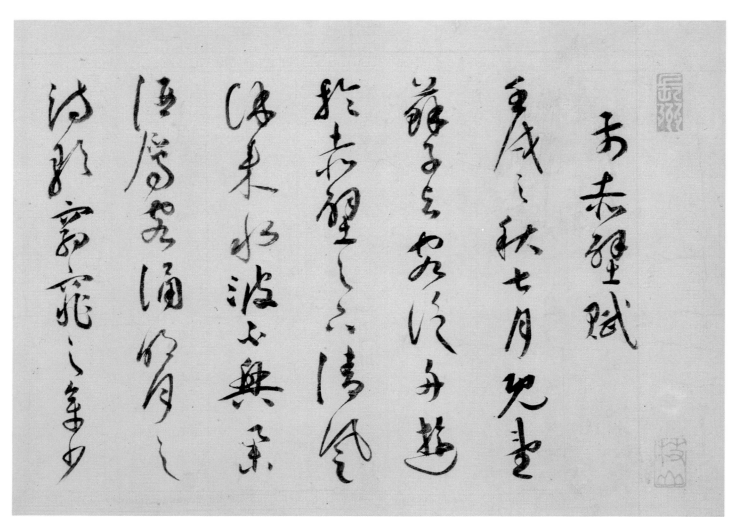

75. Zhu Yunming: *"Red Cliffs Ode."* Ming dynasty.
Ink on paper. Tokyo National Museum.

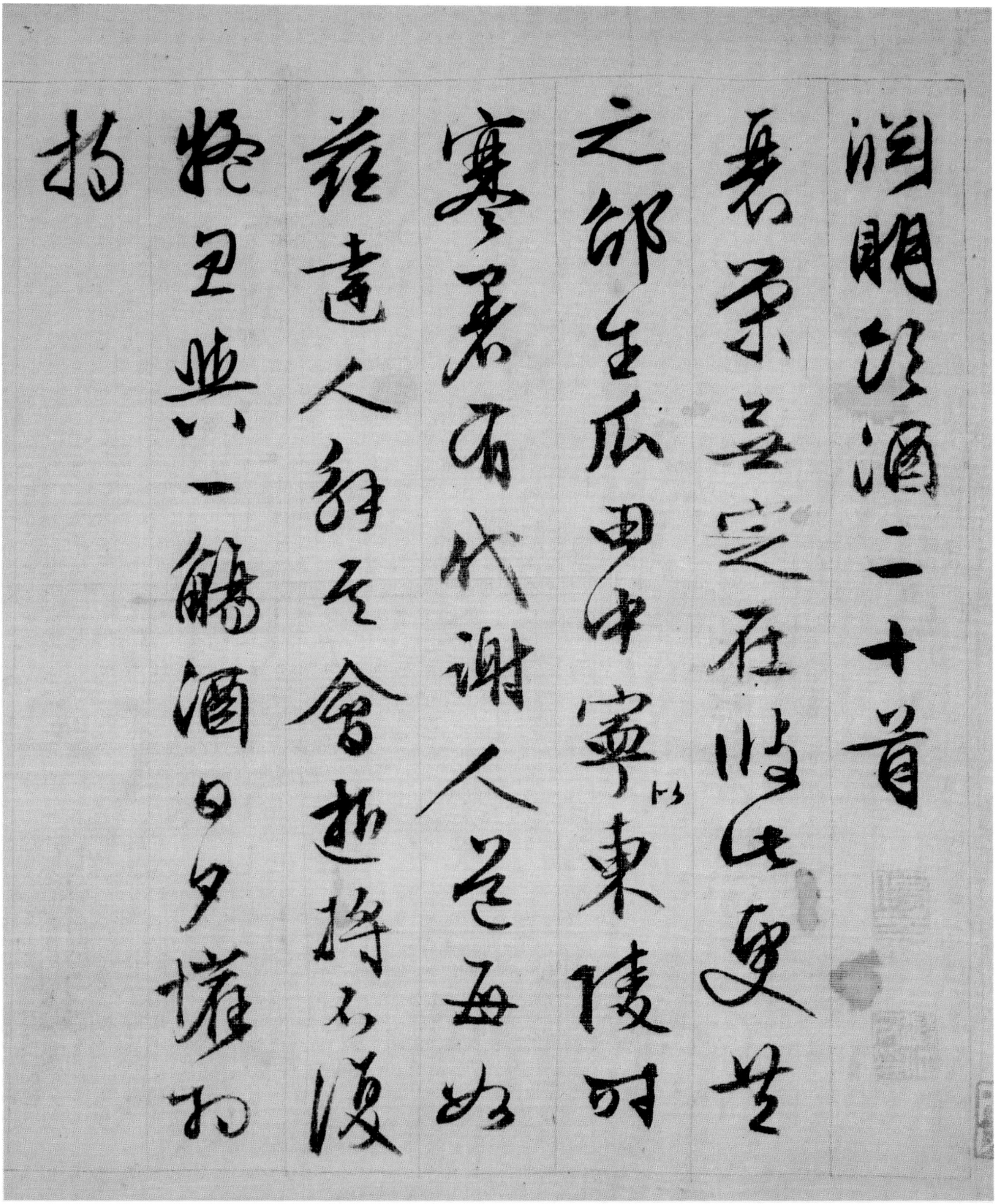

淵明飲酒二十首

衰榮無定在彼此更共

之邵生瓜田中寧似東陵時

寒暑有代謝人道毎如茲

達人解其會逝將不復

忽與一觴酒日夕懽相

持

76. Wen Zhengming: "Twelve Verses from Tao Yuanming's Drinking Poem." Ming dynasty. Ink on silk. Kyoto National Museum.

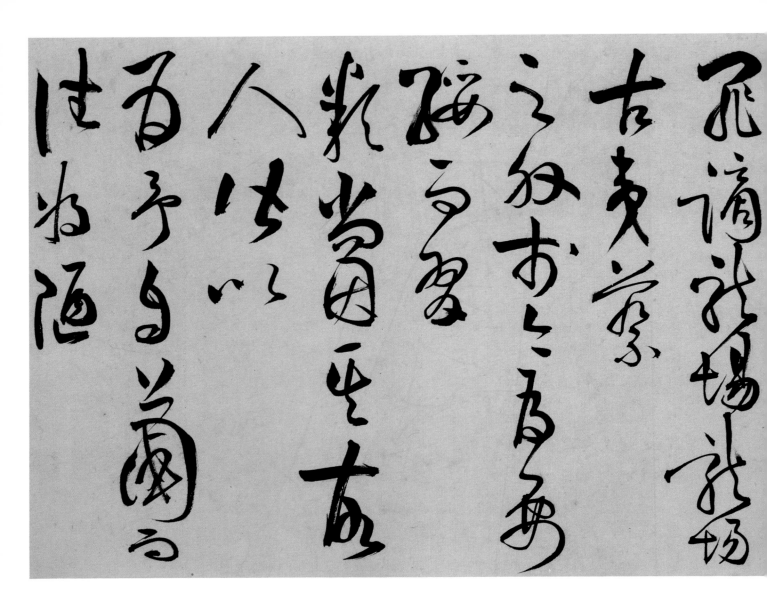

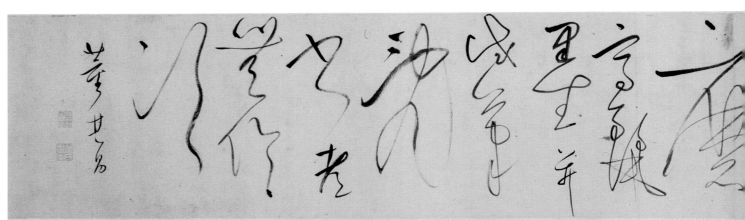

77. (*above*) Wang Shouren: "Helou Pavilion Poem Scroll." Ming dynasty. Ink on paper. Tokyo National Museum.

78. (*below*) Dong Qichang: "Semi-cursive and Cursive Calligraphy Scroll." Ming dynasty. Ink on paper. Tokyo National Museum.

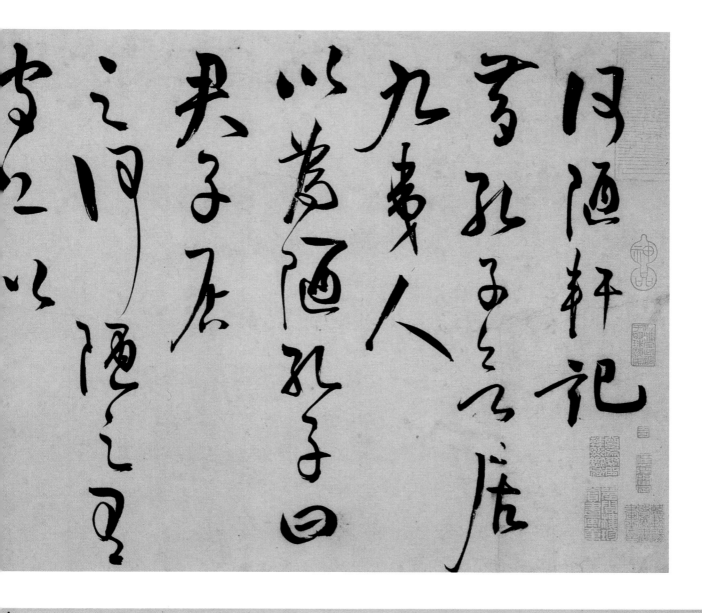

日涉軒記

曹孔子之居

九奉人

以為酒孔子曰

夫子居

之日陬之日

已以

雪邪
巖之
雲之涯山
夏見雨
宇宙之
荒卉之
子于
之伯帷
始治濠生
回之與會
漢濤生
法席
之兵軍

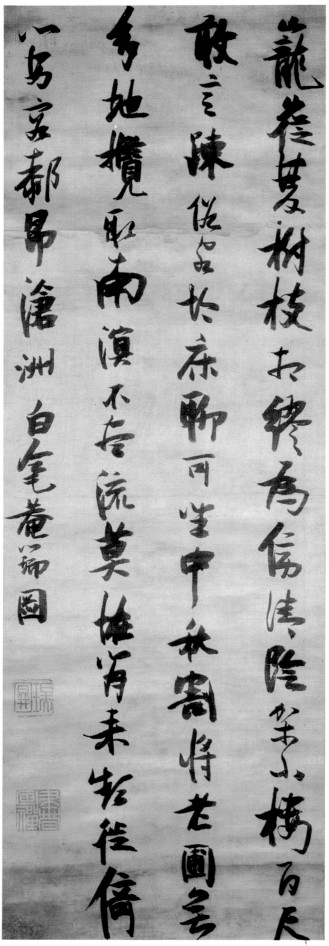

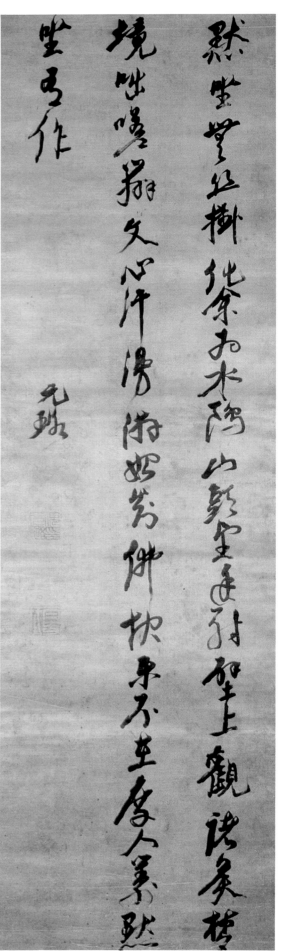

79. Zhang Ruitu: "*Building a Small Pagoda Between the Sala Trees*" Poem Scroll." Ming dynasty. Ink on silk. Kyoto National Museum.

80. Ni Yuanlu: "*Seated in Silence* Poem." Ming dynasty. Ink on polished silk. Chōkaidō Bunko, Yokkaichi.

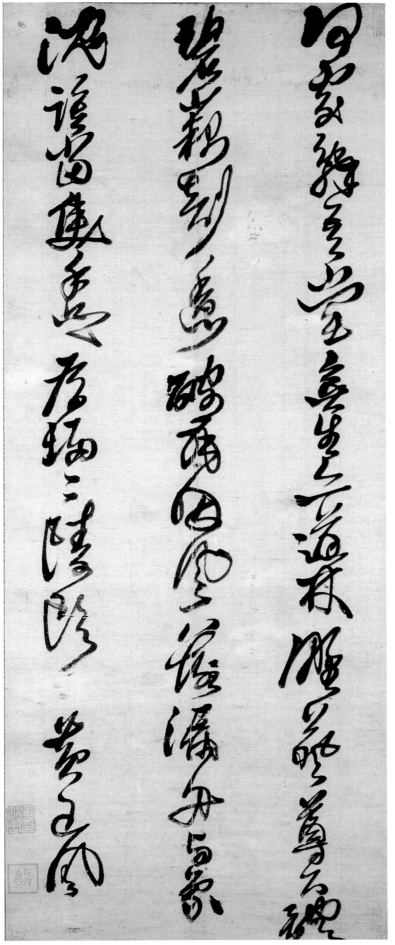

81. Huang Daozhou: "Reply to Sun Boguan's Poem." Ming dynasty. Ink on polished silk. Chōkaidō Bunko, Yokkaichi.

82. Wang Duo: "*Xiangshan* Poem." Qing dynasty. Ink on polished silk. Fujii Museum, Kyoto

83. Fu Shan: "*Wandering Hermits* Poem in Twelve Scrolls" (four shown here and on facing page). Ming dynasty. Ink on polished silk. Chōkaidō Bunko, Yokkaichi.

碧雲風...海隅...醒...水晶盤...

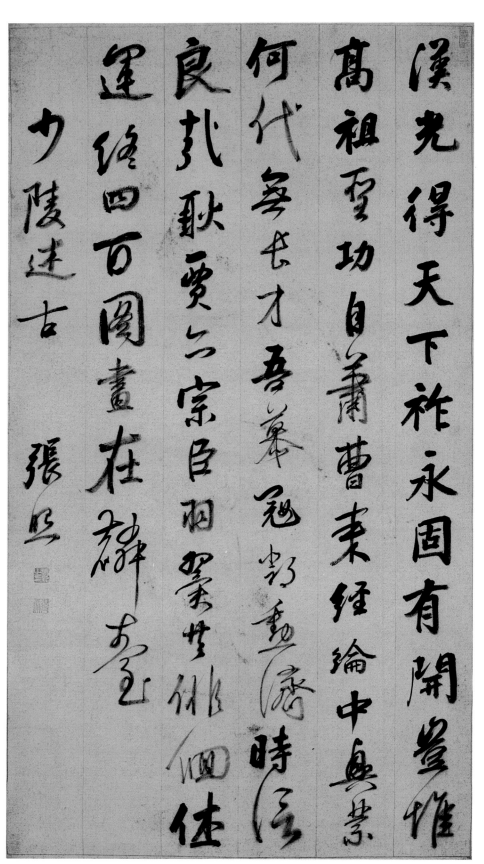

84. Jiang Chenying: "Poem." Qing
dynasty. Ink on polished silk.
Kyoto National Museum.

85. Zhang Zhao: "Ancient Poem by
Du Fu." Qing dynasty. Ink on polished
silk. Tokyo National Museum.

86. Zheng Xie: "In Praise of Ink Painting of Bamboos."
Qing dynasty. Tokyo National Museum.

87. Jin Nong: "Poem."
Qing dynasty. Ink
on paper. Chōkaidō
Bunko, Yokkaichi.

快雨堂臨晉書

黄庭経

呼吸廬間以自償保守兒堅

身受慶方寸之中謹蓋藏精

神遝歸老填壯俠以幽關流

下竟養子玉樹令可扶至道

不煩不旁迂靈臺通天臨中

野方寸之中至關下玉房之

中神門戶既是公子教我者

明堂四達法海貞貞人子丹

當我前三關之間精氣深子

88. Wang Wenzhi: "Bound Volume of Copies of Jin Calligraphy."
Qing dynasty. Ink on colored paper. Tokyo National Museum.

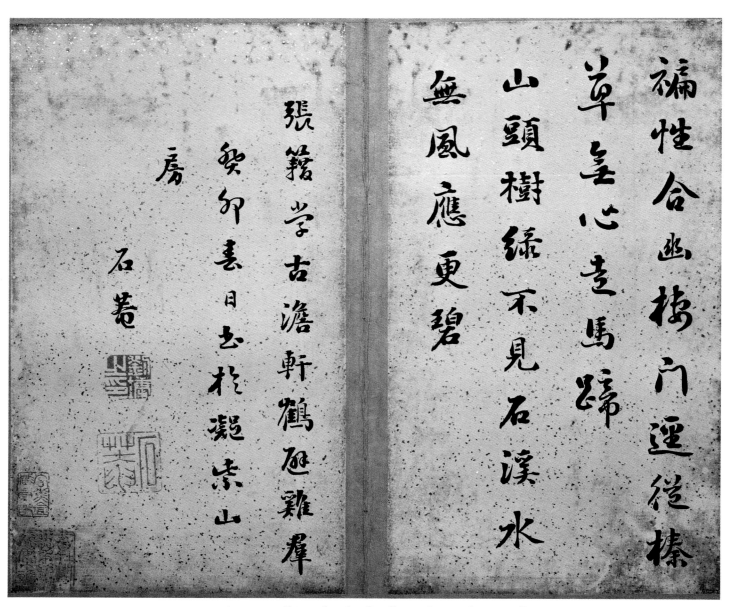

褊性合幽梅門運德榛
草盡心走馬歸
山頭樹綠不見石溪水
無風應更碧

張籍學古澹軒鶴處難羣
癸卯春日書於凝崇山房
石菴

89. Liu Yong: "Copybook of Calligraphic Techniques."
Qing dynasty. Ink on metallic paper. Private collection.

紅樹青林帶暮煙註橋常有賣魚船樊川詩
句瑩那畫亦在先生桂枝邊草堰紅棧醉

秦箬小艇初程景窗奇誰向篆端收拾得事

將至少陵詩　　陸放翁絕句

甲戌之亥　翰林院侍講學士錢唐梁□□書

90. Liang Tongshu: "Two Poems in Seven Stanzas by Lu You." Qing dynasty. Ink on polished silk. Tokyo National Museum.

少書開峯便忘
學偶靜有欣食
琴癜開得耿見

91. Deng Shiru: "Four Styles Album." Qing
dynasty. Ink on paper. Tokyo National Museum.

92. He Shaoji: "In Praise of ▶
Horse Paintings." Qing dynasty.
Ink on paper. Private collection.

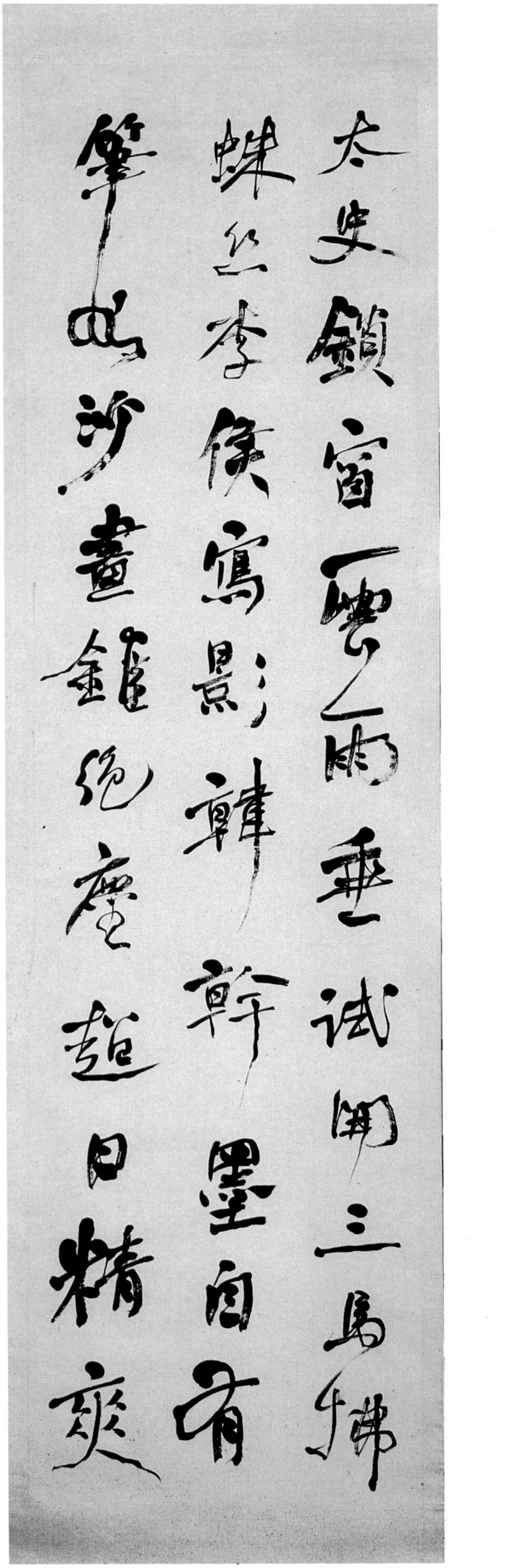

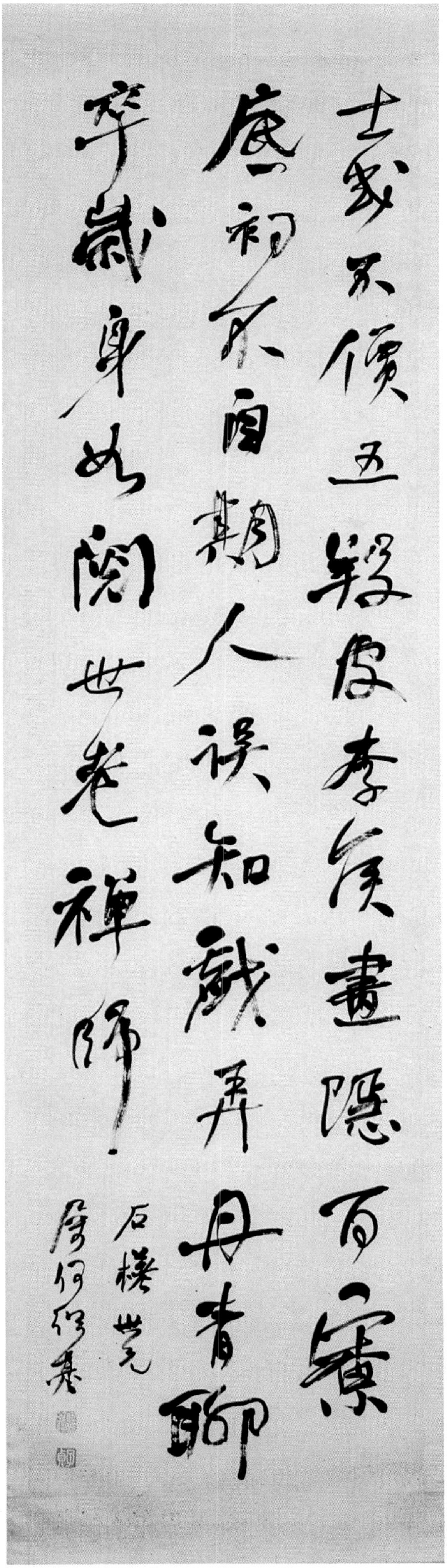

太史鎖窗雲雨垂試開三鳥佛
蛛絲李侯寫影難幹墨何有
筆與沙畫鍾絕塵超日精爽

士氣不傾五斝度李侯畫隱百二寮
度初不負期人誤知戲弄丹青聊
卒歲身如閱世卷禪師
石樓覺先
唐何紹基

大癡百歲萬雲煙富春驟影罗峻
泉是否曾經置道险十年寫是真山川

地可錐指海可測畫意诗情渺物色
本原妙霧同其沙掌力厚時培以息

隔舟舟江天裏時有巉巖插面起
浮圖野店往幽深蔺趟饱闊霜林美

我方被箧尋隱淪主人應念平之聖
笑来九月書車
晉棠觀察大人鑒　趙之謙

93. Zhao Zhiqian: "Four Scrolls." Qing dynasty.
Ink on speckled paper. Tokyo National Museum.

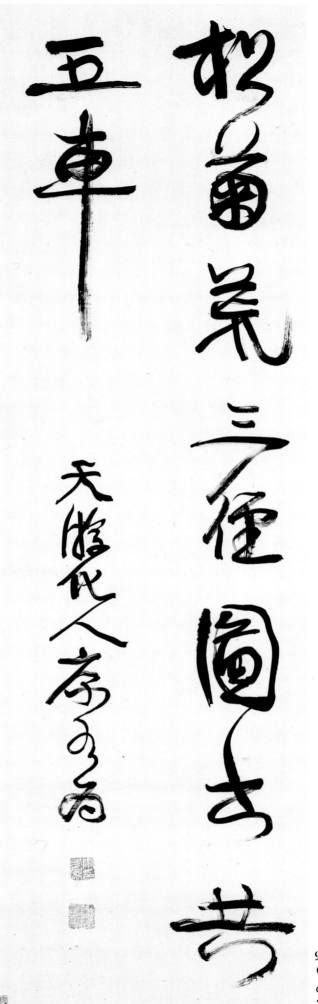

94. Kang Youwei: "Five-Character Couplet." Qing dynasty. Ink on paper. Tokyo National Museum.

桃花源記晉太元中武陵人捕魚為業緣溪行忘路之遠近忽逢桃花林夾岸數百步中無雜樹芳

95. Yang Shoujing: "Description of Peach Blossoms and Spring."
Qing Dynasty. Ink on paper. Tokyo National Museum.

# HISTORICAL SURVEY

# The Origin of Chinese Characters

With the invention of writing man took the first step toward civilization. The development of writing, however, seems to have been intimately linked to the maturation in ancient times of a system of theocratic rule, which may even have been the fundamental requirement for its development. Writing first appeared in ancient China in the middle Shang dynasty, when the Shang transferred their capital to Anyang during the reign of Emperor Wu (about 1300 B.C.). From that time, inscriptions recording the results of divination concerning imperial activities were carved into tortoise shells and cattle bones. Fragments of these oracle bones dating from the reign of Emperor Wu have been found (fig. 1), but none antedating this period have come down to us.

In later records, Emperor Wu was known as Gaozong, the hero king. For three years he led campaigns against the northern tribes in the Shaanxi area, and his success in those distant campaigns is recorded on the oracle bones as well as in ancient legends that have been transmitted in written texts. In addition, the tomb of his consort, Fuhao, has been discovered in recent years, containing magnificent bronze vessels (fig. 2), jeweled ornaments of great skill and sophistication, and ivory vessels with a distinctive animal-head design carved into all surfaces. A dazzling array of artifacts has been unearthed leaving no doubt as to the high level of civilization of these ancient dynasties.

Chinese writing was born during the peak of the prosperity of the ancient dynasties. This was most likely the case in other early civilizations as well. Writing developed in Egypt and Asia Minor during the period of the glorious First Kingdom, from 3100 to 3000 B.C. Though the development of writing in China was considerably earlier than this, a unified government under a god-king had already been established, and the invention of writing is thought to have a very close relationship to this institution of religious kingship, a system common to all ancient civilizations. In all parts of the ancient world writing was originally sacred, used in the worship and service of the gods. In China, too, the scale of the imperial tombs and the funerary objects included in them show that writing was put to use first in the ceremonial maintenance of the dynasty. Whether it be the sacred writings of

Fig. 1. Tortoiseshell inscription (Shang dynasty).

Fig. 2. Rubbing from bronze vessel (tomb of Fuhao).

Egypt or the oracle-bone inscriptions of China, writing first appeared as a product of a very highly developed ceremonial life.

One school of thought seeks the source of writing in signs that we find recorded on pottery shards from ancient periods. Significant markings appear to be engraved on the polychrome pottery from Dongpo in Xi'an and the pottery from Erligang in Zhengzhou and Gaocheng in Hebei. Among these markings are figures which appear again later in oracle-bone inscriptions. Nevertheless, these are neither words nor the precursors of words. In a monosyllabic language like Chinese, each word must have a definite written form as well as a definite meaning and sound assigned to it—form, sound, and sense—in a prescribed and stable combination. In addition to simple nouns and numbers, all parts of speech and elements to express their grammatical relationship must exist. The oracle-bone inscriptions are the first writing by these standards; and, from the first, they appear as a complete system of writing.

Writing does not consist only of nouns and verbs which express concrete objects and activities. It also requires means for creating words with no physical referents and words for ideas—pronouns and negations, for example. In order to function as writing, orthographic symbols must be able to express the full range of the spoken language. Writing does not develop as a mere collection of various signs, but as an integrated system. When this method of systematization is once achieved, all the words of the spoken language can be rendered into writing at once, for unless at least a fundamental vocabulary is rendered into writing simultaneously, writing cannot function at all.

The basic method or system for the production of Chinese writing is called the *liu shu,* or six types of Chinese characters. The *liu shu* is an exegetical system that was devised by Chinese scholars to explain their own language during the Han dynasty—long after the writing system had already developed. In this system, the pictograph is taken to be the most basic type of character. An example of a pictograph is the character 帚 (*fu*), which is a picture of a broom. Actually, it is a depiction of a ceremonial broom that was used in ancient times to sprinkle sacred wine upon the altar of the ancestral shrine as an act of purification. This activity was a duty of the women of the clan, and the pictograph for woman (女, *nü*) combined with broom means wife (婦). The broom element was also a part of the character for ancestral tomb, drawn next to a diagram of the raised dais of a shrine: (帚). Over the whole was a roof (宀), reinforcing the idea of the ancestral shrine. The resulting character—寢—is a semantic combination of three separate elements that gains its meaning from their combination. These semantic combinations were one of the six types of characters described by the *liu shu.*

The character 歸 (*gui,* to return) is a combination of the elements 𠂤, 止, and 帚. In an older form, the character was a semantic combination made up of 𠂤 and 帚 alone. The character 𠂤 is a diagram of sacrificial meat offerings, which were presented at the ancestral shrine on the occasion of the departure of a file of troops. The character 𠂤 also served as part of the character 師, which meant a military unit of 2,500 troops. After a battle, the troops returned and announced the results to the ancestors at the shrine. Once again, they purified the shrine with the ceremonial broom. The meaning of the character 帚 is not restricted to the physical object, the broom. Rather, when used in other character combinations, its *ceremonial* meaning is of primary importance. Unless we understand the intimate association of character elements with religious and ceremonial occasions by the ancient Chinese and recall how these associations were exploited when combining elements to create new characters, we will fail to grasp the full import of these ancient pictographs. Nor can we forget that writing was not devised primarily for the recording of speech, but as one component of imperial ceremony. The formal perfection of both the oracle inscriptions and cast bronze writings reflects their ceremonial origins and use. The remarkably decorative nature of the sacred writing of Egypt, too, was due to the fact that it was a ceremonial, religious offering to the gods.

Things that cannot be represented within a system of pictographs by simple or compound pictographs can be represented by sound. This occurs through association and transference of pronunciation from one character to another. The character for the first person pronoun (我, *wo*) was originally a pictograph representing a saw (𢦏). The character 義 (*yi*, righteousness) is a combination of the character for saw and that for sacrificial sheep (羊, *yang*). This character *yi* came to mean that a sacrifice was in accord with the wishes of the gods. Later, however, the character *wo* fell out of use in its original meaning of saw and was borrowed to write the first person pronoun, which was homophonous. This is an example of yet another of the six types of characters—phonetic borrowings. When borrowing is accompanied by the addition of another character component that carries a definite meaning of its own, phonetic-semantic compounds are produced, such as the characters 儀 (*yi,* ceremony), 檥 (*yi,* to moor a boat), 蟻 (*yi,* ant), and 議 (*yi,* consideration), which are all phonetic-semantic compounds combining the same phonetic symbol 義 (*yi*) with different semantic elements to represent a variety of meanings.

Another sort of pictorial representation gives indications of placement, location, or direction, such as the characters 上 (above) and 下 (below), which show location relative to the palm of the hand; or 本 (roots) and 末 (branch-tips), which indicate parts of a tree (木). These are ideographs. Thus, the principles of construction of Chinese characters are pictographs, ideographs, semantic combinations, characters that borrow the sound of another character, and phonetic-semantic combinations which consist of a pictograph and a pronunciation indicator. The last type of character in the traditional Chinese system is the "extended-meaning" character. This refers to characters that are related semantically, such as 婦 (*fu,* wife), 掃 (*sao,* to clean), 寢 (*qin,* inner chamber), and 浸 (*jin,* to soak), which, although they have different radicals and pronunciations, share a semantic unit (帚) that informs the meaning of each character in a consistent manner: having to do with a broom, sweeping, or ritual purification.

The graphic representation of Chinese characters, rather than being truly pictorial or descriptive, takes a diagrammatic approach which reveals not the outline, but the meaningful structure of its object. It is this fact that has made the construction of ideographs and indicators possible, as well as the invention of considerably complex characters capable of representing sophisticated concepts. For example, the compound of the characters 左 (*zuo,* left) and 右 (*you,* right)—左右—originally referred to the activity of entreating the gods with a divining rod (工) and spells (口), producing the meaning of assistance or aid. The left-side component of these two characters (𠂇) means hand. Another character written with this combination of signs but employing alternate pictographs for hand (彐 and 寸) means to ask the whereabouts of the gods: 尋 (*xun*). All of these characters are related to religious activities. The character 公 (*kung,* public or official) is a pictograph for the courtyard of a palace. To make entreaties to the ancestral spirits there is written with the character 訟 (*song*), combining the radical for speech (言) with the first pictograph. Another character, also pronounced *song* (頌), means to intone the virtues of the ancestors in worship. The left-hand component (頁) depicts a sacrificial vessel. These compound ideographs

Fig. 3. Rubbing from bronze vessel.

Fig. 4. Rubbing from bronze vessel.

105

Fig. 5. Rubbing from
bronze vessel.

are made up of a combination of elements, yet are unified into a single character. It is impossible to ignore the very strong trend toward unity in the orthography of the Chinese character.

In calligraphy this trend toward unity is called cohesion. This is one of the unique traits of characters. From this derives the structural and formal beauty of the Chinese character. This form, together with particular materials and means of writing, ensures infinite creative possibilities. The oracle-bone writing inscribed into tortoise shells and animal bones, the metal inscriptions produced by bronze casting, and the later carvings in jade, as well as writing on silk scrolls and wooden and bamboo slats—each was able to develop in a form appropriate to the material. Moreover, in the oracle-bone inscriptions alone we find five distinct historical styles, from the Emperor Wu period up through the end of the Shang dynasty. The style of the metal inscriptions varied, too, from the Shang to the Zhou to the period of many kingdoms, and we see the development of several styles in different regions and at different times (figs. 3, 4, 5). There are of course tremendous differences among such methods as carving, casting, and brush writing, but it is above all the brush, which was employed as far back as the oracle-bone script, that fundamentally determined the form of Chinese characters. The cohesion of the character as a combination of lines, in addition to the natural movement of the brush, are the two formative factors of Chinese characters. These two factors turned out to be most appropriate in expressing the dynamic movement of artistic inspiration, and made possible the creation of a beauty derived from that movement.

The characters of Chinese calligraphy themselves continued to encourage the production of a variety of styles, even after the standardization of the seal and scribe scripts. The calligraphers of each era pursued and perfected their own ideals of beauty. Nowhere else has the art of calligraphy occupied such an elevated position as the expression of the spirit of the successive ages of man and as a prime focus of the quest for beauty. No doubt Chinese calligraphy will continue to develop, for it is an art with a great promise for the future as well as a great tradition.

# Wooden Tablets and Silk Writings

Confucius, in his devotion to the *Book of Changes* (*Yi Jing*), was said to have "worn out the string binding three times." This indicates that before the invention of paper, works such as the *Book of Changes* and the *Analects* were written on silk, wooden tablets, or strips of bamboo. But silk was precious and tablets were bulky and difficult to handle, so that both were eclipsed by the invention of paper. They are, however, excellent historical sources for the period prior to the use of paper. Incidentally, wooden tablets have recently been unearthed in several locations in Japan, but these date from after the use of paper, and most are clear examples of types of calligraphy especially suited to wooden tablets, distinguishing them in historical value from the Chinese samples.

Fig. 6. Wooden tablet.

Tablets were made from split bamboo, fired to eliminate moisture, and cut into thin strips—approximately 23 centimeters by 1.2 centimeters in the Han dynasty (figs. 6, 7). Because the central regions of China are not particularly well-suited to bamboo culture, and bamboo clumps are difficult to revive once they have failed, wooden tablets gradually replaced the bamboo. In cases when the message was too long for one tablet (the tablets from Juyan have two lines of writing each, with roughly twenty characters per line), several were joined in sequence and tied with a binding of hemp, silk thread, or leather thongs. The character *ce* 冊 (book) is in fact a pictograph of the result. Occasionally, a triangular wooden rod with writing on all three faces was used.

In modern times, the groundwork for the study of these wooden tablets has been laid by the discovery of many of these tablets by Sven Hedin, Aurel Stein, and other expeditions to Central Asia.

The Juyan tablets (pl. 8) discovered by the Scientific Expedition to the Northwestern Provinces of China in 1931 are by far the most numerous of all ancient tablets. While the archeological artifacts unearthed by that expedition were sent to Sweden, the wooden tablets were dispatched to Beijing. There they were subjected to intense scrutiny and deciphered by Drs. Ma Heng and Lao Gan. The project was interrupted by the Sino-Japanese War, and Dr. Lao Gan was able to carry one section of photographic reproductions to safety in the Nanxi region of Sichuan, where he

Fig. 7. Juyan tablet (Han dynasty).

Fig. 8. Seal-label
(Loulan).

Fig. 9. Ledger label
(Dunhuang).

published the two sections of the *Juyan Hanjian Kaoshi* (Consideration of the Juyan Han Tablets) in a stenciled edition in his own hand. Unfortunately, the number of samples treated was limited, and more complete research on the Han-dynasty wooden tablets of Juyan had to wait for the 1949 publication of his typset work, and, in 1957, the volume of photocopies.

Juyan is an oasis some two hundred kilometers north of Zhangcheng, near Karakhoto, a stop on the silk route. From ancient times it was crucially located with respect to the east-west trade. Emperor Wu of the Han, in order to block the passage of supplies to his enemies the Xiongnu from the west, ordered General Lu Bode to construct a barrier. Further, he opened a route following the Edson-gol for communication with the back-up territory, Zhangye. He established post stations along the route and staffed them with guards. The nearly ten thousand wooden tablets that have been discovered were used by these guards to report to their superiors; by the superiors to issue orders, to keep business records and accounts of provisions; and functioned as ledgers and receipts, and as a means for recording all the details of public life.

One interesting note is that these wooden tablets date from the middle of the reign of Emperor Wu of the Former Han, with the latest examples attributed to approximately 31 A.D., the time of the great military withdrawal of Emperor Guangwu of the Later Han.

The tablets are largely made of the oak, willow, and tamarisk native to the region. Dr. Lao Gan has categorized the tablets according to their contents into writings and accounts, and further divided the writings into the four categories of seal-labels, passes of safe conduct, criminal records, and orders. The accounts are divided into twelve categories, among them census registers, personal histories, ledger labels (the front cover of ledgers) and others. The seal-labels and ledger labels (figs. 8, 9) are most worthy of note. The seal-labels were a sort of container for posted documents. The document was sandwiched between these labels, and the gap between the front and back labels was filled in with clay, over which the sender's seal was impressed. The recipient, before opening the parcel, recorded his own seal to the lower right of the addressed party's name, and to the left or lower left, the date of receipt and the sender's name. The proper handling of posted communications at Juyan, the frontier of the country's defenses, was strictly observed, and the address, sender, carrier, and posting time were carefully noted for all communications passing between the outposts from Juyan to Zhangye. If there should be any problem afterwards, the responsible party would be clearly identifiable. Because of this, two thousand years later we are able to glimpse to some extent the organization of Han-period border defenses, their location and arrangement, and their means of support—all through these documents. The ledger labels, which served also as the covers for ledgers, as shown in figure 9, were distinguished by their cross-hatched pattern—though this of course varied depending upon the type of ledger. Most of the more than 10,000 fragments of documents (the slips have been folded in three, indicating that originally there were actually fewer samples) are bits and pieces of ledgers. These ledger labels, then, serve as a sort of table of contents for the wooden tablets. In organization of the tablets for research there is of course an absolute and basic necessity to organize the samples according to personal and place names, dates, style of writing, hand, and official titles, as well as the location where they were discovered, but grouping following the listings of the ledger labels is also an important method. In particular, organization following the ledger labels provides assistance in learning the details of the daily life of the troops, the activities in the local areas, and the places of origin of the outpost guards.

Traditionally, historical research on the Han dynasty has depended largely on the *Historical Records,* the *Han Annals,* and other collections of the sort. These materials are concerned almost entirely with the major political events, high-ranking officials, and intellectual elite of the central government, and although the importance placed on the outlying regions is widely recognized as the special feature of the Han dynasty, little was known of governmental activities in those areas, nor of the activities and duties of the lesser administrators. It was only due to the discovery of the wooden tablets that we have been able to learn the details of local governance—even though it is limited to a particular region—and the relationship between the central government and the outlying regions. One example of this new information concerns the practice by which the central government kept itself informed of the conditions in the outlying regions. Once yearly in central provinces and once every three years in outlying areas, the prefect of each region selected the most able of the administrators working under him and sent him to the capital with all tax, judicial, and other records to be examined by an authority of the central government. This "accounting to the superiors" was a major factor in deciding the careers of the governors and their underlings, who were judged on the basis of the accuracy of these records. Up until the discovery of the tablets, the form of these reports was unknown. The discovery of the various kinds of ledgers of lower administrators at Juyan, revealing the strict form and the thorough cross-checking these reports were subjected to (there are cases recorded in the tablets in which an official of the central government points out inconsistencies with reports from as far as ten years back), showed that the secret of the regional policies of the Han dynasty was to be found in this thorough record-keeping system and strict examination of these records. When it was learned that this was a beaurocracy much like today's, not only was the organization of the defense of the frontier revealed, but it was of great help in understanding the nature of the Han rule and of the age.

With the establishment of the People's Republic of China, archeological investigations were carried out at important sites in several regions. In particular, in the 1970s many wooden tablets were unearthed—this time from central China. In addition to wooden tablets, armory stations and other military facilities were unearthed and investigated, and future progress in this area can be anticipated. Though at present they are still being collated at the Gansu Museum (in Lanzhou), it has been revealed that some forty volumes of bound writings dating from Wang Mang's rule (9–23 A.D.) to the beginning of the later Han have been found in one room of an armory station. These will no doubt contribute greatly to the progress of the categorization of both the old and the new ledgers. The general methods of research used in studying the Juyan tablets up to now have been: 1) research focusing on new facts and materials found within the tablets themselves; 2) comparison of the tablets with other bound materials that have been previously known, for the purpose of correcting and supplementing the written materials; and 3) attempts to reconstruct Juyan in its Han-dynasty incarnation by combining the fragmentary tablets and slips. The discovery of these new tablets will contribute greatly to all of these goals, but it is doubtful whether the conclusions reached up to now or the reconstructed layout of Juyan will be modified in any substantial way.

Other newly discovered wooden tablets, those found within the central area of China, can be divided into books and memorials. Among the books, the *Ceremonies and Rituals (Yi Li)* consisted of 496 slips. It is arranged differently from the printed version of the text, and as a work of the Han dynasty, prior to the invention of paper, is of great import. Still, it is not a very clean manuscript and seems to be of limited use in *Ceremonies and Rituals* studies. It is interesting to note that these bamboo slips are from 55.5 to 55.6 centimeters in length, or two *chi* four *chun* by Han measure. We find several ancient citations of the Confucian classics written on slips of this size.

A military commander is entombed at Yinqiaoshan. Many works of military strategy, such as the *Sunzi* (Work of Master Sun), the *Six Stratagems* (*Liu Tao*), and the *Yu Liaozi* (Work of Master Yu Liao) have been unearthed here. The most important of these is the *Sun Bin Military Manual* (*Sun Bin Bing Shu*). This work is listed in the *Han Annals,* but was subsequently lost, and its relationship to the *Sunzi* was much debated through the years. This discovery, then, represented the appearance of a legendary work. Of the other materials, the *Qin Law Tablets* (*Qin Lü Jian*) have attracted the most attention in scholarly circles. A bailiff from Yanxian by the name of Xi, who died in the thirtieth year of the reign of the First Emperor (233 A.D.), was entombed here. The bamboo slips include a record of events of his life, and extracts from the Qin codes such as the *Eighteen Versions of the Qin Codes* (*Qin Lü Shiba Zhong*), the *Jiao Codes* (*Jiao Lü*), the *Miscellaneous Essays on the Qin Codes* (*Qin Lü Zazhao*), and other works that must have been most familiar to him during his lifetime. Since there is very little Qin-period material available to us, these represent an important find. In addition to the *Shuihudi Qinmu Zhujian* (Bamboo Tablets of the Qin Tombs at Shuihudi), which contains photographs, explanations, and commentaries on the bamboo slips, many other works of research and dissertations on the material have appeared in Japan. The Qin writings are quite different from the Han legal codes, and are rather difficult to decipher. Their definitive interpretation waits upon further research, but should the majority of the Qin legal codes be discovered, we may well find a considerable difference between the natures of the Qin and the Han dynasties.

A major category of writings are the funerary testaments, or catalogues of objects that have been buried with the deceased. The larger part of the wooden tablets unearthed from tombs in China proper belong to this category. Although they are valuable in ascertaining the type of tomb, and are valuable reference materials for archeological studies, very few of them are directly relevant as historical sources. Still, these funerary testaments and other silk writings prove valuable as evidence for the characters used in the Chu period (B.C. 740–330). Until now, Chu characters have been found mainly on bronzes, with a few samples on silk, but have not been thoroughly deciphered because of a lack of materials. For this reason, future archeological finds in the area are much anticipated.

Silk writings would be expected to be another valuable source of writing, but the perishability of silk resulted in extremely few preserved examples. Stein discovered a third-century ceremonial banner with Kharosthi writing, and immediately after World War II, the well-known sample of writing on silk was discovered in the Changsha region. There have been difficulties in deciphering this silk writing, but it is thought to be a description of twelve gods of Chu-dynasty shamanism.

At present, no new facts concerning the history of calligraphy have come to light as a result of the discovery of the new tablets. The tablets from Shuihudi in scribe script indicate that it is logical to assume that this style had come into practical use in place of the small seal script by the end of the Qin dynasty. Even though the number of samples is small, we find Jin-period tablets in block script, suggesting that the block script was first employed in the Three Kingdoms period (c. 220–c. 280). There is little to conclude beyond the tentative reaffirmation of these hypotheses.

# Qin Stone Inscriptions and Han Steles

Shi Huangdi of Qin, known as the "First Emperor" (221–209 B.C.), quashed the uprisings of the warring states and unified China, but after only a few decades of his rule, rebellion arose and his reign was ended by General Liu Bang. Liu Bang then founded the Han dynasty and made Chang'an his capital. At the start, the Han dynasty followed the policies of its predecessor, the Qin, but then it went on to victory over the Xiongnu (Huns) and proceeded to concentrate national power through Confucianist policies which resulted in the tremendous development of the nation. The emperor's throne was temporarily usurped by Wang Mang, but he was soon overthrown, and the rule of the Former Han and Later Han combined held sway over China for more than 425 years. During this time there were tremendous advances in learning and the arts, and Han culture is synonymous with the golden age of Chinese culture. It was against this glorious background that Chinese calligraphy enjoyed its first great flowering.

The unified systematization of writing took place under the Qin dynasty. The small seal style was developed and put into use, marking the first time a style of writing prescribed by the government came into general use. At the same time, the scribe script, a more abbreviated style of character than the small seal, was first developed for the lower administrators of prisons, whose activities and functions had increased. It was known in Chinese as the *li* script because its simplified characters facilitated official work with a script that could be written by "unskilled laborers," taking the character *li* from a compound of that meaning. For formal documents, the small seal script was still employed, but on ordinary occasions, this abbreviated scribe script was used.

At the time, there were eight styles of characters: large seal (*dazhuanshu*), small seal (*xiaozhuanshu*), enclosed seal script (*moyinshu*), engraving script (*kefushu*), serpent script (*chongshu*), ornamental script (*shushu*), spear script (*shushu*), and scribe script (*lishu*). Among these, those in actual use were the large and small seal and scribe scripts. The others were special variations for use in very limited circumstances. The Han dynasty inherited this practice, and while the seal styles were first adopted for use, the scribe script gradually came to be more generally accepted and the seal scripts abandoned except

Fig. 10. Taishan stone inscription (Qin dynasty).

*111*

Fig. 11. Yi Ying Stele (Han dynasty).

Fig. 12. Kong Zhou Stele (Han dynasty).

Fig. 13. Tomb Steles of the Western Peaks of Mt. Hua (Han dynasty).

for special uses. As the majority of officials came to use the scribe script for all practical purposes, the ability to write well in *li* —dubbed "official script" —was made a condition for attaining government posts. As a result, the use of the scribe script prevailed.

As silk writings and wooden tablets of the Former Han dynasty have been unearthed in recent years, an intermediary or hybrid style somewhere between seal style and scribe script has come to light. Already in this period there is evidence of the style of using the brush known as *bozhe* (breaking-wave), in which the stroke extends down and then flips to the right in a way that resembles surf breaking. Recently several splendid examples have been found, including wooden tablets and a silk sample of the *Laozi* (pl. 6), found in the early Former Han emperor's tomb at Mawang mound in Hunan. Even among the wooden tablets from the western territories, discovered long ago, there are samples of very clear breaking-wave strokes in chronologies of the Former Han. This stroke is a product of the formalization of the small blot at the end of a stroke and was born from part of the natural process of writing with a brush.

During the time of Wang Mang, the eight styles of the Qin were reduced to six but were substantially unchanged. The prevailing styles are well known to us due to the stone carvings that exist to this day. Carving words in stone is an attempt to create a lasting work and impress one's name upon the pages of history. This practice had its beginning in the Zhou dynasty, and we have the examples of the Taishan stone memorial (fig. 10) and the Langye terrace stone memorial by the First Emperor of the Qin. Examples of stone carvings from the Former Han employing seal and scribe characters with almost no other decoration still exist. The stone carving at the Lu Lingguang palace remains (149 B.C.), the Qunchen Shangchou stone carving (131 B.C.), and the Lu Xiaowang carving (56 B.C.) show an older style in which the evolution of the seal and scribe scripts is not yet complete—but these are not as valuable as the tablets and silk writings mentioned above.

From the time of Wang Mang and the beginning of the Later Han, a standard form for stone carvings appears, and it is at this time that the finest examples of Han scribe characters develop. There are thought to be two basic sources for these stone memorial steles. One likely source is the pillars that supported the sacrifice in the ancient court rituals of worshipping at the ancestral mausoleums. This serves to explain the pointed heads of this type of memorial—the point was meant to hold the sacrifice. The other source is said to be the four pillars that were set at the corners of an emperor's grave. Ropes connected these pillars to the coffin, to permit lowering the emperor's casket into the grave. This is thought to be the origin of those early stone steles that had rounded heads. A curved groove is found near the rounded top of this type of stele. This was called the *yun*, or "halo," and was for attaching the rope. As a rule, examples from the early period have a hole in the center called the *chuan* through which the rope was threaded. The *yun* is a vestige of this. From the original pointed and rounded tablets, a style of stele with three sections—the *chishou* (hornless dragon ornament), the *guifu* (tortise base), and the main section of the stele—developed, with a stele cap at the top of the main section. Most frequently the title of the stele was inscribed here in seal characters, leading to the alternate name of "seal cap" for this part. With this development, the standard form for stone steles had been arrived at.

The stone steles reached their peak during the reigns of Emperors Huan and Ling of the Later Han, when *feng bei*, "steles praising the virtues," were erected in the hundreds. "Standing steles" (*li bei*) was the name to describe the memorial steles installed at family graves as a show of Confucian filial piety, but among them we also find steles raised for special occasions or praising the other Confucian virtues. Most of these inscriptions were composed by well-known historical personages and written by great calligraphers, but it was not the custom of the time to record the name of either the author or the calligrapher, though a few signed steles have come down to us. The examples from the peak period of stone steles are all excellent in composition and execution, and were obviously constructed with the greatest skill and care. With the spirit of Confucian discipline, each character is painstakingly executed with great and unfaltering dignity. In this respect they are far superior to the ink-written characters that have been unearthed from this period. More than one hundred of these steles still exist. Among them are the "Yi Ying Stele" (*Yi Ying Bei*, c. 153, fig. 11), the "*Liqi* Stele at Confucius' Tomb" (*Kongzi Liqi Bei*, c. 156, pl. 9), the "Zhang Jing Stele" (*Zhang Jing Bei*, c. 159, unearthed in 1958, fig. 18), the "Kong Zhou Stele" (*Kong Zhou Bei*, c. 164, fig. 12), the "Tomb Steles of the Western Peaks of Mt. Hua" (165, fig. 13), the "Shichen Steles" (*Shichen Qian Hou Bei*, c. 168, 169, fig. 13), the "Xiping Stone Classic" (*Xiping Shi Jing*, c. 175, fig. 15), the "Cao Quan Memorial Stele" (*Cao Quan Bei*, c. 185, pl. 10), and the "Zhang Qian Memorial Stele" (*Zhang Qian Bei*, c. 186, pl. 11). The most admired of these from ancient times has been the "*Liqi* Stele." Wang Zhu of the Qing dynasty presented a detailed discussion of this piece, claiming to find five sections and eight distinct styles of writing in this stele. These characters are superior in both cohesion and execution, and the forceful and inspired carving is a masterpiece among the Han steles.

The form of mature Han scribe script is known as *bafen*, so named because the strokes resemble the strokes in the character *ba* (八, eight). The original form of the *bafen* style is to be found in the "Tomb Steles of the Western Peaks of Mt. Hua" and the "Shichen Steles." The "Xiping Stone Classic," which was inscribed with a Confucian text and stood in the courtyard of an academy, is said to have sections done by the calligrapher Cai Yong. As its role as calligraphy commissioned to embody proper order to the Confucian scholars of the world suggests, it is a little stiff and stultified, though it was to become a model for the *bafen* calligraphy in scribe-script Han works. In the "Cao Quan Stele," expertise in the *bafen* style is more evident, and a certain grace comes through. This tablet, together with the "*Liqi* Stele," is representative of the masterpieces of Han steles.

In addition to the Han steles, characters chiseled into stone cliffs and large boulders also deserve our attention. This practice was called *moyai*, or "cliff-smoothing." Exposed to the elements, these works contrast sharply with the formal stele inscriptions. In order to bring to life this rough natural material, characters were generally increased boldly in size, and displayed a rough simplicity and freedom that was of a different order from the well-ordered steles. Examples of these boulder and cliff inscriptions include the "Stone Inscription Commemorating the Opening of the Baoxie Road" (*Kaitong Baoxiedao Keshi*, c. 66, fig. 16) and the "Stone Gate Verses" (*Shimen Song*, c. 148, fig. 17). Both of these, in their respective environments, are works of power and scale.

Though the orthodox calligraphy of the Han period is to be found in the steles, we must not forget that it was during this time that cursive script was first recognized as a form of calligraphy. Cursive script originated as an abbreviated yet legitimate style for drafts and manuscripts. Previously, during the period in which seal script was used, a cursive-seal hybrid that was an abbreviated form of the seal script existed. With the invention of scribe script in the Han dynasty, an abbreviated form of it called "mixed" scribe script developed. Both of these were abbreviated rather than officially recognized forms, and their use was restricted mainly to practical tasks such

Fig. 14. Shichen Stele (Han dynasty).

Fig. 15. Xiping Stone Classic (Han dynasty).

Fig. 16. Inscription Commemorating the Opening of the Baoxie Road (Han dynasty).

Fig. 17. Stone Gate Verses (Han dynasty).

Fig. 18. Zhang Jing Stele (Han dynasty).

Fig. 19. Stele Recording the Virtues of Pei Cen (Han dynasty).

as record-keeping and correspondence. The earliest cursive characters are known as old cursive. This evolved into full-fledged cursive characters, with their quick brushwork and frequent use of the breaking-wave (*bozhe*) stroke. This script was called *zhang cao*, or "essay cursive." Influenced by scribe script, cursive characters incorporated the breaking-wave stroke and became essay cursive. There is a connection between the breaking-wave stroke in the wooden tablets still in existence today and the essay cursive characters. The name *zhang cao* is a later, Han-dynasty apellation, referring to a type of script used in special essays presented to the court. Toward the end of the Han dynasty, as cursive script became widely used, the calligrapher Zhang Zhi took an interest in and revitalized it. Originally invented for writing quickly in an abbreviated fashion, cursive evolved into a beautiful form of calligraphy. For the first time, a script was created for the purpose of the leisurely enjoyment of the art of writing, thus leading to the later maturation of calligraphy as an art. For this reason, the cursive script of the Han dynasty is of major importance. It also posseses its own unique beauty.

We have many samples of Han-dynasty calligraphy. Characters can be found on mirrors, ceramics, lacquerwork, roof tiles, roof-tile ornaments, and other objects. Among these objects, seals have perhaps the highest artistic value and deserve the most attention as calligraphy. In contrast to the "old seals" of the Zhou and Qin dynasties, these are known as Han seals, a label that broadly encompasses seals from the Wei and Jin dynasties, too. A distinction is made between official and private seals. The official seals were engraved with the official's title, and were presented to him upon his appointment. Attached to a ribbon, these were always worn as a sort of identification, and were stamped on all documents. After retirement, this seal was to be returned. The personal seal was inscribed with the family name. In addition, there were pictographic seals and seals inscribed with felicitous words. Strict regulations regarding official seals—their style, the shape and material of the seal, its inscription and the sort of ribbon with which it was worn—were promulgated, with strict distinctions according to official ranks. The characters of the seals were known as "bent seal" characters, because in order to fit the lesser seal characters onto the surface of the seal, they had to be bent and reduced in size. Here another aesthetic realm was opened, and as the ancestors of the later seal inscriptions, we will examine the Han seals later at length.

## The Calligraphy of Zhong Yao

From the Later Han to the Wei, the old seal and scribe scripts evolved into the block, semi-cursive, and cursive scripts. Zhong Yao played an important part in this transition. He was a master of the three ancient styles of calligraphy: *mingshi* script, *zhangcheng* script, and *xingxia* script. These styles corresponded to the *bafen* script used in stele inscriptions, the scribe script used in documents, and the semi-cursive script used in personal correspondence. We have several works reputed to be his, such as the "Xuanshi Memorial" (*Xuanshi Biao*, fig. 21), but they are probably copies by Wang Xizhi. Though from the Song dynasty they have been regarded as the work of Zhong, we cannot accept them as such. It is far better to try to identify his works through their resemblance to his stone inscriptions that have been preserved. The "Memorial Awarding an Honorary Name to Gong Qing" (*Gong Qing Shang Zunhao Zou,* fig. 20) and the "Imperial Accession Memorial" (*Shouchan Biao*) are also thought to be Zhong's works. Though we cannot be absolutely certain of these, we do know that his works must have resembled these. When we consider how reverenced Zhong's writings were in the Jin and Song dynasties, we can see that the *bafen* style, with its forceful beginnings and endings of strokes, might have been influenced by Zhong's style. The block-script calligraphy dating from the removal of the Northern Wei capital to Luoyang, the epitaphs of the sixth century, and in more finished form, works such as the "Epitaph for Sima Bing" (*Sima Bing Muzhi*) must have followed in the style of Zhong's works.

Fig. 20. Memorial Awarding an Honorary Name to Gong Qing (Wei dynasty).

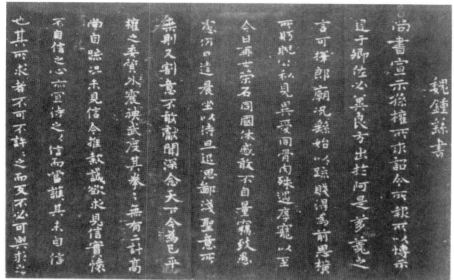

Fig. 21. Xuanshi Memorial, Zhong Yao (Wei dynasty).

# The Masterpieces of Wang Xizhi and Wang Xianzhi

Under attack from the northern tribes, the Jin dynasty was defeated by the Han (later the Zhao) in 316 B.C., and was temporarily eliminated, but just two years later Sima Rui, a member of one of the clans of the Jin, gained control of Jiangnan and ascended to the throne. Thus the Jin was revived, and its capital established at Jiankang. With the establishment of the capital, many of the nobility moved to the Jiangnan region, where they later established their hold on the reins of power. With the cooperation of the local wealthy families in the picturesque and beautiful land south of the Jiang river, they produced a magnificant culture. In addition to having a firm hold on power, the aristocrats who settled in the Jiangnan region possessed large estates and lived luxurious lives. The region known as Dongshan in Huiji had a concentration of these aristocratic estates, and the local nobility passed their days in all sorts of elegant entertainments. The Jiangnan area was known for its magnificent scenery, and it is somehow appropriate that the art of calligraphy should have developed so in this region. Here the aristocrats were able to refine their tastes, and, in their rivalry, the art of calligraphy attained an outstanding degree of maturity. Patronage of and excellence in the arts was also spurred on by the desire to confirm the superiority of Jin civilization in the face of the native gentry. After the founding of the capital, a period of stability and peace commenced, and within the aristocratic society calligraphy flourished. There were many within this group who were excellent calligraphers, but perhaps the greatest number of masterpieces must be counted among the works of Wang Xizhi and his son, Wang Xianzhi.

Wang Xizhi (303?–61?) was from Langye, Linyi. His father, Wang Kuang, was the cousin of Wang Dao, who was the Prime Minister during the flight of the Eastern Jin to the south; as advocates of the move, both were praised. Wang Xizhi, then, was from one of the leading families of the Eastern Jin aristocracy and from his childhood was nurtured and pampered as the heir of the Wang family, with great prospects for the future. He was appointed to the office of General of the Right, and was governor of Huiji, and as a result is usually known as General Wang. He is said to have begun his study of calligraphy at the age of sixteen under the tutelage

Fig. 22. Yue Yi Treatise, Wang Xizhi (Eastern Jin dynasty).

Fig. 23. Imperial Court Classic, Wang Xizhi (Eastern Jin dynasty).

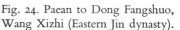

Fig. 24. Paean to Dong Fangshuo, Wang Xizhi (Eastern Jin dynasty).

Fig. 25. Orchid Pavilion Preface, Wang Xizhi (Eastern Jin dynasty).

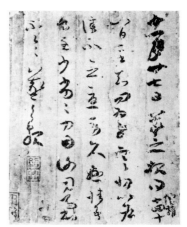

Fig. 26. Album, Wang Xizhi (Eastern Jin dynasty).

Fig. 27. Album, Wang Xizhi (Eastern Jin dynasty).

of a relative named Wang Yi. There were said to be other calligraphers whose work surpassed his youthful efforts, but in his later years, as Censor of Huiji, his calligraphy reached the highest stage of accomplishment. When looking at his work, we must keep in mind the path of development of calligraphy prior to the Wei and the Eastern Jin. He was praised by the critics of his time as the successor to Zhang Zhi of the Han and Zhong Yao of the Wei. His work rests on the foundation of accumulated calligraphic pieces from the Han and Wei. The fact that Wang is said to have often studied the works of Zhong Yao is further proof of this. The story of Prime Minister Wang Dao, who tucked Zhono Yao's work, the "Xuanshi Memorial," into his bosom as he fled south illustrates this continuity. For this reason Wang's calligraphy received such a positive reception among the southern aristocrats, was appreciated by many, and even taken as a model by some contemporaries.

One of the reasons for Wang's reputation as a skillful calligrapher was his ability to write well in each calligraphic form—*bafen*, scribe script, semi-cursive, essay cursive, and the ornamental "flying white" script, (*feibo*), written with large white spaces as if there were not enough ink on the brush. However, the samples of his work that have survived consist largely of a transitional, late scribe script very close to block script, and semi-cursive script, with a very few examples of essay cursive. The "Yue Yi Treatise" (*Yue Yi Lun,* fig. 22), the "Imperial Court Classic" (*Huang Ting Jing,* fig. 23), and the "Paean to Dong Fangshuo" (*Dong Fangshuo Huazan,* fig. 24) do exist in small block script, but these are printed versions from copybooks and are far removed from the originals. The foremost semi-cursive work is his "Orchid Pavilion Preface" (fig. 25), but the original is said to have been entombed with Emperor Taizong of the Tang at Zhaoling, and the present work is a Tang copy or perhaps the copybook of a famous calligrapher. It is impossible to ascertain its original appearance.

Samples of semi-cursive and cursive script (figs. 26, 27) exist in the form

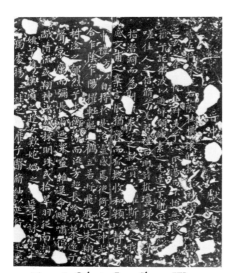

Fig. 28. Ode to Luo Shen, Wang Xianzhi (Eastern Jin dynasty).

Fig. 29. Album, Wang Xian-zhi (Eastern Jin dynasty).

of epistles in those styles or a mix of the two, the reason being that epistles were a much admired form of literature from the Han period on. Since the beauty of calligraphy is most convincingly represented by the semi-cursive and cursive scripts, epistles came to be regarded as very important examples of the calligraphic art. The epistles of Wang have been transmitted to us through various copying techniques and a special method known as *tamo*, a type of ink rubbing. The "Sang Luan Album" (*Sang Luan Tie,* pl. 16) and the "Kong Shizhong Album" (*Kong Shizhong Tie,* pl. 17) are the best of these *tamo* reproductions, followed closely by the "Feng Ju Album" (*Feng Ju Tie,* pl. 18). [It is a common practice to select as a title characters from the opening lines of a calligraphic work. They serve only to identify the work, and are usually untranslatable.—Ed.] Most of the rest of the examples are not of this quality. In contrast to samples written in ink, more than half of Wang's epistles have been handed down in the form of rubbings. One of the oldest of these is the "Shiqi Album" (*Shiqi Tie,* pl. 19). Most of Wang's epistles are included in the Song-dynasty "Chunhua Pavilion Copybook," but genuine works and forgeries are intermingled there, and it is very likely that the forms of the originals transmitted in these copybooks are imperfect. The beauty of Wang's calligraphy is best seen in the "Sang Luan Album" and the "Kong Shizhong Album." Here we find the sophisticated grace of the aristocrats of the Eastern Jin. He has been able to capture a quiet, extremely elegant and refined spirit, with the luminescence of the incorporeal form of a Taoist fairy.

Wang Xizhi had seven children, and among them it was his seventh son, Wang Xianzhi, who, following after his father, excelled in calligraphy. Together they are known as the two Wangs. Wang Xianzhi, too, left us a small-block–script rendition of the "Ode to Luo Shen" (*Luo Shen Fu,* fig. 28) and epistles in semi-cursive and cursive scripts (fig. 29). The epistles are rubbings which appear in collections of rubbings and printed copybooks, and the greater part of them are included in the "Chunhua Pavilion Copybook." His calligraphy is to be especially noted for its cursive script, which is superior even to Wang Xizhi's in spirit and charm. We have no work of Xianzhi's comparable in authenticity to Xizhi's "Sang Luan Album," but of the works that exist in Japan, the "Di Huang Tang Epistle" (*Di Huang Tang Tie,* pl. 20) is the best and the closest to an original. The title, again, derives from three characters in the first line.

The entire Wang family excelled at calligraphy, but all others were eclipsed by the two Wangs, and very few of their writings have come down to us. In addition to the Wang family, famous calligraphers were to be found in the Xie, Yu, Chi, and other families, but the works of most have not survived. Only those examples in the "Chunhua Pavilion Copybook" are available to us, and there are many doubts about the authenticity of even these.

At the southern court the writings of the Wangs were collected and studied. In particular, the gentry of the Song, Qi, and Liang dynasties appreciated the works of Wang Xianzhi. The "Wansuitongtian Era Album" (*Wansuitongtian Jin Tie*) handed down by the descendants of the Wang family in the Tang dynasty contains only a few examples of the calligraphy of these descendants—almost none survived. The "Thousand-Character Essay in Block and Cursive Scripts" (pl. 31), by Wang Xizhi's seventh-generation descendant Zhiyong, has been transmitted to Japan in its original form, and in it we can find a single example of Xizhi's calligraphic work handed down within the Wang family.

# Stone Inscriptions of the Six Dynasties

The Six Dynasties period can be broadly defined as the 350 years from the fall of the Han in the first half of the third century to the unification of China under the Sui in the latter half of the sixth. After the fall of the Later Han, Cao Cao founded the Wei in the north, Sun Quan the Wu in the south, and Liu Bei the Shu in the west, with their respective capitals at Luoyang, Jianye and Chengdu. This was the Three Kingdoms period. In Wei, the Prime Minister Sima Yan held power, and his son Zhao attacked and conquered Shu. Following this, Zhao's son Yan established the Jin dynasty. This occurred in the latter half of the third century. Afterwards, Yan defeated the Wu and unified China, but in only two generations, during the reign of Emperor Huai (307–13), northern tribes had occupied Luoyang and Chang'an, and the Jin fled to the Jiangnan region, where they regrouped at Jiankang. This was the famous revolt of the Yongjia era. The Jin state prior to this is known as the Western Jin and after this the Eastern Jin. General Liu Yu of the Eastern Jin founded the kingdom of Song in the first half of the fifth century. A succession of states rose and fell from this time on—the Qi in the latter half of the fifth century, the Liang in the first half of the sixth century, and the Chen in the mid-sixth century. These are called the southern kingdoms, and the six kingdoms from Wu on which made Jiangye their capital are called the Six Dynasties.

While the Eastern Jin was centered in Jiangnan, five different nomad peoples, the Xiongnu, the Jie, the Xianbei, the Pi, and the Qiang, established sixteen independent kingdoms in the north. Until Tuoba Gui, a member of the Tuoba subgroup of the Xianbei tribe, founded the Northern Wei in the fourth century and unified the north, these different kingdoms rose and fell. The general apellation for all of those kingdoms is the Five Tribes and the Sixteen Kingdoms. In the first half of the sixth century, the Great Minister of the Northern Wei, Gao Huan, struggled for control of the kingdom with Yuwen Tai, and each presented a candidate for emperor, splitting the kingdom into the Eastern Wei and Western Wei. Gao Yang, the son of Huan, later founded the Northern Qi, while Tai's son, Jue, founded the Northern Zhou. The period of the various northern kingdoms from the time of the Northern Wei, together with the southern kingdoms, is called the Northern and Southern Dynasties period. This division of north and south was later unified by the Sui dynasty.

## Stone Inscriptions

Stone inscriptions of the Six Dynasties period are found on steles, epitaphs, monuments, and precipices. Steles were built in great numbers in the Later Han dynasty, inscribed with the biographies of their subjects and set on graves. Others, describing glorious deeds, were set up in mortuary temples. Due to the economic misfortunes of the empire under the Wei, the construction of stone mausoleums, statues, and steles was prohibited, and a sharp decrease in their numbers resulted. In their place, epitaphs became more popular. Recently, many epitaphs from the northern dynasties have been unearthed—enough, in fact, to permit counting them year by year. These are very important in the study of the calligraphy of the northern dynasties.

Monument inscriptions tell of the origin and reason for commissioning the Buddhist statues or other monuments they are found with and are thought to have first appeared around the fourth century, when the carving of Buddhist statues became so popular in the Western Jin. The most famous of these are to be found in the Longmen caves. The first examples were constructed upon the occasion of the removal of the capital to Luoyang by the emperor of the Northern Wei, Xiaowen. The first caves were located at Yique Longmen, in close proximity to the new capital, and excavation on other caves continued at this site over a period of years. The calligraphy of the "Duke Shiping Monument Inscription" (*Shiping Gong Zaoxiang Ji*, pl. 23) is representative of these inscriptions. There are many other important works, collectively referred to as the twenty works or the fifty works. When all the samples of writing are assembled, they amount to a tremendous volume and are a real treasure trove of calligraphic materials from the Six Dynasties period up to the Tang.

The carving of inscriptions on precipices was already practiced in the Later Han. Cliff surfaces were polished and a large area for the inscription prepared. The distinct feature of this style of writing is the directness of the large characters, freed from the constrictions of more standard forms. During the northern dynasties, many such works in various categories, such as Confucian mottos praising virtuous rule, signatures, poems, and Buddhist sutras, were inscribed on natural rock surfaces. The most famous of these are the works of Zheng Daozhao and his son Shuzu, members of the Han aristocracy during the reign of Emperor Xiaowen of the Northern Wei. The "Zheng Xi Stele" (fig. 30), dedicated to Daozhao's father Xi, survives at Yungfenshan, together with the "Confucian Didactic Verses" (*Lunjingshu Shi*, pl. 24), and others.

During the mid-Qing dynasty, Ruan Yuan composed the *Treatise on the Northern Steles and Southern Copybooks* (*Beibei Nantie Lun*) and the *Treatise on the Northern and Southern Schools of Calligraphy* (*Nanbei Shupa Lun*), and declared that the northern-dynasty steles were the more orthodox, devaluing the southern albums. Later, the same viewpoint was emphasized by Bao Shichen and Kang Youwei, and this greater attention paid to the northern steles led to a greater interest among calligraphers in these examples. It is certainly true that the Six Dynasties-period samples of calligraphy that have come down to us in copybooks were all copies from after the Song period, and any number of copies, tracings, and replications stand between the original and their present forms—which may themselves have been less than genuine. From the point of view of the history of calligraphy, these

Fig. 30. Lower Zheng Xi Stele, Zheng Daozhao (Northern Wei dynasty).

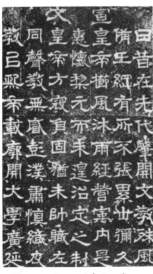

Fig. 31. Imperial Academy Stele (Jin dynasty).

works present a number of problems. Because of this, nothing can surpass the stone inscriptions, which permit us to learn of the calligraphy of a period from which no other authentic originals survive. The steles and epitaphs, in particular, were compositions of renowned men of letters, since for the most part they were commissioned to commemorate men of distinction. Carved with precision in fine-grained stone, they accurately reproduce the original form of the characters, and as such are as valuable as any ink-written specimens.

## The Evolution of Writing Styles in Stone Inscriptions

At present, most examples of stone inscriptions are to be found in the Luoyang and Jianye (Nanqing) areas, as well as Shandong. Luoyang was the capital of the Later Han, Wei, and Western Jin dynasties. It was abandoned during the confusion of the Five Tribes and Sixteen Kingdoms period, but after the unification of the north, the capital moved back to the south from the reign of Emperor Xiaowen, and Luoyang was to be one of the cultural centers of the Six Dynasties period. Jianye was first established as the capital of the Wu state during the Three Kingdoms period. Afterwards, it remained the cultural center of the south through the Eastern Jin, Song, Qi, Chen, and Liang dynasties. Shandong is interesting from the viewpoint of the history of calligraphy as a place where the calligraphy of both north and south has been preserved in harmony, but for the present we will limit our discussion to the evolution of styles in the calligraphy of Luoyang and Jianye.

Almost all of the steles and epitaphs from the Luoyang area of the Wei and Western Jin states are in the *bafen* style, demonstrating that at this time the traditions of the Han continued and the *bafen* style of the earlier period remained the official style of the time. The distinctive trait of the *bafen* style is the force of the beginning and ending of the strokes and the sharp ending of the long, downward strokes. Many fine examples of this from the Later Han can be seen. However, towards the end of that period, this force diminishes and changes to a more flowing beauty, as in the "Memorial Stele of Cao Quan, Magistrate of Geyang" (*Geyang Ling Cao Quan Bei,* pl. 10). The steles of the early Wei dynasty are represented by the "Memorial Awarding an Honorary Title to Lord Gong" and the "Imperial Accession Memorial." Both of these are important steles relating to the founding of the state and must have been written by famous calligraphers of the period. Both are forceful and dynamic compositions that are clearly influenced by the style of the Later Han works. The *bafen* calligraphy visible in such Western Jin works as the "Imperial Academy Stele" (*Huangdi Sanlin Biyong Bei,* fig. 31) and the "Epitaph for Zuo Fen" (*Zuo Fen Muzhi*) emphasizes a heavy stroke, with considerable strength put into the brush at the start and finish of the stroke. This is not the general strength and vigor to be seen in all of the Later Han works, but an additional emphasis on just those parts, designed to bring out the special features of the characters. Examples such as this are evident as early as the "The Tomb Monument of Dong Wuhou Wang" (*Dong Wuhou Wang Jibei,* fig. 32) from the Wei period, and this style spanned the later Wei and Western Jin dynasties in Luoyang. After the 150–year interruption in the history of calligraphy in the Five Tribes and Sixteen Kingdoms periods, most of the grave inscriptions of the Northern Wei, from the "Zhang Meng Long Stele" (*Zhang Meng Long Bei,* fig. 33) and the "Gao Zhen Stele" (*Gao Zhen Bei,* pl. 21) through the "Epitaph for Yuan Zhen" inscription (*Yuan Zhen Muzhi*) and the many other Northern Wei Yuan-family tombs are written in an

Fig. 32. Dong Wuhou Wang Stele (Wei dynasty).

Fig. 33. Zhang Meng Long Stele (Northern Wei dynasty).

Fig. 34. Yuan Clan Epitaph (Northern Wei dynasty).

Fig. 35. Wang Xingzhi Epitaph (Eastern Jin dynasty).

Fig. 36. Stele for Gu Liang, Prefect of Jiuzhen (Wu dynasty).

already systematized form of block-style characters. The transition from *bafen* to block script is an important one. It may have resulted in part from Emperor Xiaowen's policy of sinicization, or from the general evolution of calligraphy—we cannot be precisely sure. The block-style script of Luoyang exhibits strong beginnings and endings of strokes and, in its earliest period, a strength and an excellence that marks it as a special product of the northern kingdoms. Not from the standpoint of the form of the characters, but from the style, we can see it was produced in the period when the *bafen* calligraphy of the Western Jin was moving in the direction of block script. This style can be seen even in the relatively early samples of calligraphy, the Longman cave sculpture inscriptions. The rough simplicity of the monument inscriptions opened up new possibilities for calligraphy. Together with the grandeur of the cliff inscriptions of Zheng Daozhao in Shandong, this can be regarded as a distinctive feature of Northern Wei calligraphy. Later, in the last years of the Northern Wei, in such works as the "Epitaph for Wang, Wife of Yuan Yang" (*Yuan Yang Qi Wangshi Muzhi,* fig. 34), we can see a gradual diminishing of forcefulness, as the block script takes on a gentler grace. This is no doubt due to the influence of Wang Xizhi and the southern-court style on the northern calligraphers.

Compared to Luoyang, the number of surviving steles and epitaphs at Jiangye is smaller. Not enough evidence to document changes in styles is to be had—in fact, we are limited to the Liang dynasty (502–56) imperial tomb steles. The recently excavated epitaphs of the Wang family, such as the "Epitaph of Wang Xingzhi" (*Wang Xingzhi Muzhi,* fig. 35), are of help here. They are all written in scribe script, lack the unique *bafen* techniques of beginning and ending strokes, and show little variation in thickness. A short distance from Jiangye, in the state of Wu, that feature is obvious in such works as the "Prefect Jiu Zhen Gulang Stele" (*Jiu Zhen Taishou Gulang Bei,* fig. 36) and the "Epitaph for Liu Ke" (*Liu Ke Muzhi*). The fact that the epitaph of the Wang family was written in scribe script in spite of the fact that Wang Xizhi was a master of block script indicates that the scribe script was still the official script of the time; its special feature was an absence of variations in stroke width. The Wu-period "Divine Omen Stele" (*Tianfa Shenchen Bei,* pl. 12), distincitively written in a scribe-style script, can be understood as an attempt to create an even more striking impression within this tradition.

# Buddhist Manuscripts

The art of printing developed in China from the second half of the tenth century. Before printed books spread throughout China, it was the custom to use scrolls that had been copied by hand. The early Buddhist scriptures also took this form. Mahayana Buddhism promised benefits and blessings for infinite lives to come to those who made copies of its scriptures. This created considerable interest in manuscript copying among a broad class of people and was very effective in encouraging the spread of Buddhism. From the Three Kingdoms period far on into the future, the copying of scriptures took place on a large scale wherever Buddhism permeated. The surviving copies of Buddhist sutras dating up to the Song dynasty, when printing was invented, are referred to as "old sutra copies."

Most of these ancient copies are written in ink on hemp paper, mulberry paper, or rice paper, but copies on dyed paper written with gold dust, illustrated manuscripts, copies written in ink mixed with human blood, and stone inscriptions of sutras are also to be found.

Fig. 37. Da Lou Tan Jing (Tang dynasty).

Surviving ancient sutra copies were until recently limited to but a few examples—those brought to Japan. Most are Sui- and Tang-dynasty sutras, now located in the Shōsō-in Treasure House in Nara. The *Pusa Chutai Jing* (pl. 30), dated 550, and the *Da Lou Tan Jing* (fig. 37), dated 673, are in the Chion-in in Kyoto. However, several expeditions by Westerners in the late nineteenth and early twentieth centuries unearthed a great quantity of scriptures from the western border regions of China. Most of these several thousand rolls were discovered in cave no. 17 at Dunhuang. With this great find of scriptures, research concerning and appreciation of ancient Chinese Buddhist manuscripts suddenly increased tremendously.

These Buddhist manuscripts are original works of the period, with no adulterations or tampering by later copyists. Thus, the discovery of a large number of these manuscripts permits us to view the process of evolution of calligraphic styles over a long period and in considerable detail. They play a truly valuable role in the history of Chinese calligraphy as both works of art and historical documents. Nor can we fail to pay tribute to them as valuable materials in Buddhist studies.

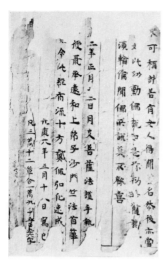

Fig. 38. Zhufo Yaoji Jing (Jin dynasty).

Fig. 39. Foshuo Huan Pujian Jing (Qi dynasty).

Fig. 40. Daban Niepan Jing, Volume 11 (Liang dynasty).

The typical process of making a Buddhist manuscript began with gluing together the necessary lengths of paper and preparing a roll. This paper might or might not be marked with columns. Those with columns were of two kinds: sutras with seventeen regular, even, small-block characters per line, and those with a variable number of columns and characters per column. The characters of the second type of manuscript were written in a functional block, semi-cursive, or even cursive script. The first format is frequently seen in sutras and *sastras* (philosophical discourses), while the latter was employed in commentarial literature. Many Buddhist manuscripts close with a dedication or postscript stating the reason the sutra was copied. The main types of manuscript copies are "sutras of offering," which are copied as offerings to ancestors or parents; "sutras of dedication," which are dedicated to the peace of the nation, its rulers, and all sentient beings; "library sutras," copied by those who wish to provide faithful and carefully edited versions of the scriptures to temple libraries; and "devotional sutras," copied as a part of the person's religious practice.

Buddhist manuscripts were copied by everyone from the highest levels of society, such as the emperor and his retainers, to the common people. Many of the attached postscripts include a date, though these must be studied with care, for sometimes the postscripts are appended long after the sutras were originally copied or even intentionally ante-dated to make the sutras look older and increase the antique value and prestige of the work. Because of this, erroneous attributions have arisen when the dates in postscripts were accepted uncritically. The Stein manuscripts in the British Museum and the Pelliot collection in the Bibliothèque Nationale in Paris as well as the manuscripts in the private libraries of collectors and antiquarians have all undergone rigorous scrutiny and are dependable research materials. Focusing on the scriptural passages of these manuscripts, we can determine the calligraphic standards of different periods as manifested in the manuscripts and use these conclusions to place other, undated works within this continuum.

Of course, Buddhist manuscripts were copied for a variety of reasons, in many different environments, and by copyists with a wide range of skill and sincerity of purpose. Not all of them have been done with care. When looking at them as calligraphy, we must also consider that most of these manuscripts were unearthed in the western border regions. During the eighteenth and early nineteenth centuries, calligraphic studies were carried out relying on stone inscriptions and copybook albums. The mass of Buddhist manuscripts brought the early history of calligraphy out into the light of day and supplemented the evidence of the inscriptions and rubbings, as well as providing the opportunity for their correction against original manuscripts. Today, Buddhist manuscripts are regularly used as research materials in the study of Chinese calligraphy along with the inscriptions and copybook rubbings.

The copying of Buddhist manuscripts is part and parcel of the specific religious character of Buddhism. Buddhist scriptures differ from secular works in the manner of expression, the spirit of the work, and the techniques used. The standard form of a sutra, with the scriptural passages in Buddhist manuscript style and an attached postscript, was recognized as an established format in the Northern and Southern Dynasties period. Let us examine the manuscripts with authenticated inscriptions and, based on those dating from this period, identify then-current trends in calligraphy. At present, we can identify twelve works from the southern court and ninety-two from the northern dynasties. Perhaps no definitive conclusions are possible from this number of works, but no other likely method of research presents itself.

The northern and southern dynasties span a roughly 150-year period from

439 to 589. The southern dynasty actually lasted nineteen years longer, continuing south of the Hua River, with Jiankang as its capital. The northern dynasties, in contrast, rose and fell in a succession of states north of the Hua. In these historical conditions, the aristocrats of the capital of the southern dynasty claimed exclusive possession of traditional Chinese culture. Calligraphy, too, was one of their pastimes, and the works of the two Wangs were especially revered, dominating the currents of fashion and contributing to the creation of an intensely refined and graceful style. Occasionally someone transferred to the distant provinces would take an interest in the ancient scribe-script techniques, but on the whole these had little influence on the calligraphic styles of the southern dynasty. Nevertheless, among the sutra copies there are some examples which share features of the older style of brushwork, as for example the *"Vinaya Preface, Volume One"* (*Lü Xu Juan Shang*, pl. 28), copied in 523.

Upright steles were strictly prohibited in the southern dynasty, and, as a result, there are very few remaining inscriptions in metal or stone. As for copybooks transmitting the writings of the calligraphers of the southern dynasty, none were compiled until 990, and even these were not much more than catalogues of manuscripts. By that time, there had been so many alterations that the reliability of these albums is much in doubt. There are so few surviving samples of calligraphy of the southern dynasty that even a few rolls of sutra copies are a great help in supplementing this insufficiency. Viewing the sutra copies of the southern dynasties, it is clear that the culture reached its peak during the Qi and Liang dynasties, and the art of calligraphy, too, exhibited a new maturity, reaching an apogee of refined elegance and grace. A considerable number of fairly complex techniques had likewise evolved, and these special features of southern-dynasties calligraphy are all visible in the sutra copies. A soft, rounded brush appears to have been used in making these manuscript copies.

The northern dynasties were ruled by non-Chinese peoples, in contrast to the south, which was governed by a Han Chinese gentry. A succession of northern states rose and fell, following each other in a complicated progression. When the Han aristocracy evacuated to the south and left the governance of the north to the "barbarians," they took with them the elegant classical culture they had created during their rule north of the Hua. As a result, the culture of the northern dynasties was of a much lower level, hardly comparable to the dregs of Han culture. In fact, in many ways its rise signaled a disruption in the transmission of the older culture that had dominated prior to the north-south split. Nevertheless, a much richer store of calligraphic works survives from the northern dynasties. Worthy of special note are the many works discovered from the second half of the eighteenth century onward. Toward the end of the Qing dynasty, the calligraphy of the northern dynasties was highly esteemed, partly as a byproduct of the great popularity of studies of stone and metal monuments.

The first of the northern dynasties, the Northern Wei, endured longer than any of the others and imparted a very special character to developments in calligraphy. Up to the end of the fifth century, a rough and embryonic style derived from scribe script predominated and can be found even in sutra copies. However, at the beginning of the sixth century, calligraphy received a new stimulus from the south, and writing styles exhibit a change. Consistent with the conscious efforts of the government to sinicize the north, an effort was made to import the refined southern style of calligraphy and have it take root among the northern aristocrats. The natural spirituality and considerable sophistication of technique of the "Zhang Meng Long Stele" and the "Gao Zhen Stele", dating from 520 to 525, is also paralleled in the sutra copies of the period. Among these, one

Fig. 41. Foshuo Pusa Cang Jing, Volume 1 (Northern Wei dynasty).

Fig. 42. Dazhidulun Jing, Volume 85 (Sui dynasty).

Fig. 43. Ceng Jia Zha Jing (Sui dynasty).

Fig. 44. Miaofa Lienhua Jing,
Volume 2 (Tang dynasty).

group of sutra copies regarded as completed from 512 to 515 by a copyist at Dunhuang exhibits a unique brilliance. An official scripture-copying bureau had been organized by the governors of the western regions and produced several works worthy of note. The characters in this group of copies are written with a considerable degree of force, but the brushwork retains a natural, measured, and compact feeling. It is of very high quality as a whole. A style of calligraphy distinct from these sutra copies and the "Zhang Meng Long Stele" and "Gao Zhen Stele" that they resembled was current at the same time. This other style avoided emphasis on technique. Both types of calligraphy were accurate reflections of the spirit of Northern Wei culture.

After the first several decades of the sixth century, the vigor of Northern Wei calligraphy diminished and gradually moved toward a gentler, softer style. The "sutras of dedication" of the governor of Gua province and Prince of Dongyan, Yuan Tairong, are representative of this trend. The further softening of Northern Wei calligraphy toward the end of the dynasty is probably due to the increased influence of the works of the two Wangs imported from the south, though there had not yet been time enough to incorporate and digest these models. The differences in national character as well as the political conflict in which the north and south stood also prevented a free exchange of influences.

Soon after the collapse of the Northern Wei, the Eastern and Western Wei governments were established. The calligraphy of this period can be considered a continuation of the trends of the Northern Wei. The *Pusa Chutai Jing,* transmitted to Japan at this time, is an excellent example of calligraphic technique. After the fall of the Eastern and Western Wei, and through the succession of dynasties such as the Northern Qi and the Northern Zhou, the softness of calligraphy remained unchanged, and, in fact, the calligraphy of the north came to greatly resemble that of the south. Still, some works from after the Northern Wei did retain the characteristic vigor of the north and, finally moving beyond scribe-script techniques, became the predecessors of what is known as the Sui-sutra style of calligraphy. The block scripts of Sui and Tang were also components of this new style.

The calligraphic style of the sutra copies of the southern dynasties is distinguished by a refined elegance derived from the calligraphy of the two Wangs. In contrast, the northern dynasties start from a firm grounding in scribe-script techniques. The results of centuries of scribe-script evolution were inherited by the northern calligraphers and combined with the fresh, natural spirit of the non-Chinese dynasties. Their brushwork is compact and cohesive, revealing its origins in the scribe script. This maturity in spirit and technique gradually evolves into a softer, gentler direction. The unique style of the sutra copies of the northern dynasties was largely a product of the Northern Wei dynasty, which also best represents this style. Nevertheless, we must not overlook the influence of Zhong Yao, who built the groundwork for and contributed to the maturity of Wang Xizhi's style, or the introduction of southern calligraphic styles into the north. To a greater or lesser extent, these influenced Northern Wei calligraphy. Though the styles of north and south were largely separate and unrelated, the way had already been prepared for the appearance of the forceful and beautiful formality of the block script which was to appear with the unification of the empire under the Sui.

# The Sui, Tang, and Five Dynasties

The Sui dynasty (581–619) lasted a brief thirty-eight years, but, because it unified north and south China for the first time in many years and paved the way for the following Tang dynasty, it is of great historical import.

Calligraphy in the Sui dynasty gradually evolved from the wide variety of styles current in earlier ages to a uniform, ordered, and graceful style that foreshadowed the block script of the Tang. Yang Jian (Emperor Wen), who founded the Sui, was an illiterate "northern barbarian" who lacked cultivation in the arts, but his son Yang Guang (Emperor Yang), whatever his faults, was a man of letters in comparison to his father. He was particularly fond of the calligraphy of Zhiyong and his disciple Zhiguo. Zhiyong was a monk who lived during the Chen and Sui dynasties, the seventh-generation descendant of Wang Xizhi. He made over eight hundred copies of the "Thousand-Character Essay" that had been handed down in the Wang family and donated them to various temples in Zhedong. The "Thousand-Character Essay" that has been preserved in Japan (pl. 31) enjoys an especially high reputation as calligraphy. Zhiguo studied under Zhiyong and prided himself on having perfected the essence of Wang Xizhi's calligraphic technique. His calligraphy is on view in his postscript to Wang Xizhi's "Feng Ju Album" (pl. 18), and is also included in the "Chunhua Pavilion Copybook." Other calligraphers of the period that have gained mention in contemporary sources are Yu Chuo of Huiji Yuyao (Zhejiang Province), Fang Yanqian (547–615) of Qinghe (Hebei Province), and Shi Ling, the teacher of Chu Suiliang of the Tang dynasty. However, no works that can definitely be attributed to these men have come down to us.

A relatively large number of Sui-dynasty works are extant, including both traditionally renowned works and newly discovered materials. These can roughly be divided into two categories: 1) refined and graceful works in the style favored by the southern court, and 2) classic works that continue in the tradition of the Wei and the Jin, or the northern-dynasties style. As a matter of record, the southern-dynasties style of calligraphy had begun to spread to the north by the end of the Northern and Southern Dynasties period, and a gradual syncretization was occurring. It is therefore unreasonable to divide calligraphic works of the period strictly by their region of

Fig. 45. Longcangsi Monastery Stele (Sui dynasty).

Fig. 46. Epitaph for Dong Meiren (Sui dynasty).

origin, though this division continues to be useful in a very general sense. Representative of the southern style are the "Longcang Temple Stele" (*Longcang Si Bei,* fig. 45), the "Qifa Temple Stele" (pl. 32), and the "Epitaph for Dong Meiren" (*Meiren Dongshi Muzhi,* fig. 46). Recently, the "Epitaph for Li Jingxun" (*Li Jingxun Muzhi*) has been discovered. Representing the second, northern, style we have the "Tomb Stele of Confucius by Chen Shuyi" (*Chen Shuyi Xiu Kongzi Miao Bei*), which is a fine example of Wei and Jin scribe script, the "Tomb Stele of Cao Zhi" (*Cao Zhi Miao Bei*), and the "Statue Inscription of Du Qianxu and Others" (*Du Qianxu Den Zaoxiang Ji*), which preserve the calligraphic style of the northern dynasties.

There is, then, considerable variation in Sui-dynasty calligraphy between old and new, north and south. However, the southern style was to come to be the mainstream of Sui calligraphy, finally evolving into the block script of the early Tang. Still, an undeniable difference remained between the block script of the Sui and the Tang. The Sui block script was rather compressed, slender, and written with a sharply pointed brush. The stiff and dignified feeling of Sui block script is unmistakable.

## Tang-Dynasty Calligraphy

The Tang dynasty (618–907) was founded by Li Yuan, who emerged from a pack of candidates for power towards the end of the Sui and later, assisted by his son Li Shimin, succeeded in establishing his own rule. The Tang was an unprecedentedly enduring dynasty in Chinese history, lasting 290 years until it was overthrown by Zhu Quanzhong in 907. During this period, the aristocratic society that had existed from the Northern and Southern Dynasties period was reestablished on a new basis, national policy was unified, and a glorious aristocratic culture flourished.

In calligraphy, the style of Wang Xizhi, which had been so highly valued for so long, contributed to the creation of the ideal of beauty for block script. Emperor Taizong, Li Shimin (598–649), was at the center of this development. Taizong was an ardent admirer of Wang Xizhi's calligraphy and did not spare any expense in acquiring his works. The works of Wang Xizhi and Wang Xianzhi in the imperial possession ran into the hundreds. Among these, Taizong was most proud of his copies of Wang Xizhi's "Yue Yi Treatise" in block script and the "Orchid Pavilion Preface" in semi-cursive script. These he had copied and traced many times to present to members of the aristocracy whom he favored. In the beginning, Wei Zheng and Yu Shinan (558–638) were in charge of the care of Taizong's collection, a task that later was delegated to Chu Suiliang (598–658).

Taizong also established the "Department for the Propagation of Literacy" (*Hong Wen Guan*), and employing Ouyang Xun (557–641) and Yu Shinan, both calligraphers following in the Wang Xizhi tradition, had them instruct the children of the nobility in block script. A "Documents Department" was also installed in the Guozi Ministry, equivalent to a national university. One of the subjects in that department was dubbed "Interpretation of Characters," and its content was described in the Tang Codes as "textual studies, interpretation of literary passages, and investigation of characters, in addition to learning to excel at the various styles of calligraphy." Following this development, the criteria for selection for bureaucratic posts came to include talent for calligraphy along with "appearance, speech, and judgment." The required skill for calligraphy was prescribed as "beautiful block script" in the "Standards for Selection" of the *New Tang Annals* (*Xin Tang Shu*).

Ouyang Xun, Yu Shinan, and Chu Suiliang were the most active calligraphers at this time when the art of calligraphy had achieved such an elevated status. Together they are known as the three great masters of the early Tang. Occasionally Xue Ji (649–713) is included to make four great masters. Both Ouyang Xun and Yu Shinan were born in the kingdom of Chen in the south, and served first at the Sui court, switching their loyalties to the Tang later. Both were great masters of block script. The "Huang-fu Dan Stele" (*Huangfu Dan Bei*), the "Huadu Temple Stele" (*Haudu Si Bei*, pl. 37), the "Fang Yanqian Stele" (*Fan Yanqian Bei*), the "Jiucheng Palace Spring Inscription" (*Jiuchenggong Liquan Ming*, fig. 47), and the "Wen Yanbo Stele" (*Wen Yanbo Bei*) are representative works of Ouyang Xun. The block script "Confucius' Tomb Stele" (*Kongzi Miaotang Bei*) and the semi-cursive "Epitaph of Princess Runan" (*Runan Gongzhu Muzhi*), and the "Jishi Album" (*Jishi Tie*) give us a good idea of Yu Shinan's talents. The calligraphy of Ouyang and Yu Shinan is even today regarded as a model of block-script technique. Their relative excellence has been debated since ancient times. Zhang Huaiguan of the Tang wrote in his *Critique of Calligraphy* (*Shu Duan*) that Ouyang was better in that he excelled in all types of scripts, but Yu Shinan actually surpassed him in the dignity of his work, which "incorporated both firmness and suppleness, and was rich in invention." Yu Shinan had studied with Zhiyong and was perhaps the most orthodox inheritor of Wang Xizhi's tradition, but did not possess the mastery of such a broad range of expression as Ouyang Xun.

Fig. 47. Jiucheng Palace Spring Inscription, Ouyang Xun (Tang dynasty).

Chu Suiliang, on the other hand, first studied under Shi Ling and later under Yu Shinan. He was an excellent student and took Wang Xizhi as his model. His block script was sensuous and full of movement. The "Yique Buddhist Image-niche Stele" (*Yique Fokan Bei*, fig. 48), the "Master Mengfa Stele" (*Mengfa Shi Bei*), the "Fang Xuanling Stele" (*Fang Xuanling Bei*), and the "Yan Pagoda Prefaces to the Holy Teachings" (*Yan Ta Sheng Jiao Xu*, pl. 38) are representative works by Chu Suiliang. Ouyang Tong (died 691), the son of Ouyang Xun, carried on his father's tradition and is the author of the "Master Daoyin Stele" (*Daoyin Fashi Bei*) and the "Epitaph of Quan Nansheng" (*Quan Nansheng Muzhi*). The style of Chu Suiliang was inherited and passed on by Xue Ji, Jing Ke, Xue Yao, and others.

Fig. 48. Yique Buddhist Image-niche Stele, Chu Suiliang (Tang dynasty).

After the death of Emperor Taizong, many steles were erected in tombs adjoining the imperial mausoleum. Among these are several that can be identified as the works of Ouyang, Yu Shinan, and Chu Suiliang, revealing just how highly regarded the great calligraphers of the age were by the imperial household.

Taizong himself was a student of Wang Xizhi's calligraphy, and has left us several impressive semi-cursive-script steles, including the "Jin Ci Inscription" (*Jin Ci Ming*) and the "Hot Spring Inscription" (*Wen Quan Ming*, pl. 35). He also attempted the "flying white" ornamental script, which is found on the seal cap of the "Jin Ci Inscription" stele, making him the precursor of all later imperial calligraphers of note.

The reign of Empress Wu (690–705) was a dark and bloody period that opened and closed in strife and disorder. The Empress seems to have devoted considerable energy to calligraphy. The "Stele for Crown Prince Shengxian" (*Shengxian Taizi Bei*) is her work, and she also composed many dedicatory titles for various temple and monastery stele inscriptions. It was during this period, however, that certain traditional attitudes regarding calligraphy began to wane, and a new style to emerge. The comment of Li Sizhen in the *Later Works of Calligraphy* (*Hou Shu Pin*) signals the appearance of this new attitude: "the scholars of old all followed their teachers' methods exclusively, while nowadays calligraphers simply follow their own instincts. They lack any natural excellence, and depend far too much on their whims." In this climate, Sun Guoting (648?–703?) composed the

Fig. 49. Paean to Dong Fangshuo, Yan Zhenqing (Tang dynasty).

Fig. 50. Lushansi Monastery Stele, Li Yong (Tang dynasty).

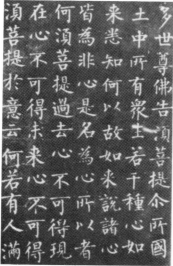

Fig. 51. Jingang Jing, Liu Gongquan (Tang dynasty).

*Treatise on Calligraphy* (*Shu Pu,* pl. 43) and tried to uphold both the theory and practice of the traditional calligraphy since Wang Xizhi. In his work, he assembled and summarized the theories of calligraphy from the Han, Wei, and Six Dynasties periods. In addition to this valuable contribution, he was, as a calligrapher, able to achieve the spirit of Wang Xizhi's cursive calligraphy—no small feat in itself.

However, toward the middle of the eighth century, from roughly 713 to 755, the ancient aristocratic society began to lose its momentum and the traditional styles of calligraphy since Wang Xizhi degenerated into formalism and lost a good deal of their inspiration. In their place, what was called "wild cursive"—the first two masters of which were Zhang Xu and Huaisu (born 725)—appeared. They often drank heavily to rid themselves of inhibitions and allow their true feelings to come out before taking up the brush. Then, facing a large folding screen or wall, they wrote bold, free-flowing script in a burst of activity, filling the writing surface from top to bottom, side to side. Such scenes have been recorded in the poetry of the time. The autobiographical albums of Zhang Xu (*Zi Yan Tie*) and Huaisu (*Zi Shu Tie,* pl. 47) represent only one small aspect of that style of calligraphy to us today. Wild cursive was practiced, too, by certain monks from the end of the Tang through the Five Dynasties period. The appearance of wild cursive, together with the *yipin,* or "eccentric masterpiece" paintings, a little later are adventurous expressions of the human spirit during a transitional period.

Yan Zhenqing (709–85), who lived in the middle of the Tang dynasty, not only mastered the traditional Wang Xizhi-style calligraphy, but enjoyed an intimate association with the wild-cursive calligraphers. He combined these two traditions to create a glorious new style of calligraphy full of life which was to be a major force in the emergence of the new calligraphy of the Five Dynasties and Song periods. Many of his works in block, semi-cursive, and cursive are available for inspection today. The "Eulogy for a Nephew" (*Ji Zhi Wengao,* pl. 46), "Eulogy for Bo Fu" (*Ji Bo Fu Wengao*), and the "Contest for Rank Draft" (*Zheng Zuowei Wengao*), works in the latter two styles, are known as the three drafts. The "Poem of Parting for General Pei" (*Song Pei Jiangjun Shi*) is a combination of the three standard scripts plus scribe script.

Li Yong (678–747) predates Yan Zhenqing slightly. He wrote several semi-cursive stele inscriptions in the tradition of Wang Xizhi, including the "Lushan Monastery Stele" (*Lushan Si Bei,* fig. 50) and the "Li Sixun Stele." Liu Gongquan (778–865) comes after Yan Zhenqing, and was much influenced by him. He created an even more vigorous style of calligraphy, and his stele printings were extremely popular among the aristocracy of the time. The *Jingang Banruo Jing* (fig. 51)and the "Xuanbi Pagoda Stele" (*Xuanbi Ta Bei*) are his compositions.

Several works in the scribe and seal scripts were produced in the Tang dynasty, including the scribe-script "Taishan Inscription" (*Ji Taishan Ming*) and the "Stone Terrace *Classic of Filial Piety*" (*Shitai Xiao Jing*) of Emperor Xuanzong (685–762). Shi Weize composed the "Chan Master Dazhi Stele" (*Dazhi Chanshi Bei*) in scribe script, and we also have, in seal script, Li Yangbing's "Title Inscription for the Banruo Terrace" (*Banruotai Taiti*).

Several especially excellent epitaph inscriptions have been unearthed recently. These include the epitaph of Zhang Tinggui (746), by Xu Hao in scribe script; of Princess Yongtai (706, pl. 45), Wei Jiong (708). Wei Xu (718), and Zhang Jiuling (740); Han Zemu's "Epitaph of the Lord of Nanchuan Xian" (*Nanchuanxian Zhu Muzhi,* 752), and the semi-cursive epitaph inscriptions for Prince Hui (810) and Zheng Derou (848).

# Calligraphy of the Five Dynasties Period

In the roughly fifty years between the collapse of the Tang and the establishment of the Song, five kingdoms rose and fell in central China—the Later Liang, the Later Tang, the Later Jin, the Later Han, and the Later Zhou. The south divided into a succession of ten different states: the Early and Later Shu, the Wu, the Southern Tang, the Min, the Chu, the Jingnan, the Southern Han, the Wuyue, and the Northern Han. The capital of the Southern Tang was located at present-day Nanjing, that of the Wuyue in Hangzhou, and the Early and Later Shu at Chengdu. All of these kingdoms were prosperous and peaceful, and experienced a cultural boom of sorts. The rulers of the Southern Tang, in particular, were interested in the arts and literature, and it was during their reign that writing implements saw considerable improvement, including the development of Dengxin Hall paper and Li Tinggui ink. The Dengxin Hall Album" (*Dengxin Tang Tie*) and the Sheng Yuan Album" (*Sheng Yuan Tie*) were also published at this time.

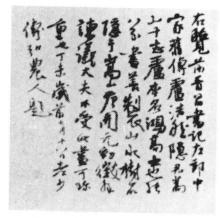

Fig. 52. Colophon to Lu Hong's Caotang Shizhi Du, Yang Ningshi (Five Dynasties).

The new style of calligraphy that had arisen during the mid-Tang stagnated somewhat during this period. Yang Ningshi (873–954) lived at this time, and breathed some life into the old forms. He was actually a man of great integrity; but due to the chaotic times he pretended to be mad and was called "Yang the Supernatural." In calligraphy, he was much influenced by Huaisu and Yan Zhenqing. His remarkable cursive script was unique and was highly praised by the Song-dynasty masters Ouyang Xiu, Su Shi, and Huang Tingjian. According to historical accounts, he was especially gifted at wall calligraphy, and the walls of the Buddhist temples and Confucian shrines of Luoyang were covered with his work. Of course this calligraphy was very difficult to preserve, and most of it is lost to us. A few examples survive in albums such as the "Jiu Hua Album" (*Jiu Hua Tie*) and his colophon to Lu Hong's *Caotang Shizhi Du* (fig. 52).

In addition, we have block script carved into jade tablets—the "Lament for Wang Jian Tablet" (*Wang Jian Ai Ce,* 918, fig. 53) discovered in 1942 in Chengdu, Sichuan Province and the "Lament for Li Pian" (*Li Pian Ai Ce,* 943) unearthed from Zutangshan in Jiangningxian, Jiangsu Province, in 1950. Wang Jian was a ruler of the Early Shu, and Li Pian of the Southern Tang. These pieces are valuable examples of Five Dynasties-period block script.

Fig. 53. Lament for Wang Jian Tablet (Five Dynasties).

# The Northern and Southern
# Song Dynasties

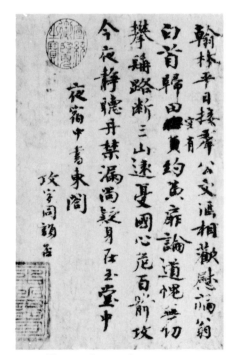

Fig. 54. Poem, Ouyang Xiu
(Song dynasty).

A great transformation took place in calligraphy from the Song dynasty onwards. In order to understand this fully, we must discuss a variety of historical developments, such as the improvement of writing implements and materials and the spread of printing as well as cultural phenomena such as the development of preface and postscript literature, the rise of studies of stone and metal inscriptions, and the influence of Chan Buddhism, which challenged all sorts of conventions. However, in this limited space, let it suffice to point out that the development of printing, in particular, freed calligraphy from the practical role it had played earlier as the only means of written communication. That new development likewise produced a definite change in the attitude of the Song Chinese toward calligraphy.

Ouyang Xiu (1007–72) is renowned as the predecessor of the literati, or gentleman-scholar, school of the Northern Song, and the author of the pioneering work of the metal and stone inscription school, the *Collected Ancient Catalogues of Postscripts* (*Ji Gulu Bawei*). He was a proponent of the idea that "the calligraphy of so-called professionals does not survive. Only the work of those with a fine insight into human nature passes down to later generations." This belief in the cultivation of insight into human nature was further developed by his disciple Su Shi (1036–1101) and Su's disciple Huang Tingjian (1045–1105). A poem in his hand is on display in figure 54.

In the Song, the official imperial collection of the calligraphy of the Wangs, the "Chunhua Pavilion Copybook" (992), was published, establishing their calligraphy as the model from the Tang period on and marking the point of departure for all others. A school of neo-classicists who revered these works, though not uncritically, and the literati school, which raised their banner in support of new techniques different from the Wangs', arose at this time.

Of the four great Song masters, Cai Xiang (1012–67) and Mi Fu (1051–1107) belonged to the first group, and Su Shi and Huang Tingjian to the second. The phrase, "Su-Huang-Mi-Cai" ("Cai" referring originally to Cai Jing), linking the four great masters of the Northern Song, was already established by the Ming dynasty. Not only is this a euphonious arrangement of tones in Chinese, but it preserves the proper chronological order. However, to the Ming Chinese, who had finally managed to liberate themselves from foreign rule and establish a Han Chinese dynasty, Cai Jing (1047–1126), who cooperated with Huizong in abandoning the dynasty to "barbarian" invaders, was unacceptable and fell out of favor as a calligrapher. He was replaced by Cai Xiang, his senior from the same region, and the order of the phrase was changed to "Cai-Su-Huang-Mi" to preserve the chronology, though at the sacrifice of sonority.

Cai Xiang passed the imperial examinations in 1030. At just this time, Fan Zhongyan was banished and Ouyang Xiu, who urgently pleaded to spare him, was also implicated. Cai Xiang wrote a poem, *"Four Sages and One Scoundrel"* (*Si Xian Yi Buxiao Shi*), fondly recalling the merits of the two, and copies were in great demand among the people of the capital. Ouyang Xiu's praise of Cai Xiang's calligraphy, then, was not based entirely on its artistic merits. Cai first studied the work of Zhou Yue, who was a master of the beautiful palace, or *yuan*, style of calligraphy. Following that, he studied Yan Zhenqing's calligraphy. His inheritance from Yan's style is quite evident in his large and small block-style characters (fig. 55). Cai also studied the calligraphy of Yang Ningshi of the Five Dynasties. In fact, the Ming-dynasty master Dong Qichang (1555–1636), in his post-script to a letter by Cai, remarked, "The superiority of Cai's calligraphy and his freedom from conventional standards are due more to his study of Yang than of Yan." Though it is important to note that Cai studied the calligraphy of Yang, who preceded Su and Huang in the literati school, the main object of his study was the methods of the two Wangs and the cursive script of the Jin masters. The "Tao Sheng Album" (*Tao Sheng Tie*), located in the Taipei Palace Museum, is Cai's most representative work and easily merits Su Shi's fervent praise as the best in China. In the early Song, debilitated and drained as it was by the strife that had continued since the Five Dynasties, Cai's calligraphy reigns supreme.

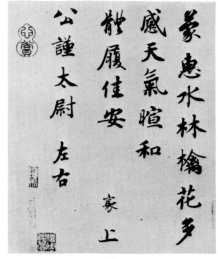

Fig. 55. Epistle, Cai Xiang (Song dynasty).

Su Shi took the name Master Dongpo after he was demoted and sent to Huangzhou. Not only is he one of the eight great calligraphers of the Tang and Song, but he was also a model of the scholar-bureaucrat class that was to be the patron of culture in the Northern Song. Though a gifted statesman, he became a victim of factional strife. Su Shi was the leader of the Northern Song literati school as well as its most accomplished practitioner. The credo of this school was "reverence for the meaning."

In his youth, Su Shi studied the "Orchid Pavilion Preface" and was also attracted to the work of Yan Zhenqing and Yang Ningshi. Critics have felt his work resembles Xu Hao's (703–82) and that his brushwork owes much to Li Yong (678–747). From the fact that he instructed Mi Fu to study the methods of the Jin masters, we may conclude that as a learned man he also viewed and studied the calligraphy of many of the old masters. Still, as he himself says in his theoretical writings on calligraphy, "Beautiful brushwork piled high as a mountain means nothing. Only after extensive reading and study does one attain divine excellence." The confidence with which he remarked, "Though I have not studied calligraphy, I excel at it," is an expression of his belief that calligraphy was not a compendium of techniques, but could only be perfected when a truly cultured person used it to express his humanity. The influence of Yan can be seen in his works that have come down to us, but the main province of the calligraphy of this truly free spirit was the poetry of his own composition, such as the *"Cold Meal in Huangzhou Poem Scroll"* (pl. 49), and works which demonstrate his "technique of no technique" such as the *"Hermit Li Taibo Poem Scroll"* (pl. 50). The memorial in figure 56 is another distinctive work.

The next of the four Northern Song masters is Huang Tingjian. He, too, was a typical example of one of the new officials. He was from a poor family

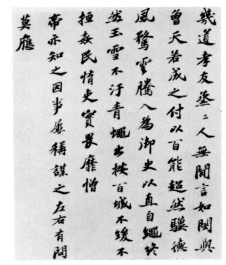

Fig. 56. Essay, Su Shi (Song dynasty).

and as a child even considered becoming an apothecary. He attained the third rank as a sole result of his own studies, but he did not have the character for worldly success and, like Su Shi, was caught up in factional strife and ended his life in the obscurity of exile.

Huang Tingjian's theories concerning calligraphy are basically the same as Su Shi's, though he elaborated on the theories of his predecessors by discussing the idea of humanity in terms of *yun*—harmony, or elegance: "Wang Zhu's works were beautiful, but lacking in *yun*; Zhou Yue had vigor, but lacked *yun*. The fact that these masters' works suffered a lack of *yun* was not due to any lack of study of calligraphy, but to spiritual short-comings." He also despised anything popular and declared that the work of the two Wangs was not desirable because it was popular as an official style.

Huang Tingjian's studies were probably very similar to Su Shi's, but his study of Zhou Yue's work at an early age, his great scorn for any hint of "vulgarity," and his particular fondness for cursive calligraphy are unique. Indeed, cursive script was the most appropriate form for the expression of his "free and flowing inspiration," as he called it. The "*Cold Meal* Poem Scroll Postscript" (*Hanshi Shichuan Ba*, pl. 53) in semi-cursive script is also an excellent piece of writing, as is the work featured in figure 57. But it is in such works as the "Li Taibo's *Recalling Past Wanderings* Poem Scroll" (*Li Taibo Yi Jueyou Shichuan*, pl. 52) that we can see Huang's unique genius. We must also note that this kind of cursive script was first made possible by the soft, sheep-bristle brush favored by Huang.

The last of the four masters, Mi Fu came from a background different from Su and Huang. He became a member of the Secretariat of the government not through the civil examination system, but through a connection on his mother's side, and when a calligraphy and printing school was instituted at Huizong's court, he became a specialist with the official title of Doctor of Calligraphy and Painting.

He had little interest in political affairs, did not get involved in any factional strife, and probably never studied for the national examinations. With little interest in the events of the world, he concentrated his energies on the collection and appreciation of ancient paintings and calligraphy and the study of the art.

In his early years, his work was criticized as being "imitative" and "pastiches of ancient characters," which proves that he could not escape the influence of his time—not one in which merely studying and carrying on the traditions of the ancient masters would suffice. He studied the works of Yan and proceeded to the calligraphy of Ouyang Xun and Chu Suiliang, mastering through Chu the old methods of the southern court. He sought to reach the classical excellence of the Jin masters, but in contrast to the classicists of the Tang period, he investigated the works of all the old masters from the two Wangs onward. In his *History of Calligraphy (Shu Shi)* he writes, "I continued to study the ancient writings until my hair had turned to white, but no ink originals from the Wei remained, so I was forced to begin from the Western Jin." And he argued, "Viewing Li Wei's "Fourteen Jinxian Albums" (*Jinxian Shishi Tie*) a certain vulgarity of the two Wangs becomes apparent, and it is clear that Xie An is of a higher quality." These conclusions are partly due to the fact that in this period, the original works of the two Wangs had become extremely scarce, and the versions of them appearing in the "Chunhua Pavilion Copybook" and other copybooks no longer presented the true appearance of the ancient works. His critical writings, the *History of Calligraphy* and the *Catalogue of Masterpieces (Baozheng Daifang Lu)*, show that in addition to being a good calligrapher he was very objective and thorough in his criticism of ancient calligraphy and painting. This represents a direct contrast to the intuitions

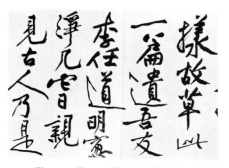

Fig. 57. Essay, Huang Tingjian (Song dynasty).

of Huang Tingjian of the literati school. For that reason, Zhu Xi (1130–1200) of the Southern Song wrote, "Huang Tingjian's learning was all theoretical, whereas Mi Fu was correct because he spoke from a true understanding of characters."

Mi Fu, so devoted to painting and calligraphy, nevertheless only left a few works in block script, such as the "Thousand-Character Essay in Small Block Characters" (*Xiao Kai Qian Wen*) and the "Eulogy for the Empress Dowager Taxing" (*Taxing Huangtaihou Wanshi*). This reveals just how predominant semi-cursive and cursive script had become in the Song dynasty. The work in figure 58 is an excellent example of his cursive script.

Fig. 58. Poetry scroll, Mi Fu (Song dynasty).

The first generation of Southern Song calligraphy was initiated by Emperor Gaozong (1107–87). Like his father, Huizong, whose calligraphy can be seen in figure 59, he had a very poor reputation as a statesman. However, he devoted special energies to his calligraphy and has even left us a work of critical scholarship. He began by studying Huang, and advanced from Mi Fu through the two Wangs. In general, the tastes of a ruler come to be shared by his ministers, and, in Gaozong's case, this influence was especially strong because his rule lasted thirty-five years and his taste governed the calligraphy of the Southern Song.

The works of the two Wangs spread to a wider audience with the distribution of the Northern Song-dynasty "Chunhua Pavilion Copybook" and its printed versions. To study calligraphy at that time meant to study the calligraphy of the two Wangs, and all officials possessed a stone carving of the "Orchid Pavilion Preface"—so popular were their works. As a result, the research on the "Chunhua Pavilion Copybook" begun in the Northern Song by the likes of Mi Fu, Huang Bosi, and Liu Cizhong was further developed by the Southern Song masters such as Jiang Kui (1155–1231), Cao Shiwan in his *Systematic Record of Copybooks* (*Fatie Puxi*), and Sang Sichang in his *Consideration of the Orchid Pavilion* (*Lan Ting Kao*), eventually surpassing the Northern Song efforts. Such masters as Yu Yunwen and Zhao Mengxian (1199–1264) appeared in this climate of adoration of the two Wangs. Even the rather unorthodox calligraphy of Wu Shuo and Zhang Jizhi (1186–1266) expresses a small aspect of this trend. These trends were amalgamated by Zhao Mengfu (1254–1322), who lived from the end of the Song to the beginning of the Yuan.

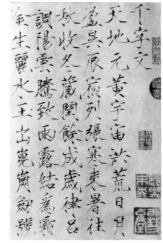

Fig. 59. Thousand-Character Essay, Huizong (Song dynasty).

Gaozong also loved the calligraphy of Mi Fu, whose heir, Mi Youren, (1072–1151) ably carried on the Mi-family tradition and was a sharp critic as well. When an office of calligraphic studies was instituted in 1122, he was appointed to the post. Gaozong published a special collection of Mi's calligraphy. Wu Jie, Fan Chengda (1126–93) and Yang Wanli (1124–1206) were students of Mi's calligraphy.

Huang Tingjian was the representative calligrapher of the period and, as the representative of the literati school, as well as the founder of the Jiangxi poetry school, had many followers. Among them were Fan Chengda, Zhang Xiaoxiang (1133–70), and Jiang Kui (see fig. 60). Wang Sheng (1076–1150) and Lu You (1125–1210) studied the Tang masters Huaisu and Zhang Yu, who had been the guiding principles of Huang's calligraphy. An example of Lu You's work can be seen in figure 61.

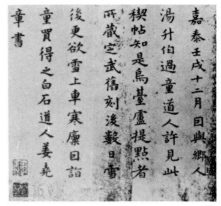

Fig. 60. Colophon to Orchid Pavilion Preface, Jiang Kui (Song dynasty).

A limited progress was also made in the study of scribe and seal scripts. The *Albums of Ancient Inscriptions on Bronze Ding and Yi Vessels* (*Lidai Zhong Ding Yi Qi Kuanshi Fatie*) of Bi Shanggong and Hong Kuo's *Scribe Script Dictionaries* (*Li Jie, Li Xu*) were composed. The *History of Metal and Stone Inscriptions* (*Jin Shi Shi*) of Zhao Mingcheng also enjoys a good reputation as a successor work to the metal and stone inscriptions studies of the Northern Song.

Zhang Jizhi was a famous calligrapher at the end of the Southern Song

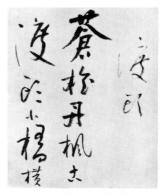

Fig. 61. Poems, Lu You (Song dynasty).

135

who had a profound relationship with the Chan clergy. The Chan ideal, which did not recognize any canons of authority, found expression in his work and is responsible for the uncertain reputation that has been accorded Zhang's work since its creation.

In general, Southern Song calligraphy was at a low level, but research on calligraphy was extremely popular, and the bases from which the later stele school and the copybook school would develop and flourish in the Qing dynasty were already laid in the active research of the Song.

# Chan Calligraphy of the
# Song and Yuan Dynasties

*Moji* (Japanese, *bokuseki*) originally meant an ink writing that was neither a copy nor a rubbing, but a hand-written original. This term appears as early as the *Biography of Fan Ye* (*Fan Ye Chuan*) in volume sixty-nine of the *History of the Song Kingdom of the Six Dynasties* (*Song Shu*), where it refers to Fan Ye's personal writings. From the Song dynasty, then, it came into wide use in the meaning of the writings of a well-known personage. We see frequent uses of the term in, for example, volume thirty-two of the *Record of Taizong's Reign* (*Taizong Shilu*), in an entry of the third month of 985, where it reads, "Pan Zhaoqing presented three *moji* of Chu Suiliang, Ouyang Xun, and Yu Shinan to the court"; and in another record of the period, in an entry of the sixth month of 997, "*Moji* of Taizong were presented to famous mountains and sites of the land." It is also frequently used in the literature of prefaces and postscripts. Although the distinction between writings and originals is unclear in this case, the term was probably loosely used in most cases to describe the famous works of a calligrapher. Whatever the case, in China *moji* referred to an original, hand-written work, but not to any specific category of calligraphy. In contrast, the writings of Chan monks were labeled *bokuseki* by the tea and Zen masters of Japan of the Muromachi period. Even today in Japanese histories of calligraphy *bokuseki* refers exclusively to the writings of Chan monks, which are treated as a separate category. This distinction is made because Chan-inspired calligraphy is very different in nature from other types of calligraphy. It is highly idiosyncratic and breaks many of the traditional rules of calligraphy. Included in the category of Chan calligraphy are the writings of the likes of Zhao Mengfu and Feng Zizhen who though laymen associated with Chan monks and whose calligraphy shows a Chan influence, as well as correspondence actually addressed to Chan monks. Strictly speaking, then, the religious import is more important than the calligraphic style in the writings of Chan monks. The writings of the Chan monks of the Song and Yuan dynasties are especially highly regarded and known as "old *bokuseki*" in Japan.

The Chan school is a product of Chinese soil and is perhaps the most Chinese sect of Buddhism. This school criticizes the Sanlun, Faxiang, Hua-

Fig. 62. Sermons of Dahui, Wuan Puning (Song dynasty).

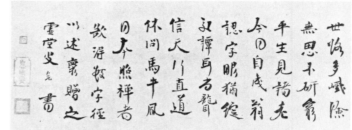

Fig. 63. Poem, Xutang Zhiyu (Song dynasty).

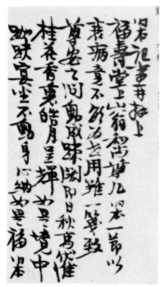

Fig. 64. Poem, Zhongfeng
Mingben (Yuan dynasty).

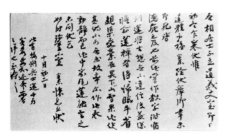

Fig. 65. Letter, Dahui Zonggao
(Song dynasty).

yan and other doctrinally-oriented schools of Chinese buddhism as being lost in the interpretation of doctrines and textual passages and missing the essence of Buddhism. In contrast, Chan teaches freedom from the restrictions of language, reaching the true nature of the mind through sitting in medition, and attaining a state of enlightenment identical to the Buddha's. Bodhidharma is regarded as the first patriarch of the school, but it didn't truly become active until the reign of Empress Wu at the beginning of the eighth century. The two masters Shenxiu and Huineng appeared at this time and founded the northern and southern schools of Chan. The northern school declined after the middle of the Tang dynasty, but the southern school, having gained the support of regional military and influential families, developed from the end of the Tang through the Five Dynasties period (9th–10th centuries) into five schools, the Weiyang, Caodong, Linji, Fayan, and Yunmen schools. Later the Linji sect further divided into the Huanglong sect and the Yangqi sect, and together these were known as the five schools and seven sects of Chan. Soon after this the Weiyang and Fayan schools ceased to exist. The Yunmen school flourished during the Northern Song. Later, the Huanglong sect made its appearance, and during the Southern Song the Yangqi sect began to flourish, continuing on into the Yuan dynasty. Relations between Japan and China, which had been in limbo since the cancellation of the tribute missions, resumed from the middle of the Southern Song. As a result, most Japanese monks who visited the Song studied the Yangqi sect of Chan and brought it back to Japan. This is the reason that most of the Chan calligraphy presently in Japan are the works of monks of this sect.

While undergoing this series of periods of activity and decline, the Chan sects made positive efforts to reach out to the aristocracy and the scholars that were rewarded with unstinting patronage. The Chan sects flourishing in the Jiangnan region in the early Song made their entry into the capital of Kaifeng with the construction of the Shifang Jinyin Chan Hall in 1049, during Renzong's reign. Following that, in 1080, during Shenzong's reign, the Huilin and Zhihai Chan Halls were built in the largest temple in the capital, the Ta Xiangguo Monastery. To the south of the capital the Fayun Chan Temple was built, and "all those in the realm with an inclination for Chan flocked to the capital" (Huizong's preface to the *Continued Transmissions of the Lamp, Xu Deng Lu*). Zongben, the founder of the Huilin Chan Hall, received the title Chan Master Yuanzhao from Emperor Zhezong, and was instructed to "make the Chan school prosper, and lead it well." The chief priest of the Falun Temple, Foguo Weibo, was said to "enter the palace frequently and to have sat on the imperial throne three times to preach the subtle teachings of the Buddha at the Emperor's request."

The incursion of the Chan school into the capital coincided with the rise of the new scholar-administrator class, and the birth of the new culture that they produced. The hereditary aristocracy of the Tang dynasty disappeared and was replaced at the reigns of power by the new class of scholar-officials, who attained their posts through the difficult new civil service examinations.

Fig. 66. Verses, Wuxue Zuyuan.　　　　　　　　Fig. 67. Parting Verses, Gulin Qingmao (Yuan dynasty).

They were also the most educated class at the time and thus took a leading role in cultural activities, too. They abandoned the old, formalized types of study, literature, and the arts in favor of new, freer, and more personal forms of cultural activity. The peak of this movement was the Qingli era (1041–48) of Renzong's reign, when Fan Zhongan and Ouyang Xiu were leaders in the political world trying to effect governmental reforms, and those arts and sciences that appeared in this period are known as the "reformed studies of Qingli." Following this, Su Shi, Huang Tingjian and later Cheng Hao and Cheng Yi went on to carry Song culture to its apogee. The scholar-administrators of the Song dynasty showed a great interest in Chan, which also challenged authority and tradition, and many practiced Chan as lay followers. Their active advocacy of Chan gave their poetry and painting a new perspective. The most famous examples of this are Su Shi, who was close to Donglin Chancong and Foyin Liaoyuan, and Huang Tingjian, who studied Chan under Huitang Zuxin and Sixin Wuxin.

As its relationship to the court and government become closer, the Chan church gradually became bureaucratized, and civil administrative systems were introduced into Chan temple organizations. The imperially designated head priest presided over the temple—his administrative unit. In the Southern Song, the "five schools and ten temples" system was instituted as public policy, and the practice of promoting head priests up the heirarchy of temples by imperial decree was exactly parallel to the process by which administrators rose in the ranks of government service. At the "dharma-assemblies" of the various temples, the same sort of documents used in government departments were produced, the *beng* (announcement), *shu* (report), and *qizha* (epistle). At this point, the Chan monks began to write the formal essays of the bureacracy, or *pianli,* in alternating lines of four and six characters. The copying of these essays was also instituted, and thus the Chan school, which originally advocated "not depending upon words," came to be intimately involved with writing and official documentation, and a unique Chan literary culture was produced.

Of course, "not relying on words" refers to avoiding becoming bogged down in the literal meanings of the words of the Buddhist texts and does not enjoin complete abstention from the use of language. On the contrary, from the Tang dynasty on, words were freely used to express the realm of enlightenment and to lend a helping hand toward that direction. Beginning with the third patriarch Seng Can's *Testimony to Faith* (*Xin Xin Ming*), Yongjia Yuanjie's *Odes to Enlightenment* (*Zheng Dao Ge*), Shitou Xiqian's *Reaching Equanimity* (*San Tong Qi*), and other works, many "records" in the colloquial language, collections of sermons, sayings, and discussions were composed and passed down as instructions for practitioners. Students of Chan, lest they miss any word of their teacher's discussions, took to recording them in earnest. Foyin Liaoyuan, known through his association with Su Shi, strongly criticized this trend, quoting the old story of the Chan master Yunmen Wenyan, who, discovering one of his students was recording his words,

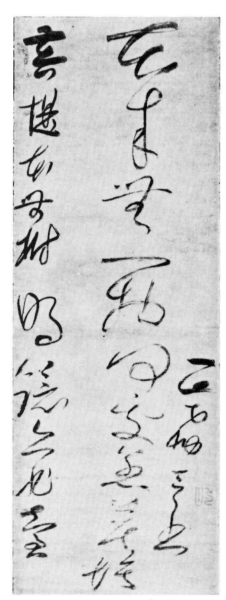

Fig. 68. Verses on the Six Patriarchs, Yishan Yining (Yuan dynasty).

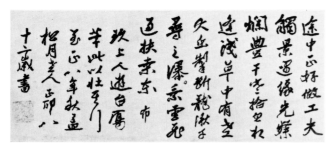

Fig. 69. Parting Verses, Yuejiang Zhengyin, (Yuan dynasty).

Fig. 70. Linji Sect Sermon, Chushi Fanqi, (Yuan dynasty).

drove him out of the monastery shouting, "Do you plan to sell me?" Adding his own comment, he said, "Scholars of later generations fishing for words will be like someone trying to inflate a net by blowing into it. If this isn't stupidity, its madness." Tahui Zonggao burned his teacher Yuanwe Keqin's composition, the *Blue Cliff Record* (*Bi Yan Lu*), and reprimanded students for their habit of recording everything. These anecdotes, however, show how respect for the written word was growing in Chan monasteries.

The custom of writing out one's sermons and passing them on to disciples became popular in the Southern Song. It is recorded in the "Postscript to *Yuanwu's Sermons*" (*Wuzhun Shifan Chanshi Yulu*, volume five) by Wuzhun Shifan that "from the time of Master Yuanwu, records admonishing and instructing students became popular." Since this seems to indicate that Yuanwu of the Northern Song was the first to make this practice popular, the "Yuanwu Keqin Diploma" (*Yuanwu Keqin Yinkezhuang*, pl. 56), the oldest existing Chan calligraphy, becomes extremely important as a Song-dynasty Chan document.

The written sermons that disciples received from their masters were not only remembrances of their teachers but also served as a license or certificate of sorts. As such, they were carefully guarded and passed from disciple to disciple. There is an interesting account related to this in the biography of Wuzhun Shifan: "When Po'an passed away, Mi'an Xianjie's dharma-robe and portrait were given to Shifan, but he refused them, and took only Yuanwu's calligraphy and Mi'an's sermons." We cannot be sure if Yuanwu's calligraphy and Mi'an's sermons mentioned here are the same "Yuanwu Keqin Diploma" and *Mi'an Xianjie's Sermons* (*Mi'an Xianjie Fayu*) that we have today, but the former has a postscript written by a Yuan-dynasty personage, indicating that at least up to the Yuan dynasty it had been transmitted from disciple to disciple within the Yangqi sect, and we cannot discount the possibility that it had passed through the hands of Shifan. At any rate, the passage above shows that together with the robe and the portrait of the master, his original writings were highly respected as proof of religious credentials, and this Chinese Chan custom is probably the source of the veneration of Chan calligraphy—especially sermons—in Japan.

When Japanese monks studying in China were to return home, they received from their teachers written sermons or farewell verses, or had a portrait of the master painted, and after having him write a few verses on it, brought these things back to Japan. These were treated as diplomas, and thus were always treasured after their return home as momentos of their teacher. In addition, they served as proof of their "dharma lineage" and as such were passed on to their disciples.

In other words, what are called *bokuseki* in Japan were not kept merely as samples of calligraphy or objects of beauty, but as, for their inheritors, the Buddha's teaching. In the appreciation of Chan calligraphy, this remains a crucial point that must be understood.

# Zhao Mengfu and His Followers

The calligraphy of Su Shi, Huang Tingjian and Mi Fu, after having thoroughly explored and ingested classical influences, exhibited a considerable degree of individual character. These three masters had a definite influence on the world of calligraphy after them, but the most extreme exponents of this style were guilty of self-indulgence and extravagances that led to the decline of this school. There were many other Southern Song calligraphers, but none that can compare with those three masters.

The Yuan dynasty, of course, was founded by the Mongol people. At the beginning of the dynasty, the Mongols took great care to preserve their own nomadic customs, and made no positive attempts at cultural exchanges with the Chinese. However, after the defeat of the Southern Song and Mongol dominance over all of China, they gradually began to be absorbed into the Chinese culture, and it wasn't long before certain Mongols and men of the northwest regions began to show ability in cultural pursuits as well.

Zhao Mengfu (1254–1322) was from Huzhou (Wuxing) in Zhejiang Province. As the eleventh-generation descendant of Tazu of the Song, he was fortunate in birth and gifted in learning, and served in important capacities under several early Yuan-dynasty emperors. As the heir to the Song emperors, who had been so gifted in artistic ability, he showed great talent. Not only did he excel in calligraphy and painting, but he was also a skilled poet, an excellent seal engraver, possessed of sharp critical faculties and no little musical talent.

Zhao Mengfu studied exhaustively the calligraphy of earlier ages, conducting extensive research into even seal-scribe and essay-cursive scripts. His disciple Yang Zai said of him, "He studied seal script from the stone drums and Chu spells, scribe script from Liang Hu and Zhong Yao." Song Lian of the early Ming dynasty wrote of him, "At first he studied Gaozong of the Southern Song, later Zhong Yao, the two Wangs and their followers, and finally Li Yong." But his studies did not stop here, for he incorporated the special traits of the calligraphy of many Tang masters into his writing, with the influences of Yan Zhenqing and Huang Tingjian especially evident. Liu Guan remarked that "In his early years he took pleasure in copying

Fig. 71. Essay, Zhao Mengfu (Yuan dynasty).

Zhiyong's "Thousand-Character Essay," verifying that the warm, flowing beauty of Zhiyong's calligraphy was an undercurrent in Zhao Mengfu's formal, majestic style. Zhao's semi-cursive script owes a great deal to Wang Xizhi's "Orchid Pavilion Preface" and "Holy Teachings Preface" (*Shengxiao Xu*), and his cursive script mainly to the "Shiqi Album." Wu Rongguang of the Qing dynasty discusses Zhao's style by dividing it into periods, saying, "Zhao's calligraphy passed through three stages. Prior to the Yuanzhen era (1295–97), it remained within the bounds of Gaozong's standards. During the Tade era (1297–1307), he concentrated on the "Orchid Pavilion Preface," and from the Yanyou era (1314–20), he incorporated the methods of Li Yong and Liu Chengxuan. However, most of all he made use of the stele inscriptions." This sort of division is open to much debate, which we cannot pursue here. In conclusion, Zhao studied the calligraphy of many different eras and endeavoured to combine and use the best of everything.

The *History of the Yuan* (*Yuan Shi*) described Zhao Mengfu's calligraphy as among the masterpieces of all time, saying that "His *seal, bafen,* scribe, block, semi-cursive, and cursive scripts were absolutely unparalleled, and he was known throughout the empire for his calligraphy." Yu Ji also remarked, "Zhao's calligraphy exhibits his mastery of the brush and his great learning. When looking at his calligraphy, one can see that his hand is responding to what he knows in his heart, and he always writes with the meaning in mind. Unless one has both erudition and natural talents for calligraphy, one cannot reach profound artistic heights," saying in effect that because Zhao was able to make his great learning a foundation, he was able to fully exploit his natural gifts for calligraphy, reaching the greatest extremes of delicate sophistication. In fact, his remarkable achievements in many different artistic arenas are due to this wedding of natural gifts and erudition. Some will no doubt dispute the paean, "No calligraphy equalled his for five hundred years past or future, or for ten thousand leagues in any direction," but when we consider his remarkable display of talents in such a variety of arenas, this praise cannot be totally discounted.

It is also a simple matter to detect defects in Zhao Mengfu's calligraphy. The Ming-dynasty master Dong Qichang, comparing his own work to Zhao's, wrote, "My calligraphy is unlike Zhao's, with its columns squeezed together and all its characters the same. Zhao's passion often resulted in vulgarity, while my calligraphy has a spiritedness that results in superior form. Zhao's calligraphy is contrived, while mine flows and is direct in expression." Many others have also pointed out that Zhao's calligraphy is monotonous and lacking in backbone, with a feeling of over-ripeness. These criticisms are best taken as faulting Zhao for the very qualities, mentioned earlier, for which he was praised.

From an entirely different perspective, many criticized him because, though of the Song imperial line, he cooperated with a barbarian dynasty. Fu Shan, one of the loyal opposition during the Ming dynasty, said, "When the person is disparaged, his calligraphy is also despised." And Weng Fanggang remarked, "There is no beauty to be found in flattery. This is not the proper nature of calligraphy. It results in a corrupt style." These volleys, delivered from the standpoint of critics who held that not only calligraphy but all arts are a reflection of the integrity of the personality of their creator, can probably not be avoided in Zhao's case.

Of the many examples of Zhao Mengfu's works that have come down to us, the most brilliant are the "Three Gates Record," the "Miaoyan Temple Record" (*Miaoyan Si Ji*) the "Dan Ba Stele" (*Dan Ba Bei*), and the "Chou Yanzhong Stele" (*Chou Yanzhong Bei*), all in large characters. In small semi-cursive and cursive script, we have the "Postscript to the Album

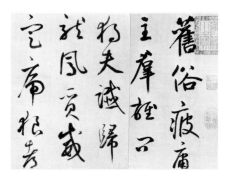

Fig. 72. Vision of the God of Fortune,
Zhao Mengfu (Yuan dynasty).

of Huaisu's Writings" (*Huaisu Lunshu Tie Ba*), the "Thirteen Postscripts
to the Orchid Pavilion" (*Lan Ting Shisan Ba*), and others. The "Biography
of Ji'an" (*Ji'an Chuan*, pl. 68) is quite well known for its excellent small
block script. Almost one hundred stone carvings are preserved in the *Huan
Yu Catalogue of Steles* (*Huan Yu Fang Bei Lu*) alone. In general, the pieces
represented in copybooks are inferior, but the *Ode to the Spirit of Luo River*
(*Luoshen Fu*) in the "Yunqing Hall Album" (*Yunqing Guan Tie*) is rich in
spirit.

The reason that those in the world of calligraphy at this time, under the
advocacy of Zhao Mengfu, headed in the direction of Jin and Tang calligraphy—mainly that of the two Wangs—and put their energies into a
sudden classical revival was that they naturally tried to preserve traditional
Chinese culture under the extreme pressure of the Mongol policies. However, since this was largely a negative, defensive posture, the classic revival
had little positive energy and, at the very least, was lacking in creativity.
Nevertheless, the achievement of Zhao Mengfu in gathering together and
passing on to the next generation the aesthetic tradition beginning with the
two Wangs, which had fallen into decline and might otherwise have been
completely lost, was, together with his similar role in the world of painting,
an important event in the history of Chinese art. If it had not been for his
activities, it is possible that neither Wenzong's Kuizhang Archives nor
Emperor Shun's Xuanwen Archives would have been built, and the rich
literary and cultural flowering in Jiangnan during the later Yuan and early
Ming might not have occured.

Through the Yuan dynasty, men like Deng Wenyuan, Yu Ji, Zhang
Yu, and Wang Meng carried on in Zhao's tradition, while Xianyu Shu,
Kangli Kuikui, Yang Weizhen, and Ni Zan are usually regarded as little
influenced by him. However, as both groups were classical revivalists who
studied the Jin and Tang works, they showed a great deal in common with
Zhao Mengfu. His calligraphic style was still very popular in the early
Ming, and Song Ke, Jie Jin, Shen Du, and Shen Can all studied his calli-
graphy.

This style even spread to Korea and Japan—particularly the former, as
Chu Gen Wang of the later Kŏryo kingdom became intimate with Zhao
in Beijing. As a result, his style was to hold sway over the Korean peninsula
for some two hundred years. This is what is known as *shu* style, the name
deriving from a dialect pronunciation of a section of the character for
Zhao's name. His style was also much favored in printed characters such
as those which were carved into wood printing blocks.

The reasons for the great popularity of Zhao Mengfu's calligraphy were
no doubt that it was based on the orthodox tradition of the two Wangs,
that is was beautiful and elegant, and that it was clear and easy to read. The

Fig. 73. Du Fu's Poetry, Xianyu
Shu (Yuan dynasty).

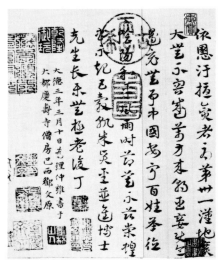

Fig. 74. Copy of the Ji Jiu Glossary, Deng Wenyuan (Yuan dynasty).

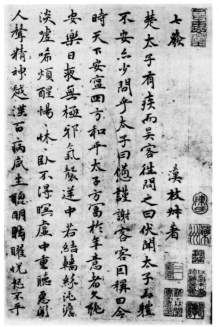

Fig. 75. Essay, Yu Ji (Yuan dynasty).

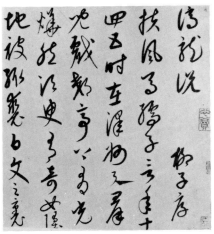

Fig. 76. Essay, Kangli Kuikui (Yuan dynasty).

style of Dong Qichang, which "prized extremes and oddities," stands in direct opposition to Zhao Mengfu. If an extreme and odd style of calligraphy had prevailed at this time, the art might have fallen into a degeneration from which it would have been difficult to rescue.

If we are pressed to find one calligrapher who can compare to Zhao Mengfu, it would be Xianyu Shu (1257–1302). He was originally from Yuyang in Hebei Province. Later, he retired to Xihu and lost himself in his leisure pursuits. The *Brief introduction to the History of Calligraphy* says that "he was able to create original shapes for characters as he wished, excelled in both semi-cursive and cursive, and Zhao Wenmin regarded him very highly," but he was also criticized for tendencies toward vulgarity. He associated closely with Zhao Mengfu and they even exchanged poems. An example of his work can be seen in figure 73.

Deng Wenyuan (1259–1329) was from Mian district in Sichuan. His calligraphy (fig. 74) was modeled after the two Wangs, and he later studied Li Yong. In the mid-Yuan dynasty it was said, "Naming the accomplished calligraphers, we come down to Deng, Xianyu, and Zhao," though the first two did not of course compare with Zhao.

Wenzong of the Yuan was intoxicated with Chinese culture, and collected a great many ancient implements, works of calligraphy, and paintings, storing them in the Kuizhang Archives and devoting himself to their appreciation. Yu Ji and Ke Jiusi worked under his direction in this effort. Yu Ji (1272–1348) was from Chongren in Jiangxi Province. He was the greatest calligrapher of the Yuan court and accomplished in all the arts. The *Brief Introduction to the History of Calligraphy* says of him, "His block, semi-cursive, and cursive script were all masterful, and his ancient-style scribe script was the best of the period." His semi-cursive script can be viewed in figure 75. Ke Jiusi (1290–1343) was from Taizhou in Zhejiang. He is famous for his ink paintings of bamboo, and he also studied the calligraphy of Ouyang Xun. Another who served in the Kuizhang Archives and the Xuanwen Archives was Kangli Kuikui (1295–1345), of the Kangli tribe in the western region. His calligraphy (fig. 76) is often ranked next to Zhao's, for he had mastered the brushwork of the Jin masters. People fought for scraps of his letters, so treasured was his calligraphy.

Wu Qiuyan was from Hangzhou in Zhejiang. He was skilled at seal script, and his *Xue Gu Bian* is treasured as the first specialist work on seal carving. Zhou Boqi (1298–1369), who was also accomplished in seal script, was from Poyang in Jiangxi. He was much favored by Shun Di and entrusted with various posts in the government, but afterwards, invited by Zhang Shicheng of Suzhou, he switched his loyalties. Zhang Sicheng had occupied the rich region of the lower Changjiang. He welcomed scholars, and many arrived at his court, escaping the chaos at the end of the Yuan dynasty and passing on the cultural boom of the former dynasty to the Ming.

Zhang Yu (1277–1348) was from Hangzhou in Zhejiang. He had a high reputation as a sage and was also an excellent poet whose calligraphy was said to be free from all vulgarity. Yang Weizhen (1296–1370) was from Shaoying in Zhejiang. Giving up on worldly success, he exiled himself to Songjiang and for over thirty years reigned over the literary boom of the later Yuan. His calligraphy was said to be forceful and wild. Ni Zan (1301–74) was from a wealthy family in Wuxi, Jiangsu Province. Squandering his fortune in his devotion to calligraphy and painting, he retired from public life. He is numbered as one of the four masters of Yuanli, and one of the great masters of the southern school of painting. His calligraphy (fig. 77), which was modeled after the Jin masters, was very graceful. These three were devoted masters of the arts who ended their lives in retirement from the public realm. They have been taken as models of "men of culture" through the ages.

Zhao Mengfu's presence during the Yuan can be compared to Wang Xizhi of the Jin and Yan Zhenqing of the Tang. The first drew together the traditions of the Han and Wei dynasties, and the second combined the virtues of the calligraphy of the northern and southern dynasties. Zhao, taking the Wei and Jin masters as his teachers and studying closely the Tang and Song masters, combined the virtues of all. It is a shame that he has left us no writings on his theories of calligraphy and painting and also that very few of his postscripts remain. This, with only a few exceptions, is an unfortunate fact of the Yuan dynasty. We have only two specialist works on calligraphic theory, Zheng Yun's *Yan Ji* (The Ultimate), and Chen Yiceng's *The Secret Teachings of the Hanlin Academy* (*Hanlin Yaojue*). The former is an extremely difficult work and is usually read following Liu Youding's commentary. We do have a collection of biographies of calligraphers in Tao Zongyi's *Brief Introduction to the History of Calligraphy,* but the theoretical development of Yuan-dynasty calligraphy is largely unexplored.

Fig. 77. Poetry, Ni Zan (Yuan dynasty).

# The Ming Literati

The Ming dynasty (1368–1644), succeeding the Mongol-ruled Yuan dynasty, was the first Chinese dynasty in over one hundred years. For the next 270 years the Chinese would rarely be threatened by invasion. This period of peace contributed to the regeneration of the Chinese cultural tradition that had continued from the Han, Wei, and Six Dynasties period up through the Tang and Song, and led to its fullest fruition.

For convenience's sake, Ming calligraphy can be divided into three periods. In the first period, from 1368 to 1487, the classical revival of Zhao Mengfu of the Yuan continued. In the middle period, from 1488 to 1566, many new calligraphers appeared. In the final period, from 1567 to 1644, a revolutionary new calligraphy was created.

The most telling features of Ming calligraphy appeared during the middle period. A literary movement flourished at this time, and devotion to calligraphy and painting became widespread. In the process, the revolutionary calligraphy of Su Shi, Huang Tingjian and Mi Fu of the Northern Song attracted attention. Zhang Bi (1425–87) of Huating in Jiangsu was the precursor of this development. He excelled in a wild and free "wild cursive" script, which he wrote while inebriated, and is famous for the comment, "the fullness of nature is my teacher." Also in Suzhou, Shen Zhou (1427–1509) wrote in the manner of Huang Tingjian. Wu Xuan (1435–1504) excelled in Su Shi-style calligraphy (fig. 78), and Li Yingzhen (1431–93) studied the Jin and Tang masters, though he prized variations and was not content to merely follow old methods faithfully. Chen Xianzhang (1428–1500) from Xinhui in Guangdong is known as the one who laid the foundation for Wang Yangming's philosphy, but he also wrote in a distinctive, highly developed hand, using bundles of reeds as a brush (fig. 79).

Shen Zhou, Wu Xuan and Li Yingzhen were all from Suzhou. Later, Zhu Yunming (1460–1526) and Wen Zhengming (1470–1559) were active in that region. Both are famous calligraphers of the period. Zhu Yunming was the son-in-law of Li Yingzhen and was influenced by his work, but he also often copied the Wei and Jin calligraphy. He excelled in small block, semi-cursive, and cursive scripts. Zhu produced a new style of his own and was said to be "foremost calligrapher in the land." In this later years, he was

Fig. 78. Poetry, Wu Xuan (Ming dynasty).

Fig. 79. Poetry, Chen Xianzhang (Ming dynasty).

praised for his wild cursive, at which he was also very accomplished. Wen Zhengming studied under Li Yingzhen, preserving a continuity from the Song and Yuan back to the Jin and Tang. He was very good at small block script, and was known as the best semi-cursive and cursive calligrapher since Zhao Mengfu. He turned to Huang Tingjian's style as he grew old and left several works that show this influence (fig. 80). However, he did not excel in calligraphy alone. He was a master of painting and poetry as well, blessed with a fine critical sense, and interested in many different pursuits: in sum, a man of the highest refinement. This kind of person was known as a "man of letters," or a literatus. Shen Zhou, who preceded Wen Zhengming, was of this mold, as were all who made names for themselves as calligraphers during this period. Most of them came from Suzhou, Jiangsu and Zhejiang.

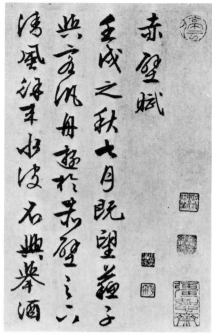

Fig. 80. Red Cliffs Ode, Wen Zhengming (Ming dynasty).

These literati were of many different types, and it is difficult to define them as a class. In ancient times, the term meant learned men and referred to writers. Eventually, it came to mean anyone gifted in literature or the arts, and especially those involved in the actual creation of works of art or literature. Closer consideration would reveal that in China, where mastery of writing was the mark of the official class, there were many who were both "men of letters" and officials at the same time. On the other hand, the two vocations were in some senses contradictory, and many redirected their activities from one arena to the other during the course of their lives. From the Song period, the number of literati who withdrew from official life increased. In the Yuan dynasty, there were many individuals who preferred private life to public service. They chose a life among the city populace over retirement in the wilderness and devoted themselves to the arts. The men who came from Suzhou during the Ming were the inheritors of that tradition.

The appearance of the literati suggests a social environment that approved of and encouraged the growth of such a class. The Jiangsu and Zhejiang regions were the major rice-growing areas since the Song and the Yuan dynasties, Suzhou being the center of this area. The population of the region was dense, and, in the Ming dynasty, it became a textile producing region. As a major producer of cotton and cotton cloth, it achieved considerable economic development. But this was not all. Suzhou was well known for its beautiful scenery and many famous sites. From ancient times, many cultured people had been drawn to the "water capital," as Suzhou was known. Now, from this new economic springboard, the people of Suzhou experienced a rise in the level of education, culture, and creature comforts, and the region became a cultural and economic center to rival Beijing.

One special feature of this region was that many of the gentry of the region did not seek official rank or, if they did, retired from office early and chose to associate instead with the numerous other literati that lived in the region. Shen Zhou and Wen Zhengming were just such cases. This shows, perhaps, that the arts enjoyed an existence quite separate from official life. In other words, the economic development and educational advancement of the people of Suzhou had created a leisure culture within which the appreciation of works of calligraphy and painting and their pursuit and collection were nurtured. Against this larger background the literati pursued their elegant and refined pastimes. Eventually, as they cultivated eccentricities, the movement degenerated into dilettantism and professionalization. Wen Zhengming, who "ruled over the alliance of elegance in old Suzhou for thirty years," managed to avoid this extreme and remain true to his art. He excelled in poetry, calligraphy, and painting over the span of a long lifetime of ninety years, but it was his refined personality more than anything that prevented him from falling into lifeless professionalism. He persisted in creating for his own enjoyment, which was the true spirit of the movement.

147

Fig. 81. Epitaph for Xu Gong, Wen Peng (Ming dynasty).

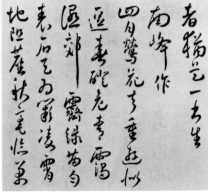

Fig. 82. Poetry, Wang Chong (Ming dynasty).

It was this erudition and his integrity as a scholar that led Tang Yin, known for his eccentricity, to say of him, "Just being next to him, one is overawed."

The Wen family all excelled in the arts. Wen Zhengming's children, Wen Peng (1498–1573) and Wen Jia (1501–83) made names for themselves in calligraphy, and Wen Peng is famous as the father of modern seal carving (fig. 81). The many who inherited and continued Wen Zhengming's style formed a "Wen School," and of these Chen Shun (1483–1544), Wang Chong (1494–1533; see fig. 82 for a sample of his work), and later Zhou Tianqiu (1514–95) are the best known. Still, towards the end this school, too, headed towards professionalization. In opposition to the Wen school, Feng Fang (died 1576?) appeared in the Zhejiang area, but his school was overshadowed by its rival.

One point that cannot be overlooked in relation to the calligraphy of the literati is that it grew out of the life of leisure and was inseparable from that lifestyle. Originally, calligraphy was practiced as one of the de rigueur accomplishments in the salon of the literati. That salon, or more accurately, study, was equipped with brushes, ink, inkstones and paper, copybooks and rubbings of monument inscriptions, ancient bronze vessels, and arrangements of flowers, stones, and sand. There, calligraphy went on with other activities, such as the preparation of tea, the appreciation of rare incense, entertaining guests, and muscial performances. This kind of life of leisure was first cultivated among the hermits who lived in the wilderness during the Southern Song and, refined and crystalized during the Yuan and into the Ming, reached its peak from 1522 to 1620. It was in this context that calligraphy and painting came to be the supreme pleasures, and the collection, appreciation and discussion of famous works, together with personal printings of selections of them, became popular. Xiang Yuanbian was a famous collector with a marvelous and important collection. The popularity of collecting encouraged a flood of forgeries, but appreciation of calligraphy was directed more toward grasping the essence of the work than distinguishing between authentic and forged works.

Copybooks and albums were published by Hua Xia and Wen Zhengming in the early 1500s. Other well-known collections by the likes of Wu Ting and Dong Qichang appeared by the late 1500s and early 1600s. Famous works, mainly from the Jin and Tang but extending to the Song and Yuan, were assembled in these copybooks. These were enjoyed as curios, but selections were also made on a scholarly basis and to establish and document the editor's own calligraphic style.

A variety of forms of presenting, displaying, and mounting works of calligraphy developed at this time. Prior to the Ming, the horizontal scroll predominated. During the Yuan the vertical scroll to be hung on the wall for viewing came into being, becoming more and more popular throughout the Ming. In addition, a variety of other formats for calligraphic works were accepted, including calligraphy on folding fans and books. On all of these, seals were used to stamp the author's name. Other seals, carved with felicitious passages, were stamped in the compositions' upper right corner. The earlier trend toward excelling in the three arts of poetry, calligraphy, and painting resulted in the practice of writing poems on paintings and compiling volumes of composite works. These were of many types, such as collections made by a group of artists in one sitting, collections of the calligraphy and paintings of individual masters, and collections by genre—such as fan calligraphy or letters. In addition, gold-flecked paper and, towards the end of the Ming, shiny white silk paper and other textured, embossed papers came into use in addition to the traditional silk papers. All of these developments arose from the treatment of calligraphy as a salon art in the leisure-oriented lives of the literati.

At the end of the Ming, Dong Qichang (1555–1636) was active in Song-jiang, which is adjacent to Suzhou. In contrast to Wen Zhengming, he entered government service as a member of the Hanlin Academy and, in later years, as the Minister of the Department of Rites in Nanqing. He was a greedy and selfish man, devoted to acquiring wealth, who assiduously bought up as many works of painting and calligraphy as he could and was so disliked that his property was looted and burned twice. Still, his gifts in the arts were on the par with Wen Zhengming, and his profound and extensive learning and · perspicacious art criticism even superior to Wen, earning him the title, "the master of the arts for one hundred generations." His art criticism was his most memorable achievement. His theories concerning the northern and southern schools of painting are well-known. Discussing the calligraphy of Su, Huang, and Mi, whose attention was drawn to the surpassing elegance of the calligraphy of the Jin masters through Yan Zhenqing of the Tang, and all of whom valued creativity more than the traditionally technique-oriented calligraphy, Dong wrote, "the Jin masters emphasized grace, the Tang masters, techniques, and the Song masters, meaning." He defined the highest goal of calligraphy as a simple naturalness and declared that personal enlightenment was the only method to reach it. His view of calligraphy, of course, was based in his own talents as a calligrapher (see fig. 83) as well as the leisure culture of the literati which had reached its peak at that time. The naturalism championed by Li Zhuowu, originating in Wang Yang-ming's teachings that synthesized the three teachings of Buddhism, Taoism and Confucianism, was another important influence on Dong.

Contemporary with Dong Qichang, in the north Mi Wanzhong (dates of birth and death uncertain) excelled at Mi Fu-style calligraphy, and Xing Tong (1551–1612) studied the two Wangs and Zhao Mengfu, but neither could really rival Dong Qichang.

Pressures on the Ming from the Manchus to the north began to increase, but since the court adopted a policy of passive indifference, raids and minor conflicts continued and the Ming fell, leaving China under the rule of the Manchus in the new Qing dynasty. Some brilliant calligraphy was created at the end of the Ming and beginning of the Qing—the calligraphy of Zhang Ruitu (1570–1641), Huang Daozhou (1585–1646), Ni Yuanlu (1593–1644), Fu Shan (1607–84) and Wang Duo (1592–1652). Though they all reacted differently, some turning their backs on government and devoting themselves to religion, some dying as martyrs for the Ming, some stubbornly resisting the new dynasty, and some giving in to its sway, they shared a calligraphic style—continuous, or connected, cursive script written on long vertical scrolls. The despair of these men who had witnessed the collapse of their world forced them to deviate from classical standards. Their calligraphy is strange and eerie, with a strength and determination that strikes home. Because cursive script was a style developed by adapting characters freely for writing quickly and in an abbreviated fashion, it permitted creative expression and was the most expressive writing style. Cursive was the main style during the Ming period, and during this time it reached an apogee of artistic expression. At the same time, the calligraphic theories of Dong Qichang were also refined and developed by the reform school.

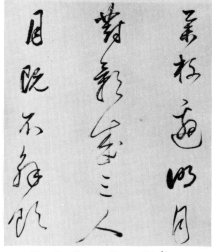

Fig. 83. Poem, Dong Qichang (Ming dynasty).

# Copybook and Stele Studies
# of the Qing Dynasty

The copybook and stele schools are not the names of groups of calligraphers, but terms that provide a bird's-eye view of the many different schools of Qing-dynasty calligraphy. The copybook school took the work of the two Wangs and Zhong Yao printed in copybooks and albums such as the "Chunhua Pavilion Copybook" as its main subject of study. Included under this heading were those who followed the traditions of Mi Fu, Zhao Mengfu, Dong Qichang, and others who inherited the tradition of the Jin masters. The stele school, on the other hand, took its direction from studies of the stone carvings dating from the Han through the Wei and northern dynasties. These had been almost totally neglected since the Song dynasty. It also included those who, in their search for the essential beauty of calligraphy, studied ancient works, including even seal script and bronze castings. However, there were many who studied both schools and broke new ground of their own. The true situation cannot be quite so simply drawn. Nor is it correct to identify the copybook school as conservative and the stele school as progressive, in a cut-and-dried fashion. Even so, the tide of the times was in favor of the stele school, which has continued to dominate up to the present. The general character of the calligraphy of the Qing, in both schools, was a neo-classical movement based on scholastic research.

## The Copybook School

The copybook school was most active from the beginning of the Qing to 1736, a period of roughly 150 years. To understand this period, it is most conveniently divided into two parts, the early copybook-school period, up to 1735, and the later, from 1736 to 1795. Further, three distinct movements can be identified within the copybook school:

1) The calligraphers who were accomplished in connected cursive script, represented by Wang Duo and Fu Shan of the late Ming and early Qing. These men differed considerably in character and means of livelihood, but their calligraphy shared in common a strength of brush, extension of

phrase, and stirring quality. The generous, otherworldly calligraphy of Bada Shanren belongs to this category. However, this style was not to survive much longer.

2) The main tradition of the early period of the copybook school, represented by Zhao Mengfu and Dong Qichang.

3) Those who are most characteristic of the later copybook school, who first studied Zhao and Dong, and later went on to the work of Su Shi, Mi Fu, and Yan Zhenqing, finally advancing to Zhong and the two Wangs. When the copybook school is mentioned, it is usually the first and second groups that are being referred to. The style of Zhao Mengfu and Dong Qichang was most predominant from 1662 to 1795. Dong Qichang's work dominated at first, because it was greatly admired by Emperor Kangxi. He himself excelled in Dong-style calligraphy, his ministers followed suit, and eventually this style even found its way onto the national examination papers. However, by the late eighteenth century the popularity of this style had run its course and was on the wane, and Zhao Mengfu's style replaced it in the hearts of the public.

Those active in the early copybook-school period, though they may have pursued the styles of others, such as the classical techniques of the Jin and Wei, the block-script techniques of the Tang, or the styles of Su and Mi, came to these sources after passing through studies of Zhao and Dong. None of them ever approached the freshness of either of these masters, however, and no new developments that would supercede their achievements were forthcoming. Several calligraphers gained some following during this period.

Shen Quan (1624–84) was a descendant of Shen Du of the early Ming. He studied Dong Qichang, who was from the same district as he, and was a favorite of Emperor Kangxi. Jiang Chenying (1628–99) was praised for his small block script in the Zhong and Wang styles, and his graceful rendition of Dong-style semi-cursive and cursive scripts. Cha Sheng (1650–1722) was declared by all the critics to have attained Dong's grace. Chen Yixi (1648–1707) worked a synthesis of Zhao and Dong's styles, and after his death his "Mengmo Tower Album" (*Mengmo Lou Tie*) was assembled at Emperor Yongzhong's command. He Zhuo (1661–1722) was a scholar of historical studies who began with Dong's style and went on to excel in the small block characters of Jin and Tang. Wang Shu (1668–1739) was a master of all styles, having studied both steles and copybooks and contributed to later scholarship with several extensive studies. A sample of his seal script is on view in figure 84.

Thus, as they entered the mid- and late eighteenth century, calligraphers were moving away from Zhao and Dong and beginning to make direct contact with Jin, Tang, and Song copybooks. The following points should also be made concerning the cultural background of the later copybook-school period. Emperor Kangxi encouraged cultural development with his sympathy for the traditional scholarship of the Chinese and, at the same time, his attempts to import and absorb European culture. Emperor Yongzheng continued in this vein, sponsoring many cultural projects.

The *Catalogue of Paintings and Calligraphy of the Peiwen Archives* (*Peiwen Zhai Shu Hua Pu*), completed during Kangxi's reign, assembled and organized the works of calligraphy and painting throughout the ages, and the foundation of the study of copybooks was thus laid. These studies reached their fullest development during the latter part of the eighteenth century. During this period, too, many works that had been in private collections passed into imperial possession, and the number of imperial possessions reached enormous numbers.

The *Shi Qu Bao Ji* was a catalogue of the government holdings in calli-

Fig. 84. Seal-script calligraphy, Wang Shu (Qing dynasty).

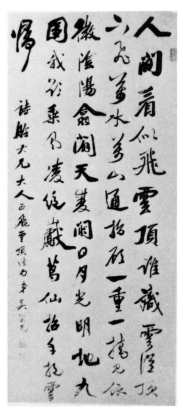

Fig. 85. Semi-cursive script scroll, Wu Yingguang (Qing dynasty).

Fig. 86. Stele in scribe script, Weng Fanggang (Qing dynasty).

graphy and painting whose compilation continued on into the early nineteenth century. A collection of famous writings, the "Three Treasures Hall Copybook" (*San Xi Tang Fatie*), was also copied and printed, and a consideration and commentary on that great work of calligraphy, the "Chunhua Pavilion Copybook," was printed.

Following the Ming practice, many collectors printed private editions of copybooks, and numerous scholarly catalogues were printed as well. The late seventeenth and early eighteenth centuries saw the appearance of Feng Wu's *Orthodox Tradition of Calligraphy* (*Shufa Zhengchuan*); in the later eighteenth century, other collections related to traditional calligraphy were published. This movement to collate and publish ancient works formed the mainstream of the copybook school, and persisted on into the later nineteenth century.

The mid-eighteenth century was the peak of the copybook school. Several calligraphers who observed the old techniques of the Jin and Tang and managed to attain the style of the Song masters were active. The following are the four who are best known.

Zhang Zhao (1691–1745) was an important minister who moved through a succession of posts, including Cabinet Minister and Secretary of the Department of Justice. He entered the world of calligraphy through Dong Qichang, but studied the famous works of calligraphy of all ages and later concentrated on Yan Zhenqing and Mi Fu. His semi-cursive script was said to be bold and graceful, and he attracted many followers.

Wang Wenzhi (1730–1802) retired from public office in his middle years and, associating with artists and writers, lived the life of one of the cultured elite. He studied Chu Suiliang's block script and Wang Xizhi's cursive. Though Zhao and Dong formed the true foundation of his style, it was still quite distinct, with a warm and beautiful character.

Liu Yong (1719–1804) had a career spanning two generations and climaxing in the high office of Grand Secretary. He studied the Confucian classics and was an excellent poet, but these achievements were overshadowed by the praises of his calligraphy. He lived a long, full life of eighty-six years. In his youth he studied Zhao and Dong, moving on to the stele rubbings of the Jin and Tang from middle age. He avidly studied Yan Zhenqing, Su Shi and Mi Fu and, grasping their essence, created a synthesis that was the very foundation of the copybook school, of which he was the great patriarch. He achieved a simplified expression in his block, semi-cursive, and cursive scripts by utilizing the white space fully and had a bold, richly suggestive style.

Liang Tongshu (1723–1815) also retired from public office early. He excelled in poetry and painting and had a fine critical sense, too, but was most accomplished as a calligrapher. He lived to be ninety-three and when over ninety continued to produce calligraphy upon request, his reputation spreading as far as Korea and Japan. He, Liang Guozhi, and Liang Yan are known collectively as the three Liangs.

From the second half of the eighteenth century, the stele school began its rise in popularity, but many such as Liang Tongshu continued to work mainly with the copybook school. Yao Nai, Qian Bojiong, Zhang Wentao, Cheng Xinwang, and Wu Yingguang (see fig. 85) are others in this group. There were also some who actually used the copybook studies for the basis of their calligraphy. Weng Fanggang (1733–1818) was a high official who reached cabinet rank. He left many marvelous achievements in a wide variety of fields, but he was particularly erudite in stone and metal inscriptions and in copybook studies. He evidenced the same kind of careful research methods in his copybook studies that were applied in studies of

Han and Tang steles and composed the "Study of the Su-Mi Library Orchid Pavilion manuscript" (*Su-Mi Zhai Lan Ting Kao*), a consideration of the bible of the copybook school, the "Orchid Pavilion Preface." Some list him together with Liu Yong, Wang Wenzhi and Liang Tongshu as one of the four masters of the copybook school. He began with Yan's techniques and is said to have studied Ouyang and Yu Ji. He is often underestimated because of the conscientious and reserved nature of his calligraphy (fig. 86).

At the peak of the copybook studies period, those who would later become active in the stele school were already emerging. But several artists who belonged to neither school were especially active during this period. Among them we must mention the Eight Eccentries of Yangzhou and the Four Masters of Xiling. Yangzhou (present Jiangsu Province, Jiangtu Prefecture) was at that time an economic and distribution center and one of the leading commercial cities in Jiangnan. This economic power attracted many artists from all over China. The Eight Eccentrics of Yangzhou were eight especially accomplished masters from among this group. They were called eccentric because they possessed a creative ability that transcended all traditional techniques and means of expression and prided themselves in their independence and escape from all the restraints of authority and power. The Eight Eccentrics were chosen largely for their painting ability, but Jin Nong and Zheng Xie were also regarded as masterful calligraphers.

Jin Nong (1687–1763) spent his life in painting, poetry, and calligraphy. As a young man, he made a name for himself as a poet, studied rubbings of metal and stone inscriptions, and developed a fine critical sense for ancient calligraphy and paintings. He associated with Zheng Xie and Gao Xiang, and was especially close to Ding Jing. He had a fierce ego, and his poetry, calligraphy, and painting show a synthesis of feeling and thought that originates in his strong belief in a classical revival.

Zheng Xie (1693–1765) was of a strongly anti-authoritarian nature and did not pander to the tastes of the time. He wasted his earnings on drink, and died in poverty. His was a semi-cursive and cursive script (fig. 87) based on Huang Tingjian of the Song, and he created an individual style of calligraphy by adapting one of the ornamental calligraphic styles.

The pioneering reformers in the seal carving world were active for the most part in the Zhejiang region and were called the Zhe school, but they were also known as the Xiling school. The leader of this school was Ding Jing (1695–1765). He tired of the elaborate seal style that had been current from the Ming dynasty and urged a return to Han classicism, a move which attracted many followers. The representatives of this school who were active during the mid- to late eighteenth century included Jiang Ren (1743–95), Huang Yi (1744–95), and Xi Gang (1741–1803). Together with Ding Jing, they are known as the Four Masters of Xiling. Among these four masters, Huang Yi also pioneered in research on metal and stone inscriptions and contributed to research on Han and Wei calligraphic techniques (see fig. 88).

These new movements like the Yangzhou school and the Zhe school were highly appraised in later generations, but at the time the calligraphers of the copybook school, which was in favor with Emperor Qianliang, were the representatives of the mainstream of the world of calligraphy.

## The Stele School

As one of the policies aimed at placating the unrest of the Chinese, the Qing rulers sponsored many vast imperial publishing projects from 1662 to 1795. *The Collection of Old and New Documents (Gujin Tushu Jicheng)* and the

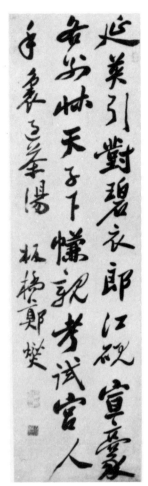

Fig. 87. Semi-cursive script, Zheng Xie (Qing dynasty).

Fig. 88. Scribe-script scrolls, Huang Yi (Qing dynasty).

Fig. 89. Scribe-script version of Du Fu's poetry, Zheng Fu (Ming dynasty).

Fig. 90. Seal-script scrolls, Qian Dian (Ming dynasty).

*Collected Works of the Four Treasuries* (*Si Ku Quanshu*) were examples of these. On the other hand, the regime, in seeking support for its authoritarian policies, feared anti-Manchu attitudes and prohibited all criticism of the government. The harsh control of public debate embodied in the censorship laws effectively nipped in the bud any participation of the intellectual class in the government. Under these kinds of pressures, the intelligentsia turned their energies to scholarly research.

This research consisted of comparisons of the ancient texts and historical records against other historical materials—the stone and metal inscriptions on steles and bronze implements, for example. However, these sources were not limited to use in scholastic research.

For example, the achievements of Gu Yanwu (1613–82) at the start of the Qing in the study of Chinese characters were inherited and advanced by Zhu Yizun (1629–1709) and Huang Yi. During that same time Zheng Fu (1622–93), at the peak of the copybook school's influence, was writing scribe script full of feeling and movement inspired by the classic simplicity of the Han steles (fig. 89). In other words, the scholars of metal and stone inscriptions also promoted the use of ancient techniques of calligraphy, and scholastic studies and calligraphy were as closely melded as two sides of a coin.

The research into ancient techniques which began in the late eighteenth century produced visible results in the early nineteenth century. The study of metal and stone inscriptions was systematized, and the practice of actually visiting, investigating, and recording finds at important sites was increasingly practiced as time passed. Major works such as Sun Xingyan and Xing Peng's *Record of Visits to the Huanyu Steles* (*Huanyu Fang Bei Lu*), Wang Chang's *Volume of Jin Stone Inscriptions* (*Jin Shi Bian*), and, in the study of Chinese characters, Duan Yucai's *Annotated Dictionary of Characters and Phrases* (*Shuo Wen Jie Zi Zhu*) were published one after another. Calligraphy, too, turned to Tang-dynasty block and Han scribe script for models and inspirations, and new developments in seal script were also seen.

There are several reasons for regarding the first two decades of the nineteenth century as the preliminary period of stele studies. The two aforementioned developments—the consolidation of metal- and stone-inscription studies as well as the beginnings of scholarly studies of Chinese characters—deserve special note. The transmission of the results of these studies to the next generation and, in the realm of calligraphy, the new developments in scribe and seal scripts also mark the period as one of ground breaking.

There are many calligraphers of this period who enjoyed reputations as scholars of stone inscriptions and Chinese characters. Qian Daxin (1728–1804) was the author of the work regarded as the model of inscription studies, the *Qianyan Hall Metal and Stone Postscript Inscriptions* (*Qianyan Tang Jinshewen Pawei*), and was also accomplished in seal and scribe scripts. Gui Fu (1736–1805) was a master of the *bafen* style of scribe script, authored the *Commentary on the Dictionary of Characters and Phrases* (*Shuo Wen Jie Zi Yizheng*), and assembled a catalogue of ancient seals. Qian Dian (1741–1806) excelled at metal-inscription style (see fig. 90), authored a treatise on the *Dictionary of Characters and Phrases,* and was a pioneer in the study of bronze inscriptions.

Deng Shiru, Yi Bingshou, and Chen Hongshou deserve mention as calligraphers of the period. Deng Shiru (1743–1805) came from a poor family in an impoverished village and devoted his life entirely to calligraphy. He made his living from his art on into his old age, but as a youth was fortunate enough to have found a patron that allowed him to study and copy the classics for some ten years, contributing to the results of his mature years. For a time he was criticized by Weng Fanggang and Qian Daxin for his stylish creations that lacked a scholarly backing, but he observed tradition correctly and diligently set himself to his work. At an early point he turned to the block

Fig. 92. Semi-cursive–script scrolls, Yi Bingshou (Ming dynasty).

Fig. 91. Eight-character scribe-script compositions, Deng Shiru (Ming dynasty).

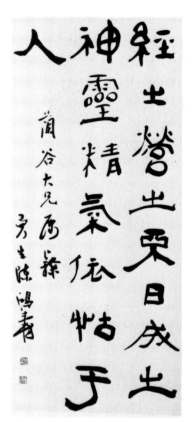

Fig. 93. Scribe-script scroll, Chen Hongshou (Ming dynasty).

script of the steles of the Six Dynasties. He created a unique scribe script, imparting nuances of dignity and even melancholy to his brushwork. His seal script (fig. 91) was said to be in the direct tradition of Li Qi of the Qin, with an elevated, antique flavor. His seal carvings, on the other hand, were full of energy and liveliness and attracted many followers who formed a school in his name. In general, he created a style that was direct, bold, polished, and unwavering. Not only did it prevail throughout the Qing dynasty, but it was one of the great achievements in the history of calligraphy. Not without reason is he known as the founder of the stele-studies school.

Yi Bingshou (1754–1815) was, more than a calligrapher, a great educator, scholar of Song studies, and regional administrator of great talent, but these achievements were overshadowed by his reputation as a calligrapher. Though he excelled at all styles, his scribe, semi-cursive, and cursive scripts were completely unique. His semi-cursive and cursive were based on Yan Zhenqing, but he occasionally combined them with seal and scribe scripts and created a distinctive style of calligraphy that made full use of the white space to achieve a feeling of liberality (fig. 92). He studied the Han steles for inspiration for his scribe script, incorporating the feeling of the stone and metal inscriptions. He also adopted a structure similar to lettering, reduced undulations, and moved the brush with considerable power. This precise "structural" feeling results in a fresh, bold character in his calligraphy.

Chen Hongshou (1768–1822) was a man of many talents, who was not inhibited by the rules in either his calligraphy, painting, or seal carving. His scribe script (fig. 93) shared the grandness of the precipice carvings, and his semi-cursive and cursive had a distinct character, too. His foundation was in copybook studies, but his work exhibits a simple, quiet, unconstrained quality different from Dong and Zhao. His seal carving earned him in-

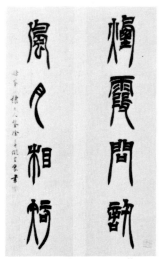

Fig. 94. Seal-script scroll, Xu Sangeng (Ming dynasty).

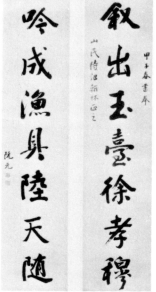

Fig. 95. Seven-character semi-cursive scrolls, Ruan Yuan (Ming dynasty).

Fig. 96. Semi-cursive-script scrolls, Bao Shichen (Ming dynasty).

clusion as one of the Eight Masters of Xiling. His remark, "The natural gift of the artist appears when he does not cultivate his art," marks him as a true member of the literati class.

From the mid- to late nineteenth century and on into the early twentieth century, the Qing was a declining empire, as external pressures mounted and internal confusion and foreign enemies mutiplied rapidly. There is little, as a result, worthy of cultural note during this period. In calligraphy, "a hundred flowers bloomed," and many variations appeared. At any rate, those studying the copybooks could no longer ignore the stele studies.

The first thing of note at the beginning of this period with regard to the theory of stele studies is the appearance of such great advocates as Ruan Yuan and Bao Shichen. Stimulated by their theories, Wu Xizai and Zhao Ziqian took up calligraphy, together with He Shaoji, who studied both copybooks and steles. Later, from the 1860s, calligraphic works spanned a much broader range of subjects than they had during the early periods of stele studies due to the popularity of the northern steles. Kang Youwei was the leader in academic works of stele studies, and other representatives of the movement included Yang Yisun (1813–81), Xu Sangeng (1826–90, see fig. 94), Yang Xian (1819–96), Yang Shoujing (1839–1915), Wu Dacheng (1835–1902), and Wu Changshi (1844–1927). Let us now investigate this movement by discussing a few of its more renowned proponents.

Ruan Yuan (1764–1849) was a high-ranking official who attained the post of Great Scholar of the Tiren Archives. He was a learned man who contributed much to his era. Mobilizing his disciples, he published many collections of works of calligraphy and painting. In addition, he left highly respected works of his own (fig. 95) as well as metal- and stone-inscription studies and historical researches. And, in association with Huang Yi, Qian Daxin, and Sun Xingyan, he published the results of more than twenty years of study, the famous *Treatise on the Northern and Southern Schools of Calligraphy* and *The Treatise on the Northern Steles and Southern Albums*. These works overturned the authority of the southern copybook school, which had been corroborated by the "Chunhua Pavilion Copybook." While granting that the fundamental techniques of calligraphy originated in the Han and Wei, he demonstrated that the mainstream of Chinese calligraphy was to be found in the stele inscriptions of the Northern Dynasties, heretofore dismissed as barbarian kingdoms. He also initiated a reevaluation of the traditional view of the calligraphy of the two Wangs as the unchallenged ideal. Ruan Yuan's theories of calligraphy were to be a source of inspiration for calligraphers from his time on.

Bao Shichen (1775–1855) was eager to serve in public office, but unable to secure a suitable post; he made his name as a scholar of calligraphy who inspired many calligraphers. Bao himself idolized Deng Shiru. He promoted Deng's work and developed a unique theory of calligraphic technique based on it. He describes a method for achieving "vividness," his ideal in calligraphy, a technique of moving and holding the brush described as "reverse beginning and smooth ending." His advocacy of the calligraphy of the Six Dynasties was a result of tracing the roots of his own style to that period, and his attempt to embody the purity of that "dense" beauty in his work (fig. 96) stood in contrast to Ruan Yuan's more scholarly motives. Thus, while studying the stele inscriptions of the northern and southern dynasties, he also sought out the calligraphy of the two Wangs and studied Sun Guoting's works repeatedly, incorporating his theories of block, semicursive, and cursive.

Ruan Yuan's advocacy of the northern steles and Bao Shichen's theories of calligraphy technique stimulated Wu Xizai, He Shaoji, and Zhao Ziqian, becoming the impetus for their individual achievements in calligraphy. All of these men, however, had their lives disrupted by the Opium Wars and the Taiping Rebellion that followed.

Wu Xizai (1799–1870) devoted his life to calligraphy, painting and seal carving. In particular, as Bao Shichen's disciple, he faithfully realized his master's theories and developed a highly sophisticated style of seal and scribe-script (fig. 97) seal carving, which Bao had not been able to attain. His seal script is graceful and even. His seal carvings opened a new avenue with their fleshy and richly expressive strokes and masterful delicacy of feeling.

He Shaoji's (1799–1873) acquaintance with Bao Shichen in his youth served as his motive for studying calligraphy. Also, as the disciple of Ruan Yuan and acquaintance of Wu Yingguang, he had access to many stele rubbings and a wide knowledge of calligraphy. He studied the seal and scribe script of the northern steles based on Yan Zhenqing and also studied metal inscriptions, perfecting his semi-cursive and cursive script by incorporating the best of all styles. He had a uniqueness that did not permit imitation.

Zhao Ziqian (1829–84) had a difficult life, aspiring to a position in the bureaucracy but failing to find one. Finally, in his later years he was able to actually purchase a post and become a regional administrator, only to die at the end of the Manchu-French War. Though he had a strong political streak, it is for his calligraphy and painting that he is remembered. Zhao first ventured into seal carving and later went on to painting. Only after this did he turn to calligraphy. He also authored scholarly works on metal and stone inscriptions. In his seal carvings he studied both the Zhe and Deng schools, combining all of the styles of the Qin and Han, and excelled in various different treatments of the seal surface, condensing a rich variety of expression into a tiny area one inch square. He first studied Yan Zhenqing's calligraphy, but went on to produce his own original styles in block and semi-cursive script after incorporating Bao Shichen's reverse beginning and smooth ending technique, and closely studying the northern steles. He also distinguished himself in seal and scribe script. It is probably fair to say that the theories of Ruan Yuan and Bao Shichen were synthesized and given form by Zhao.

Wu Changshi (1844–1927) wandered from region to region after his family was dispersed during the Taiping Rebellion. His calligraphy, painting, and seal carving, polished and refined during that time, represented the peak of mastery from the late Qing to the early Republic. His calligraphy and seal carving owe much to the stone-drum studies that he pursued throughout his life. Even his semi-cursive and cursive script were the products of an adaptation of certain stone-drum–inscription techniques (fig. 98). As he approached his later years, his style developed to full maturity, and he enjoys an especially high reputation in Japan, where he has exerted considerable influence.

If we take a broader look at the situation during the later stele-school period, we can see that a degenerate style of calligraphy gained prominence as the era came to an end. This was probably a result of the decline of Chinese society, which had been buffeted by disturbances of many sorts and was feeling the pressures of modernization and westernization.

Fig. 97. Scribe-script scroll, Wu Xizai (Ming dynasty).

Fig. 98. Copy of stone-drum script, Wu Changshi (Ming dynasty).

# COMMENTARIES ON THE PLATES

1. Oracle-bone and tortoiseshell characters. Shang dynasty. Tokyo University Research Center for the Humanities.

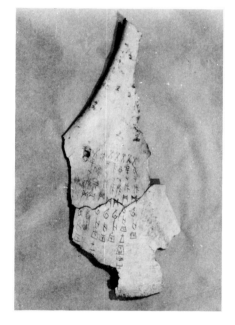

Oracle bone and shell characters are the writing inscribed on animal bones and tortoise shells used in divination during the Shang dynasty. The collection of these artifacts began when Wang Yirong at the end of the Qing dynasty discovered characters inscribed on so-called "dragon bones" being sold at the time as a cure for malaria. Beginning with the work of his disciple Liu E, the *Tie Yun Cang Gui* (Tortoise Shells of the Tie Yun Collection), works such as Luo Zhenyu's *Ying Xu Shu Qi Qian Bian* (Bone Inscriptions of the Shang Ruins, Volume 1), followed by *Jing Hua* (A Selection of Bone Inscriptions), and the second volume of the first-mentioned work were published, and over a thirty year period, twelve catalogues were completed recording roughly 10,000 fragments.

In the autumn of 1928, the Central Research Institute's Historical Linguistics Study Center was founded, and that very year the first experimental excavation of the Shang site at Xiaotun took place. As a result of this and the following fifteen excavations, approximately 13,000 bone and shell fragments were unearthed, and subsequently catalogued in four volumes. Those pieces that had been discovered prior to this and had been removed from China were also gradually catalogued. The total of all fragments amounts to almost 60,000 pieces. Recently, the National Academy of Sciences has recollated all of this data, appended categorizations by period and kind, and is in the process of publishing the *Jia Gu Wen He Ji* (Collection of Oracle Bone and Shell Writings) in thirteen volumes, eight of which have already appeared. When this is completed, it will be the standard, complete collection of oracle bone and shell writings.

Almost no new finds had occurred since the Second World War, but in 1973, 4,600 fragments were unearthed in the area south of Xiaotun, and they are recorded in the *Xiaotunnan Di Jia Gu* (Oracle-Bone and Shell Fragments from Xiaotunnan) in two volumes, published in 1980. Then, in 1977, some 17,000 fragments were found at a construction site in Fengchu village, near Qishan in Shaanxi Province. Among these, some two hundred are inscribed with characters, for a total of approximately six hundred words, in a form of writing known as Early Zhou divinatory script. They include divination passages in extremely small script of a distinctly different style from other early writings.

The oracle-bone and shell inscriptions can be divided into five periods from roughly 1300 B.C. to the end of the Shang (1122 B.C.) by the format and contents of the inscriptions. The styles of the characters themselves vary from period to period. In this formative period, writing already possessed a formally complete calligraphic character. The plate shows a divination of a ten-day period. The prospects for the next ten days were divined on the last day of the previous period. This was a ceremonial practice that served as a periodical rite of exorcism more than an actual divination of future events. A similar custom is still practiced by the Japanese Imperial Household.

2. Chu characters on silk. Warring States period. Arthur M. Sackler Collection, New York.

According to the research of Shang Chengzuo published in *Wen Wu* (Literary Artifacts), September, 1964, this writing on silk was unearthed at an ancient tomb known as Wujiazushan in the area of Changsha in Hunan. It was said to have been folded and placed inside a lacquer box. The silk measures 30 by 39 centimeters, and curious depictions of gods in red, blue and brown border the text on four sides. In the center extended passages of writing are located to the right and left, of eight and thirteen lines respectively. With approximately thirty-seven characters per line, there are a total of some six hundred characters, though the characters on the folds have worn away. The text apparently consists of spells directed to the deities, and it was probably a talisman of sorts to be buried with the dead. Many copies have been made of this remarkable piece.

We have both silk paintings and silk writings, but neither are plentiful, being very difficult to preserve. Writings on silk in tombs were preserved by a phenomena known as "fire caves." Under conditions of high temperatures and humidity, the proliferation of evaporated substances in the sealed cave prevented decay. However, these vapors were highly combustible and exploded when touched off by a spark. In the *Han Annals* it is recorded that "upon opening Ding Ji's outer coffin, flames lept out for a distance of twelve to fifteen meters." According to another account, several hundred people perished at this time.

Silk writings were preserved at Changsha due to this "fire cave" effect, thanks to the hot, humid climate of the region. In tomb no. 1 at Mawangdui a silk painting that was used as a coffin wrapper has been found. Many silk writings have also been discovered in tomb no. 3. Twenty-six different texts were unearthed, among them the *Laozi* (Book of Laozi, pl. 6) and the *Strategies of the Warring States* (*Zhangguo Ce*), most of them lost works. One of these has a picture with a commentary, which assists in tracing the evolution of Chu silk paintings. The characters are already in the Han scribe script, but the painting is from the Warring States period, and the brushwork recalls the older characters, replete with variations and abbreviations. The shape of the characters and the brushwork is somewhat similar to the recently discovered *Hou Ma Treaty* (*Hou Ma Mengshu*). This work dates from around the end of the fourth century B.C., and was a treaty carved in jade on the occasion of the succession dispute between Zhao Zhang and Zhao Shuo. The silk paintings of Chu are probably from the same period, but some problems with the interpretation of characters still remain.

3. "Gou Jian, Prince of Yue's Sword Inscription." Spring and Autumn Annals period. Ink rubbing.

This sword was unearthed in 1965 at the Wangshan Chu-dynasty tomb no. 1, located at Jiangling in Hubei. It was placed to the right of the deceased inside his coffin; 55.6 centimeters long, with a hilt of 8.4 centimeters, the entire length of the sword is decorated with a diamond pattern, and on both sides the swordguard is inlaid with dark blue glass and turquoise. The inscription is on the sword near the guard, in two lines: "Prince of Yue Jiu Qian/made this sword for his own use." This was in fact the sword of the Prince of Yue, Gou Jian, known from the disputes between the states of Yue and Wu. The characters are in bird script, with avian elaborations decorating each character.

The bird script was known long ago as bird seal script. A reference to it appears in the *Later Han Annals* (*Hou Han Shu*). There, Emperor Ling was said to be fond of literature, and to have called to his side dozens of people who excelled in bird seal script. And, in another passage, Yang Qiu was criticized as someone who recklessly gave away imperial office because he awarded posts to those who presented him with an ode or were clever at bird script. In addition to bird seal script, a serpent seal script existed, and in the *Dictionary of Phrases and Characters* (*Shuo Wen Jie Zi*) by Xu Shen, we find a reference to bird and serpent script in the introduction. These styles were used from the end of the Spring and Autumn Annals period.

Many swords, pikes and halberts of the Wu and Yue dynasties have bird seal script inscriptions, as do brass vessels from the Chu, Song, and Qi. Recently, the Guang, Prince of Wu sword, the Fu Cha, Prince of Wu sword, the Zhu Ju, Prince of Yue sword, the Zuzuo Yuanyong, Prince of Yue sword, the Sun, Prince of Chu halbert, and others have been discovered—including of course the present item. The personal names of the Wu and Yue dynasties are full of variant readings, and this rubbing contains several such alternate characters, making deciphering the inscription a difficult task.

The art of alloy casting spread throughout China from the end of the Spring and Autumn Annals period, but even among the Prince of Zhongshan ritual vessels there are already many excellent pieces. The Luan Shu wine cask (*fou*) of the Jin and the tally of Lord E are known for their inscriptions. This bronze sword was found in a Chu tomb, but most Wu and Yue implements have been found in Shou Prefecture of Anhui Province, at Xiangyang in Hubei, Hui Prefecture in Hunan, and even in distant Shanxi.

4. Rubbing of large bronze tripod inscription. Warring States period.

5. Large bronze tripod. Warring States period.

Since 1974, the imperial tombs and funerary relics of the Prince of Zhongshan at the site of the ancient capital of Lingshou have been investigated by archeological researchers of Hebei, and from more than thirty different tombs over 19,000 articles from the Spring and Autumn Annals and the Warring States periods have been unearthed. Remains from the grave of Prince Cuo of Zhongshan are the most numerous. The richly decorated tripoint ritual battle axe, beautiful ornaments of gold and silver alloys, ritual bronze vessels in perfect condition, and skilled jewelry work—all are splendid pieces of great beauty, but in particular, the nine tripods, the square and round pots with their extended inscriptions, and the chart of the entire burial grounds are invaluable research finds.

The legs of this large tripod are iron. The nine Zhongshan tripods range in size from 17.4 centimeters to 51 centimeters. Together they from a set. The inscription starts at the knobs on the lid and continues down to the body of the piece in seventy-seven lines of six characters each, for a total of some 469 characters. The inscription on the vessel describes how the Lord of Yan, Kuai Zi, relinquished his throne to Zi Xi, thereby inviting rebellion, and how Prince Cuo's predecessor, Prince Cheng, receiving the mandate of heaven, crushed that revolt, to the national glory. Following that, it praises the virtue of the assistance of the venerable loyal minister Zhou and, citing the revenge of Prince Gou Jian and his destruction of the Wu state, warns that vigilance must never be relaxed.

The extended inscription is arranged in ten lines on each face of the vessel, for a total of forty lines and 450 characters, relating how the vessel was cast from copper captured from the attack on Yan, praising the virtues of Minister Sima Ma Zhou, and expressing certainty that the national honor will be preserved by this wise minister. The inscription on the round pot consists of 59 lines and 182 characters. A memorial for the previous ruler Prince Cuo, it praises his compassion and wisdom and declares that judging from the precedent of Yan, his descendants should long rule the state.

The characters on all of these vessels are engraved in similar form. They most resemble the Luan Shu wine vessel of Jin, exhibiting a gracefully flowing style which is so decorative that occasionally the original shape of the characters and their strokes is sacrificed.

6. *Laozi.* Han dynasty. Ink on silk.

In December of 1973, archeological remains far superior to those previously unearthed at tomb no. 1 of Mawangdui at Changsha in Hubei were discovered in tomb no. 3. Among these, the discovery of a great quantity of silk writings deserves our notice. In both quantity and quality, these were on a par with the previously discovered Jizhong bamboo tablets and the Juyan and Wuwei tablets of recent discovery. They included many lost works, including the two sections of the *Laozi* (the *Book of Laozi*)—*De* (virtue) and *Dao* (the way)—and versions of the *Zhou Divinations* (*Zhou Yang*), the *Strategy of the Warring States,* and other works. Categorizing these works according to titles, we have: a) the *A* text of the *Laozi,* four sections of the second volume; b) four sections of the first volume of the *B* text of the same work; c) three sections from the second volume of the *Zhou Divinations,* the *Zhou Divinations Commentary* (*Zhou Yang Xici*); d) a variant version of the *Strategy of the Warring States;* e) the *Zuo Chan* (*Commentary on the Spring and Auutumn Annals*) and related materials; f) astrological divinations; g) three sections of criminal codes; h) two sections on *yin-yang* practices; i) a yogic breathing chart; j) a map; k) a military chart; 1) a street map; and m) miscellaneous divinatory writings.

The *Laozi* is divided into two texts, an *A* text and a *B* text. By combining the second roll of the *A* text with the first of the *B* text, one long roll can be created, twenty-four centimeters in height. The *A* text contains 463 lines of approximately 13,000 characters. The *B* text had worn on the folds and fallen into into thirty-two pieces when it was discovered. It contains 252 lines for a total of 16,000 characters.

The *A–B Laozi* text shows slight variations in words and sentences from our present texts of the same work. The greatest difference is that the two volumes on the *Way* and *Virtue, Dao* and *De,* are ordered *De-Dao*, in contrast to the present reverse order. This is in agreement with ancient references in the *Laozi* commentary sections of the *Han Feizi* and no doubt represents the ancient order of the text. Tomb no. 3 was built for someone who died in 168 B.C., so these silk writings reveal the state of the text during the Early Han. In the *B* text, notations of 3,401 characters in the *De* section and 2,426 in the *Dao* section appear at the end of each roll, amounting to the traditional "five thousand characters of the *Laozi*." The plate shows (a) lines 53–55, (b) 61–66, (c) 90–98, (with the *Dao* section beginning from the fifth line), (d) lines 78–87, and (e) 67–69. The characters reflect little scribe-script influence.

The twenty-eight related fragments of the *Strategy of the Warring States* unearthed at the same site, totalling approximately 11,200 characters, are untitled. Eleven of those sections correspond to the presently existing copy of the work, with many variations. The characters resemble Qin seal script—uniform, square in shape, and densely constructed. They are approaching the "breaking-wave" style of the wooden tablet writing.

7. Ink rubbing of the Langye Terrace inscription. Qin dynasty. Museum of Calligraphy, Tokyo.

After unifying the land, the founder of the Qin, the First Emperor, made a tour of the lands under his governance and built stone inscriptions in praise of his achievements and to communicate them to later generations. In 219 B.C., he traveled to Zouyishan in Shandong and also to Taishan and the Langye Terrace. The following year he visited Zhifu, traveling to Jieshishan in Hebei in 215 B.C. and Huijishan in Zhejiang in 210, raising memorial inscriptions at each location. There are seven stones in all. This fact, and the contents of the inscriptions, is recorded in the *Historical Records,* but all that remains today is part of a supplementary inscription made by his heir at the Langye site. The 146 characters of the Taishan stone were still legible during the Song, but after that the stone was scorched by fire, and now only a few stone fragments with characters remain.

The Langye stone was already severely eroded by the Song dynasty, and no ancient rubbings exist. However, Ruan Yuan was able to make a clean rubbing of the stone fragment with the supplementary inscription, which was one line two characters longer than the old rubbing, for a total of eighty-six characters.

The stone was ensconced in a display pavilion, but in a great thunderstorm of April, 1900, it fell into the sea. In 1921, fragments were gathered, assembled, and kept in the Education Bureau's Antiques Preservation Department. It is now preserved in the Shandong Provincial Museum.

Of the thirteen lines of inscription, the first two give the names of two ministers who accompanied the First Emperor on his visits, Yue Ying and Yang Jiu. The supplementary inscription of the First Emperor's heir, Emperor Huang, begins from the third line: "Emperor Huang declares that these stone inscriptions are all the work of the First Emperor. I have now inherited his name. However, if these inscribed words are not known as the First Emperor's forever after, but instead thought to be those of some descendant, it will not be in accord with the great virtue of his achievements. Prime Minister Li Si, Minister Qu Ji, the governor-generals and virtuous ministers entreated, 'We beg you to have monuments carved to clarify this. Thus we humbly entreat.' And so I declared, 'Let it be done.'"

The traces of the characters of the present Taishan rubbing vary slightly from this version and are not perfect in form, but show good brushwork.

8. Wooden tablets unearthed at Juyan. Han dynasty. Gansu Provincial Museum.

In ancient times, books were made from wood and bamboo in the form of tablets. Depending upon the period or locale of their origin, they were sometimes known as Chu tablets, Qin tablets, Juyan Han tablets, or Wuwei Han tablets. During the reign of Emperor Wu of the Jin, several tens of cartloads of bamboo tablets were unearthed from the tomb of Prince Xiang of the Wei at Jijun. Following that, a small number of tablets continued to be turned up in various locations, but it was in the early part of this century that vast quantities of Han and Jin tablets were discovered in the northwestern oases by Stein and Hedin. From 1930, the Chinese National Scientific Survey discovered 3,000 tablet fragments at Juyan and Wuwei, and then in 1933, some 19,637 new fragments were discovered at Juyan. They are now being collated and studied.

In recent years, the discovery of bamboo tablets has been reported in a variety of locations. Many new articles have come to light, beginning with the bamboo tablets from Yangtiange of the Chu tombs, at Changsha in Hunan; the bamboo tablets of the Han tomb at Mawangdui, Changsha; the tablets at Yinqiaoshan, from Linyi in Shandong; the tablets from Wangshan, Jiangling Prefecture in Hubei; the Han tomb tablets from Fenghuang in Jiangling; the bamboo tablets from Changtaiguan in Xinyang, Hunan; the Qin tablets from Shuihudi in Yunmeng, Hubei; the bamboo tables of Fuyang in Anhui; and the tablets from the Genghou tomb in Sui Prefecture, Hubei.

The newly unearthed tablets from the northwest have not yet been made public, but they are thought to be valuable both as historical and calligraphic evidence. This one item was included in *Han Jian Lishu Xuan* (A Selection of Scribe Script from Han Tablets, March, 1981), a collection of the best examples from Juyan, Wuwei and Kangu, enlarged and catalogued by the Gansu Provincial Museum. In the illustrated tablet, the first column of characters is a formal expression indicating that this is an official message. The style of calligraphy is also much more formal than that of ordinary official correspondence. It was probably written by the most accomplished calligrapher in the particular department, with the utmost care and courtesy. This piece represents the perfection of Han scribe script. The form of the characters is dignified, their construction cohesive, and the brushwork extremely beautiful, yet full of vigor.

9. "*Liqi* Stele at Confucius' Tomb." Han dynasty. Ink rubbing. Tokyo National Museum.

Many steles, or stone tablets, have been raised at the site of Confucius's tomb at Qufu commending those who repaired and kept up this landmark of the ancient state of Lu. By the Han dynasty, three famous steles, The "Yi Ying Stele" (153 A.D.), the "Han Chi Stele" (156), and the "Shichen Stele" (169) already existed. The "Yi Ying Stele" was known for its artless simplicity, its strength, its regularity, and solidity. The "Han Chi Stele" corresponds to the "*Liqi* Stele" illustrated here, and was regarded as a work of classical elegance, strength, and lightning swiftness. The "Shichen" also exhibts an antique grace and elegance, and is a masterpiece of cohesion, structure, feeling, and execution—one of the most orthodox models of the *bafen* style. All three are models of Han scribe script and have received the highest praise since ancient times, but this "*Liqi* Stele" in particular has been singled out among classical works as showing masterful changes of style. Wang Shu remarked, "Tensile strength like iron, ever-changing like a dragon, each character is a wonder beyond comprehension." The calligraphy of Chu Suiliang is thought to owe much to this stele.

There are sixteen rows of characters on the stele, with thirty-six characters per row. An inscription in four-character verses follows after an explanation of the reason for building the stele. The offices and names of those who worked on the repairs of the tomb are listed, running off the face and onto the back and the sides. The stele is exceptionally well-preserved and is presently stored in the Qufu stele garden.

10. "Cao Quan Stele." Han dynasty. Ink rubbing. Mitsui Bunko, Tokyo.

A stele from the reign of Emperor Ling of the Later Han (185). This stele was discovered much later, around the year 1573 of the Ming Dynasty, in Geyang Prefecture on the eastern border of Shaanxi. The stele was found broken in two, with the seal cap missing. It is now in the Xi'an stele garden.

The face of the stele has twenty lines, with forty-five characters per line. On the back, the names of fifty-seven donors are listed in five columns. The stele inscription recounts how Shu Zhenduo of the Cao clan was granted the kingdom of Cao back in the Shang period, and later, how Cao San aided the Han. Afterwords, the clan entered the western regions and dispersed. Cao Quan's military exploits in this region were renowned, and after the Zhangjiao rebellion, he became ruler of Geyang. The stele was raised by the three elders of the prefecture, the town, and his followers to praise his virtues.

The rubbing from this stele was brought to Japan at any early date. A careful printing was made from a tracing, and this sample has served as a model for many. Even among the Han steles, this piece exhibits a great beauty in the left and right flow of its strokes in the *bafen* style, and the brushwork shows a great mastery and concentration. The strokes have "strong bones," and represent the apogee of the style of Han scribe script. The names on the reverse of the stele, in contrast to the slim characters on the face, are written in a slightly heavier script.

In the inscribed passage many characters are replaced with alternative characters, often with the aim of improving the aesthetic value of the work as calligraphy.

Recently, a cinnabar ink rubbing of this stele was on exhibit in Japan. It measured 250 by 98 centimeters.

11. "Zhang Qian Stele." Han dynasty. Ink rubbing. Mitsui Bunko, Tokyo.

This dates from 186 of the Later Han dynasty. It was discovered at the beginning of the Ming dynasty in Donga, Shandong. Because it does not appear in any of the ancient catalogues, because the calligraphy itself is unique, and because there are many errors in the characters, Gu Yanwu and others have declared it to be a later forgery. However, this very square, regular style did exist within the boundaries of the Han scribe script. The "chopped off" style of some later works probably originated in these steles, and this inscription may have been an early prototype.

The face of the stele contains sixteen lines with forty-two characters per line. On the seal cap are two lines of six characters for a total of twelve, and three columns of names are inscribed on the back. This memorial stele was built to praise the virtuous rule of Zhang Qian, who had been the chief of Gucheng, and was being sent as governor to Dangyin. The characters of the seal cap which explain this are not the usual elongated strokes. They are instead a bit broader and show a new spirit.

There are numerous erroneous and variant characters in this inscription, which has put the authenticity of this stele in doubt since it was first discovered. However, any investigation of the passages included in such a standard reference work as the *Scribe Script Dictionary* would easily produce as many of the same, and we cannot conclude that this work is a later forgery on those grounds. The form of the characters places them firmly in the path of the development of the style of writing from the end of the Han to the Wei and Jin, a representative of one school of the simple, classic style that refrained from the strong "wave" brushstrokes. Still, the passage itself contains many decorative fictions and allusions to other sources.

### 12. "Divine Omen Stele." Three Kingdoms period, Wu. Ink rubbing. Neiraku Art Museum, Nara,

A stele from 276, the Wu dynasty. It is made up of three layers of stone which were originally piled on top of each other, and the contents of the inscription can only be read when all three are assembled. The date, "the first year of Tianxi," follows the title. Below that there are twenty-three lines of main text, of which eleven still exist. Sixteen characters make up one line, and including the title, there are 208 characters in all.

The *Annals of the Three Kingdoms* (*San Guo Zhi*) relates that a fissure appeared in the rock of Liyangshan near Poyang, forming twenty characters which read, "A man of Yang will become emperor, pacify the land, and a time of great peace will begin." Son Hao, the emperor, rejoiced at this divine portent. He had an inscription engraved in the stone praising the virtues of the spirits and thanking the god of good fortune. The passage inscribed refers to the investigation and the resulting fortunate divination. Hao had great faith in good omens and often changed era names in hopes of inviting divine favor. Nevertheless, he perished soon after this.

A reference to this stele appears in a Jin-dynasty account of the region: "Yanshan is to be found in the southern thirty *li* of Moling prefecture. There is a stone cave in the western peak, and to the left of the great road of the eastern peak, a square stone. It is three meters long and engraved with the praises of Wu. It was built by Son Hao." References also appear in later works. At first, this stone was located in Ziyaoshan. Later, it was installed in Tianxi Monastery, though it was returned to the Chousi Pavilion in 1091. During the Yuan dynasty it was moved to Fuxue, and in the Ming, to the Zunjing Pavilion. In 1805, it was destroyed in a fire. For that reason, there are very few rubbings, and even Yang Shoujing's exhaustive research turned up only two original rubbings and three reproductions. The seal script of Deng Wangbo was said to have been inspired by this stele.

The characters of this stele are written in neither seal nor scribe script, but a unique style. Zhu Yizun regarded it as midway between seal and scribe script, while Yang Shoujing concluded it was a hybrid of the two. The passage describes a supernatural event, and the characters are written with the "chopped off" brushwork, in a bold and impressive style suitable for a divine omen.

### 13. Lu Ji: "Ping Fu Album." Western Jin dynasty. Ink on paper. Beijing National Palace Museum.

This is a letter said to have been written by the scholar of the Jin dynasty, Lu Ji (261–303). References to this work appear early on and it was included in the Imperial Song collection as a work of Lu Ji. This copybook was originally a single quire included in the "Fourteen Jinxian Albums" in the possession of Li Wei of the Song, together with another Jin work, the "Xie An Album" (*Xie An Tie*). Mi Fu viewed this piece and mentioned it in his work, the *History of Calligraphy*. The calligraphy is in essay cursive script, and several passages are difficult to read. It is in the form of a letter to a certain Yan Xian. Whether it is actually the work of Lu Ji, it does stand as an example of a letter from the Western Jin dynasty. Since very few originals from this period have been preserved, this piece is extremely valuable. This sample of essay cursive script, too, has great significance in the history of calligraphy.

14. Li Bo: "Draft of a Letter." Eastern Jin dynasty. Ink on paper. Ryūkoku University Library, Kyoto.

During the Ōtani Expedition of 1908–9 to northwest China, two complete letters of the Governor-general of the area, Li Bo, were discovered with other documents at Loulan. This is one of them. Li Bo was an official under Zhang Jun of the Former Liang and at the time he wrote these letters he was the Governor-general Marquis of the territory. The letters were written to the ruler of the Uygurs and are extremely valuable as historical materials. Since they were written at the beginning of the Eastern Jin, which corresponds to the youth of the patron saint of calligraphy, Wang Xizhi, they are also important to the history of calligraphy. The added fact that they are ink originals makes them invaluable. Though they were written by someone in the outlying regions and differ somewhat from the calligraphy of the aristocracy of central China, there are several points of resemblance to the writings of Wang Xizhi's youth. It is important to note, at least, that there were common features in the calligraphy of the men of the Jin dynasty throughout China.

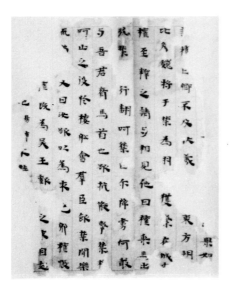

15. Anonymous: *Wu Annals,* from the *Annals of the Three Kingdoms,* fragment of the twelfth volume. Western Jin dynasty. Ink on paper. Museum of Calligraphy, Tokyo.

Most of the ancient manuscripts from northwest China are Buddhist texts, but here we have a historical text, a fragment of the *Wu Annals* (*Wu Zhi*) from the *Annals of the Three Kingdoms* (*San Guo Zhi*). As historical material from Chinese Turkestan, this is a very rare piece. It is a fragment of ten lines from the *Biography of Yu Fan* of the twelfth roll of the *Wu Annals,* copied during the Western Jin. The calligraphy resembles that of the *Zhufo Yaoji Jing,* a Buddhist sutra copied in 296. The author of the *Wu Annals,* Chen Shou, died in 297, and this text was probably copied very close to that time. This text dates from the period when the scribe script of the Han dynasty was evolving into the block script of later times, and we can see that the breaking-wave stroke to the lower right is thick and large, as is the right tip of each horizontal stroke. This is an excellent example of the style of calligraphy that flourished for a time during the Wei and Jin, developing from scribe script just as essay cursive developed from ordinary cursive script.

16. Wang Xizhi: "Sang Luan Album." Eastern Jin dynasty. Ink on paper. Collection of the Japanese Imperial Household, Tokyo.

From ancient times, the masterpieces of Wang Xizhi have been brought to Japan. The "Sang Luan Album" (*Sang Luan Tie*) deserves first place among those masterworks. This is a collection of letters consisting of seventeen lines. The first eight lines are one letter, the next five a fragment of another, and the last four another letter. The plate shows only the first section.. This was copied by the method known as *tashu,* a process in which first the outlines of the characters are traced from the original and then painstakingly filled in, resulting in a very precise copy. This piece belonged to Emperor Shōmu during the Nara period, and upon his death was donated to the Tōdai-ji with many other imperial treasures. Fortunately, it has been preserved to this day. Most likely, this was a copy made during the early part of Taizong's reign in the Tang dynasty, when the appreciation of Wang Xizhi's works had reached its peak, that found its way to Japan. The white hemp paper, often used in *tashu* copying, is lightly scored in vertical columns to prevent flaking of the ink when the scroll is rolled. Nothing comparable has been preserved in China, and we can regard it as one of the great works of Wang Xizhi.

17. Wang Xizhi: "Kong Shizong Album." Eastern Jin dynasty. Ink on paper. Maeda Ikutokukai, Tokyo.

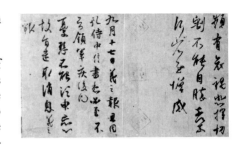

A copy of letters by Wang Xizhi of the Jin dynasty made up of three sections of three lines each. They are customarily identified by titles consisting of characters which appear in the first line of each fragment: the "Ai Huo Epistle" the "Jiuyue Shiqiri Epistle," and the "You Xuan Epistle." In the space between the first two sections, a Japanese imperial seal of the Enryaku era (782–806) is stamped three times, indicating that, like the "Sang Luan Album" (pl. 16), this too was an imperial possession—of Emperor Kammu at the beginning of the Heian period. There is very little doubt that this was also part of Emperor Shōmu's collection of copies in the Nara period, as were probably all works listed in the "Catalogue of Donations to the Tōdai-ji" of the Shōsō-in. The text matches almost exactly the version quoted in the semi-cursive script chapter of the Tang-dynasty scholar Chu Suilang's catalogue, *Youjun Catalogue of Calligraphy* (*Youjun Shumu*)—only one character is missing—suggesting that this is one of the Wang masterpieces that Chu Suiliang identified as originals in the imperial possession in the early Tang period. Since this work was a possession Emperor Taizong, it is safe to assume that meticulous copies of it were made following *tashu* methods. One of these arrived in Japan and after being in the imperial possession found its way into private hands. In the Meiji period it became part of the Maeda lkutokukai Collection. Together with the "Sang Luan Album," this is one of the great Wang masterworks without compare. Like the "Sang Luan Album," the paper is white hemp, and in order to avoid friction when rolling and unrolling the scroll, it is scored with fine lines. Even damaged areas of the paper have been faithfully reproduced, indicating just how important exact transmission of this work was felt to be.

18. Wang Xizhi: "Feng Ju Album." Eastern Jin dynasty. Ink on paper. Taipei National Palace Museum.

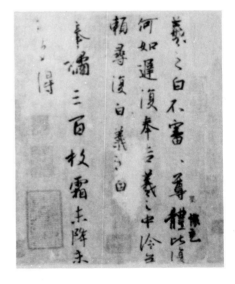

This is a copy of letters of Wang Xizhi. The two characters *feng ju* which appear in this piece have given it its name. In semi-cursive script, this piece is made up of three sections, the "Ping An Epistle" in four lines, the "He Ru Epistle" in three, and the "Feng Ju Epistle" in two. These three sections were recorded in the catalogue of the Tang scholar, Chu Suiliang, matching exactly the passages quoted here (except for the inversion of two characters, *he* and *ru*). All three works were in the imperial possession in the early Tang dynasty, recognized as original works of Wang's calligraphy. Following the calligraphy is a Sui-dynasty date, "the 27th day of the third month of the 18th year of Kaihuang (698)," as well as the seals of Zhuge Ying, Liu Guyan and Zhiguo, indicating that these pieces were also appreciated during the previous Sui dynasty. This work is also recorded in Mi Fu's Song-dynasty work, the *History of Calligraphy,* under the entry, "Tang Copy of the 'You Jun Album.'" Upon close inspection of the copy, it is clear that both the body of the work and the seals at the end have been traced together, so that the Sui dates and seals are also actually part of the Tang copy. Thus there is no contradiction in Mi Fu's title for the piece. During the Northern Song, this piece was in the collection of Li Wei, and the stamp, "Li Wei Library" can also be seen after the last section. This copy, then, was first owned by Li Wei, then passing into the possession of Emperor Huizong, and, known as "the Treasure of the Song," came into the hands of collectors of the Ming and Qing dynasties. It is now in the Taipei National Palace Museum.

19. Wang Xizhi: "Shiqi Album." Eastern Jin dynasty. Ink rubbing. Kyoto National Museum.

This is a copybook collection of Wang Xizhi's letters. The title, "Shiqi Album" (*Shiqi Tie*), is recorded in the Tang-dynasty scholar, Zhang Yanyuan's *Brief Catalogue of Copybooks* (*Fashu Yaolu*). The best-known copybook collection in Tang Emperor Taizong's imperial storehouse, it includes twenty-three individual pieces and is 3.6 meters long, in 107 lines and 942 characters. The copybook was stamped with small seals of the Zhenguan (627–45) and Kaiyuan (713–41) eras, and the names of the great ministers of the time were recorded at the end of the roll. The original still existed in the early Tang dynasty and at an early date it was given the title *Shiqi Tie* (Seventeen Copybook), after the date at the beginning of the roll. It now exists in the form of printed versions of a rubbing and it includes twenty-nine individual works. It exists in versions with and without the character "by imperial degree." Those with it are known as official texts and are regarded as the better copies. At the end of the roll, a note reads, "Those copies with 'by imperial degree' were ordered copied by Minister of the Imperial College, Jie Wuwei, and are complete official texts, inspected and approved by Minister Chu Suiliang. Sengquan." "Sengquan" is the seal of Xu Sengquan of the Liang, which is proof that this text was transmitted from the Liang royal house. The works are mostly letters to Zhou Fu in the state of Shu (Sichuan), and most of them are in a disconnected cursive script, though a few are in block script. These have long been valued as samples of Wang's cursive calligraphy. There are various texts, but this one is either a Tang or Song impression which, passing through the ownership of Qing collectors such as Jiang Shi, came into the possession of the Ueno family in Japan and is now in the Kyoto National Museum.

20. Wang Xianzhi: "Di Huang Tang Epistle." Eastern Jin dynasty. Ink on paper. Museum of Calligraphy, Tokyo.

A copy of a letter by Wang Xianzhi. The three characters of the title are taken from the text of the piece, which consists of six lines of semi-cursive script. This work is also printed in the Song-dynasty "Chunhua Pavilion Copybook." The main outlines of the characters are the same, but there is variation in details. This is probably a Tang tracing of a copy, not a direct tracing from the original. Still, Wang Xianzhi's style and skill are in evidence here and as such this is a valuable piece. This was once passed down in the family of the Ming-dynasty scholar, Wen Zhengming, who presented it to his disciple, Wang Chong. In the Qing dynasty, it came into the possession of Wu Rongguang. Later it was brought to Japan and now it is in the Museum of Calligraphy in Tokyo.

21. Anonymous: "Memorial Stele for Gao Zhen." Northern Wei dynasty. Ink rubbing. Mitsui Bunko, Tokyo.

Gao Zhen was the brother of the consort of Xuanwu, the emperor of the Northern Wei. According to the stele, he died at the age of twenty-six on April 26, 514. The stele was built at his grave site.

The original stone is now in the stele garden of Confucius's tomb at Qufu in Shandong. It was unearthed in the Qing dynasty, toward the end of the eighteenth century, from the third mound at Wei River in De District of Shandong. Many members of the Gao clan are entombed in this region, and this stele, together with two previously unearthed steles for Gao Zhang and Gao Qing, are well-known as the three Gao steles of Bohai.

Twelve characters are carved in relief into the seal cap in four lines reading, "The stele of the former governor of Ying District, Lord Yihou Gao." The characters are written in a decorative style, the beginnings and endings of each stroke ornamented with birds' beaks. The governorship of Ying District was a posthumous rank, and Yihou the posthumous name awarded to Gao. The stele passage consists of twenty-four lines in block script, with forty-six characters per line.

Even though it was unearthed from a burial mound, there are few damaged or eroded characters. The stele is quite large, being 1.86 meters by 64 centimeters. It was completed in June of 523, the same year that the Binyang cave at Longmen in Hunan was completed.

The characters conform to a strict standard with no deviation and little space between the components of each character. A strict and regular order is observed. The strokes are neither especially wide nor narrow. The brushwork is vigorous. A certain awkwardness characteristic of the Northern Wei remains, but it does not violate the general feeling of refinement—for here we have not a simple, natural style of calligraphy, but a painstakingly done piece which counts as one of the masterpieces of Northern Wei calligraphy. Since Gao Zhen was a maternal relative of the imperial family of the Northern Wei, we can assume that this is the work of one of the accomplished calligraphers of the time.

Many variant and alternate characters are used in this stele, which may be a result of the more than 1,000 new block-style characters authorized in 425, during the reign of Emperor Taiwu—or, in fact, this may be an example of the many new characters which had already come into use, occasioning this reform.

22. Anonymous: "Epitaph for Yuan Zhen." Northern Wei dynasty. Ink rubbing. Osaka Municipal Museum of Fine Art.

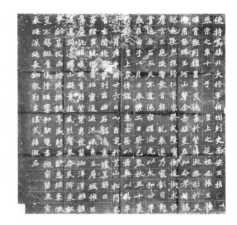

The practice of engraving epitaphs and interning them with the deceased is a distinctly Chinese custom. These epitaphs (*muzhi*) usually relate the main events in the life of their subject, and their purpose is to transmit his deeds to future generations and ensure that his name be preserved for prosperity. The epitaphs that have been unearthed from the Later Han through the Wei and Jin were simple grave markers, coffin inscriptions, or miniature steles, with very brief inscriptions. With the approach of the North and South Dynasties period in the fifth century, these epitaph stones gradually became square in shape. By the sixth century, an inscription stone with a separate cover had evolved.

Epitaphs usually took the form of a main epitaph text and a title inscription. We see early examples of this in the Western Jin, occasionally with an additional introductory inscription. The body of the epitaph usually followed in the tradition of the Han stele inscriptions, with a standard formula and order for the events inscribed. The title was in the style of the stele titles, most frequently in four-character rhyming verses. Epitaphs and titles were written by accomplished men of letters, and several have come down to us with calligraphy executed by great masters.

The epitaph stone for the main inscription ranged from 50–60 centimeters to 70–80 centimeters square. Fine lines were drawn on its surface in a grid pattern, and one character was inscribed in each grid. The most typical arrangement consisted of roughly twenty vertical columns with a varying number of characters per column. A cover stone inscribed with the family name and the rank of the deceased rested on top of the epitaph stone. Seal script was usually used on the cover stone, known as the *zhuan gai*, or "seal cover." This format of epitaph and title is found almost exclusively among remains from the Northern Wei. As with manuscripts, epitaphs from the southern dynasties are very rare. This format for epitaphs, however, was to remain in use on into the Sui and Tang dynasties.

As a forceful, vigorous, yet refined block script came into use as the main style of calligraphy in the Northern Wei dynasty, the epitaphs, which had been written in the *bafen* style from the Later Han to the Eastern Wei, gradually evolved from that lofty style to the greater grace of the block script without losing any of their force. Behind this evolution, the influence of the calligraphy of the great master of Wei calligraphy, Zhong Yao, can be felt, and the loveliness of the calligraphy of the epitaphs of the northern and southern dynasties is partly a result of this. Yuan Zhan (447–96) was the eleventh son of Emperor Gong of the Northern Wei and a relative of Emperor Xiaowen. The epitaph records the important role Yuan Zhen played in Xiaowen's decision to transfer the capital to Luoyang. Following that, he was invested with the title of Prince of Nan'an and made Governor and Protector of the North and Governor-general of Xiang district. The inscription is written in a square grid of seventeen lines with eighteen characters per line. The calligraphy, as the sharpness of the engraving shows, was done with strong, forceful brushwork. This inscription is the oldest article that has been removed from the Yuan family tomb at Luoyang, and can be regarded as a typical example of the epitaphs of the Northern Wei.

23. Anonymous: "Title Inscription of Buddhist Image Constructed by Duke Shiping." Northern Wei Dynasty. Ink rubbing. Osaka Municipal Museum of Fine Art.

Longmen is located twelve kilometers south of Luoyang in Henan Province. Here, the Ling river is flanked on east and west by a chain of mountains rising from its banks and known, respectively, as the Eastern and Western Mountains. Their sharp peaks rising on both sides resemble a great stone gate, from which the name Longmen—literally, "dragon gate"—derives. Many caves have been excavated in both mountain chains. These are known as the Longmen stone caves and are famous as Buddhist sites of the Northern Wei. In each of the some 2,000 caves, the statue of a Buddhist deity has been placed, and many religious figures are carved into the walls and ceilings. In some, Buddhist altars have also been constructed. In most of the caves, the date of the construction, its sponsors, the purpose, the course of excavation, and a religious dedication as well as inscriptions similar in form to the title inscriptions of steles and listings of the names of members of religious groups are carved in the backs of the dais or halo of the image or in the form of a separate stele or monument plaque. These are known as the "account of the image construction," the image inscription, or the image title. There are more than 3,689 image titles inscribed during the period from the Northern Wei to the Tang, of which some 2,000 are from the Northern Wei. Most of these date from 227–527, making Longmen the earliest of the Buddhist cave sculpture and inscription sites.

The excavation of the Longmen caves began with the repeated excavations and enlargements of the Guyang cave and gradually expanded to other caves. The best-known works of these title inscriptions are concentrated here. The supreme works—the "twenty works of Longmen"—are also to be found here. During the Qing dynasty, with the rise of interest in the study of metal and stone inscriptions, the image inscriptions of Longmen appeared in ever greater numbers of catalogues of works. They were assiduously studied and greatly admired by the calligraphers and literati of the stele and metal inscription school in the late Qing, from 1735 to 1850. Kang Youwei of the Qing regarded the inscriptions of Longmen as the epitome of the "square brush" style. Emphasizing the beauty of the square brush, he praised it as the most vigorous of styles and dubbed it the Longmen style, holding that it reflected the best of calligraphy. The "Title Inscription of Buddhist Image Constructed by Duke Shiping" is one of the twenty major pieces to be carved in relief. This inscription is in the form of a stone tablet, and at the top of the tablet, six characters are inscribed in two lines: "The Duke Shiping Statue." The body of the inscription is enclosed in a square frame of ten lines, with twenty characters per line. The north (right) well of the Guyang cave is divided into an upper, middle and lower section. This tablet is located to the right of the Buddhist altar, in the upper section near the mouth of the cave.

The title derives from the inscription at the top of the tablet. The text of the inscription tells us that the Monk Huicheng, since entering Buddhist orders upon the death of his father, Duke Shiping, has always expressed his gratitude to the emperor and the nation by devoting himself to the construction of these rock temples. This he did as the fulfillment of a vow to improve his father's future karma, to honor his deceased father, to secure blessings for his ancestors, and for the glory of his clan.

Though much speculation has gone on since ancient times concerning both the deceased Duke Shiping and Huicheng, nothing certain is known of their history. As is touted at the closing of the inscription—"expert passages of brilliant truths and beautiful calligraphy"—a great deal of effort was put into its design, distinguishing it from the other, less inspired inscriptions. It was also the first monument to be built inside the cave. This indicates that Huicheng was probably an important and high-ranking person, who built this monument soon after Xiaowen moved the capital to Luoyang and excavations on the rock temples began. The calligraphy does justice to Kang Youwei's description of it as stately and vigrorous. It uses many alternate characters, which has made it useful in research on the rather idiosyncratic writing of the epitaphs.

24. Zheng Daozhao: "Confucian Didactic Verses at Yunfengshan." Northern Wei dynasty. Ink rubbing. Mitsui Bunko, Tokyo.

The precipice carving on a cliff of Yunfengshan in Ye Prefecture of Shandong Province is one of the many inscriptions on that mountain. Some 3.1 meters high and 3.36 meters wide, it consists of twenty lines of varying length. Each character is twelve centimeters square, inscribed in large block script.

The first section of characters explains the purpose and circumstances of the inscription and tells us that the Governor of Guang District (modern Shandong) wrote here his own composition, a collection of poems. He was then in residence at Laicheng and discovered Yunfengshan with its striking shape fifteen leagues to the southeast. The inscription was completed in 511.

The poem is an ode in five-character lines. As with all of the poems inscribed on Yunfengshan, this one has a strong Confucian coloring. When the Confucian sage was at a loss for the proper path of conduct, he should retire to Yunfengshan and cultivate his spirit—so urges this poem. The characters *jingshu* (classic) usually refer to the Confucian Classics, indicating that this poem is to be regarded as a text for the realization of Confucian ideals. This is truly a masterpiece of one of the members of the Han aristocracy during the Northern Wei dynasty of Emperor Xiaowen.

Each character is large enough to be visible from a distance, and the overall impression is of grandeur. The characters are full and exploit the surface of the cliff to advantage. Even though they are not always perfectly aligned due to the difficulties in carving the cliff face, the attack of each horizontal stroke is strong and sharp, rising slightly toward the center and gradually tapering off with a sleek grace. Compared to the block script of the Tang dynasty, there is much interesting variation and freedom here. This, too, is a product of Confucian values, which, finding expression in calligraphy, impart a bracing feeling to the work.

This work was first introduced through a rubbing by Ruan Yuan of the Qing dynasty. Prior to that, it had gone unnoticed except for a mention in Zhao Mingcheng's *Catalogue of Metal and Stone Inscriptions,* a Song work. Later, it was praised by Bao Shichen and gained attention as a famous work. It is prized as an example of the "round brush" technique of the Northern Wei.

25. Anonymous: "Yi He Inscription." Liang dynasty. Ink rubbing. Fujii Museum, Kyoto.

This inscription was located on a cliff on the southwest side of Jiaoshan, one of the three scenic mountains of Jiang River in the Changjiang region of the eastern part of Dantu Prefecture, Jiangsu Province. Struck by lightning, the stone was split into pieces and fell into the river, where it remained up to the Northern Song. It was retrieved once during the Southern Song, but fell into the water again. In 1712 of the Qing dynasty, Zhen Pengnian had it hauled up to the top of the mountain and, rejoining the five pieces, had it placed in a display pavilion built to protect it.

This inscription was praised by the likes of Ouyang Xun and Huang Tingjian and came to the attention of many of the metal and stone inscription scholars. As the original stone lay in the Jiang river, rubbings could only be made in autumn and winter, when the river was frozen. These were especially prized and known as "water rubbings" or "not-yet-retrieved rubbings."

The inscription laments the death of Xian He and was to be a memorial commemorating his burial. Ten characters can be made out on the stone, and much debate concerning these has continued among calligraphers from the Song period on. At present, most of the evidence seems to indicate that the attribution to Tao Hongjing is the best supported. According to the inscription, it was completed in 514. Another work of Tao, the *Jing Lan Ti Zi,* dated 515 and now in the Fujii Museum, bears a marked resemblance to this, perhaps indicating that the calligrapher actually was Tao Hongjing.

The stone is of poor quality, and the inscription was never very clear. The main style of script is block, with some scribe-script characters mixed in. The characters are large and written in vertical columns from right to left. The calligraphy is appropriate to a Confucian sage, exhibiting a serenity free from any vulgarity. Together with the cliff inscriptions of Zheng Daozhao, this is a valuable calligraphic work. Kang Youwei of the Qing called it the "round brush" style of the northern steles.

26. Bei Yiyuan: "Liang Stele for Zhongwu Xiao Dan, Prince of Shixing." Liang dynasty. Ink rubbing. Mitsui Bunko, Tokyo.

This stele is a very precious artifact from one of the few royal tombs of the Six Dynasties period located in lower Danyang Prefecture six kilometers west of Xixiashan near the southern bank of the Changjiang River. This is the left stele, which stood on the right side, facing the grave. The stele cap is in the shape of a semi-circle, with square borders of the stele inscription traced inside it. Below this is a round hole, and the body of the stele rests on the "tortoise base." It is, in fact, a faithful rendition of the stele style of the Later Han and an example of a stele that consisted of conjoining left and right sections. Only one-third of the characters remain undeciperable, and many entire sections of the carving are legible.

The title of the stele is written in an accomplished block script. Xiao Dan was made Prince of Shixing District in 502, the year of Emperor Wu's accession, and Governor-general in 520. He was the seventeenth child of Emperor Wen, and died at forty-five in 522. He was posthumously awarded several high ranks and given the name Zhongwu. The stele was probably built in Liang at the same time the "Gao Zhen Stele" was built in the Northern Wei.

The stele is in thirty-six lines of block script, with eighty characters per line. At present, approximately 2,580 characters have been deciphered. Both the title and the text of the stele are carefully executed, stately works, the compositions of Bei Yiyuan. We know little of Bei Yiyuan except that he was from Wuxing and held a low court rank. Since the stele of Xiao Dan's brother, Xiao Xiu, is also Bei's work, we can assume that he was a talented block-script calligrapher of the age.

Zhu Xizu, the author of the 1935 *Report on the Findings in Six Dynasties-Period Tombs* (*Liuzhao Lingmo Chabao Gaoshu*), describes this piece as being "calligraphy which had been influenced by Zhong Yao and Wang Xizhi, and went on to influence Ouyang Xun and Xue Ji." Certainly, the calligraphy is well controlled and refined. When we compare this stele with the contemporary "Gao Zhen Stele," we are struck by the similarity in spirit and the minor differences in details. This is an excellent piece to study for grasping the differences between the calligraphy of the northern and southern dynasties. At present, this stele is protected in a pavilion constructed for that purpose.

27. Anonymous: *"Dafangdeng Daji Jing."* Qi dynasty. Ink on paper. Kyoto National Museum.

"Dafangdeng" (Sanskrit, *Mahāvaipulya*) is a general epithet for Mahayana teachings in Buddhism. The *Daji Jing* (Great Collection of Sutras) is the name of collection of Mahayana sutras that the Buddha was said to have taught in the desire and form realms after gathering together all the Buddhas and Bodhisattvas of the ten directions. This scripture is included in the thirteenth volume of the Japanese edition of the Buddhist canon, the *Taishō Daizōkyō,* in a sixty-volume format which differs in its textual divisions from this copy. The generally held theory is that the present *Daji Jing* is a compilation into sixty volumes of various translations that were in existence at that time, which was prepared in 586 by one of the monks of the Zhaoti Monastery. Thus, this manuscript, representing the state of the text prior to this compilation, is quite valuable in the study of Buddhist texts. The translation is by Tan Wuchen.

This is an incomplete text, the beginning section of which is missing. At a length of twenty-two pages, it is copied in standard Buddhist manuscript style. The postscript by the same calligrapher reveals that this copy is a "vow scripture" of the monk Wu Jiao.

The calligrapher employs a soft brush and writes without any hesitation or interruption. The strokes to the lower right are especially fluid, while the brushwork of the horizontal strokes, from the start to the end of the stroke, resembles block script. In general, it is graceful and flowing, exhibiting the influences of traditional calligraphy from the work of the Wangs onward. It can legitimately be regarded as a predecessor of the *Yong Ming Jing* (Eternal Light Sutra), and is extremely valuable as a relatively early example of a Buddhist manuscript of the southern dynasty, from which we have so few samples of calligraphy.

At this time, the capital of the Northern Wei had just been transferred to Luoyang, but the policy of sinicization had not yet begun and cultural exchange between the north and the south was limited. As a result, in the northern dynasties, an accomplished scribe-script–influenced calligraphy was practiced in contrast to the calligraphy we can see in this Buddhist manuscript of the southern court, which was a development from the calligraphy of the Jin dynasty.

This manuscript was unearthed from a border region, and it is likely that the calligraphy of the central regions was a bit more controlled in style, representing as it did the fullest development of the calligraphy of the southern dynasties.

28. Zhengfa Wujincang: "*Vinaya* Preface." Liang dynasty. Ink on paper. Private collection.

This is a copy of the *Shan Song Pini Xu,* translated by the Kashmiri master Vimalāksa during the Eastern Jin. In the *Taishō* edition of the text, it is appended to the *Shi Song Lu,* translated by Puṇyatāra of the Later Qin, corresponding to volumes sixty and sixty-one of that version. This manuscript was unearthed in Turfan in the west of China.

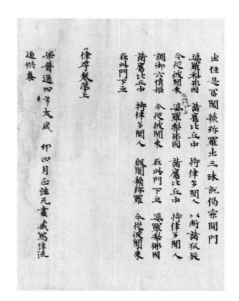

Zhengfa Wujincang, who is indicated as the copyist in the postscript, also is known to have copied the twenty-ninth volume of the *Huayan Jing* (Museum of Calligraphy, Tokyo). Both were copied in April of 523, suggesting that perhaps a large number of manuscripts were copied as a religious offering at this time.

As calligraphy, the triangular finish of the horizontal strokes first strikes the eye. This resembles the calligraphy of the later, forty-seventh volume of the *Huayan Jing* (pl. 29). This feature is evident in most Buddhist manuscript copies from the northern dynasties. After Ruan Yuan of the Qing dynasty published his critical studies, the differences between the calligraphy of the north and south came to be emphasized. Still, how can we interpret the many calligraphic techniques common to both this work and the twenty-ninth volume of the *Huayan Jing,* even though the former is ten years earlier than the latter? We are forced to admit that the north and south dynasties were in contact as far as calligraphy was concerned, and that totally independent, separate styles of calligraphy, did not, in fact, develop. Still, the structure of the characters in this work shows a more rigid, square and regular arrangement than that of the *Huayan Jing.* This is perhaps the one area in which the calligraphy of the southern dynasties can be faulted: the brushwork seems to lack strength and vigor.

A mark of sorts is visible above the final title. This greatly resembles the mark over the end title of the *Datong Fangguang Jing,* the Dunhuang manuscript dated 590, now in the Ōtani University Collection.

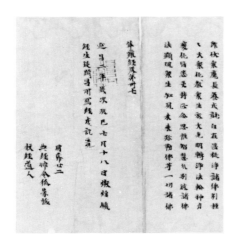

29. Zhang Xianchang: *"Huayan Jing."* Northern Wei dynasty. Ink on paper. Ōtani University Library, Kyoto.

This is a copy of the translation of Buddhabhadra of the Eastern Jin. However, though the end title of this copy identifies this as volume forty-seven, it closely resembles the fiftieth volume of the *Taishō* text. Further, the form of the final line is unnatural for a manuscript copy, and the seam between the final title and the rest is also a cause for concern. The copyist, Zhang Xianchang, is also responsible for the seventh volume of the *Loutan Jing* (Stein text no. 341). There is no dissimilarity in the calligraphy of the two works. Since the paper is only very lightly dyed, no columns are drawn.

More than eleven manuscript copies with the same format of closing inscription are to be found in existing catalogues. From them we can learn that the Dunhuang district, established from the Han dynasty, was the site of an outpost from the Northern Wei. A manuscript copying department on a grand scale was set up there, and we know that a great number of officials were set to copying manuscripts in a highly organized fashion. These efforts were divided among various specialists such as the high-ranking copyists, binders and bookmakers, and proofreaders and editors who checked the completed copies. This careful copying and production of correct versions of the Buddhist scriptures was a type of public work project, which has provided us with excellent source materials for research concerning the form of Buddhist manuscripts of this period.

The calligraphy of these manuscripts is deeply tinged with scribe-script style, and the brushwork is measured and forceful. The horizontal strokes end in a triangular finish, with considerable force in the brushstroke. We can also recognize, in the breaking-wave stroke, a forceful stopping of the stroke followed by a change in direction of the brush and a fillip. The internal structure of each character is natural and unforced, in an elevated style. The copyists of this period underwent thorough training, and created their own individual calligraphic styles. The calligraphy even suggests that perhaps a stiff brush was used to give this effect.

30. Anonymous: *"Pusa Chutai Jing."* Western Wei dynasty. Ink on paper. Chion-in Treasure House, Kyoto.

This manuscript was discovered among a group of ancient Buddhist scriptures in 1852 by the seventy-fifth head monk of the Chion-in in Kyoto. Of the five volumes of the scripture, volumes two, three and four are ancient copies from the Western Wei. The ancient library stamp of the Jinfengshan Monastery is to be found on the copy. The scripture was originally in the form of a scroll, but had been rebound into the format of a folding book. This is the oldest manuscript copy to be transmitted to Japan. The scripture was translated by the monk Zhu Fonian of Liang Province in the Later Qin.

According to the closing passage, Tao Jianhu and thirty others spent two years seeking out all of the Buddhist scriptures in the Western Wei and recorded them in their entirety. This copy is probably one of that group. It was copied in 550, but when we compare it to other copies from the same period, the form of the dating inscription is unique, which casts some doubt on its authenticity.

While it basically represents the continuation of the Northern Wei style, the calligrapher has completely surpressed the uniquely sharp strength of that style and in its place exhibits a soft line and a blunt breaking-wave stroke. The structure of each character is rather fluid, with a grace and purity that is commanding. Because in this work we can recognize the connection with Buddhist manuscript copies of the Sui, and because calligraphic materials from the Western Wei are extremely scarce, this is a valuable piece.

31. Zhiyong: "Thousand-Character Essay in Block and Cursive Scripts." Sui dynasty. Ink on paper. Private collection.

The *Thousand-Character Essay* was a rhymed composition of Zhou Xingsi, created upon the command of Emperor Wu of the Liang during the Six Dynasties period. Emperor Wu had a rubbing of one thousand characters from a Yin Tieshi inscription of Wang Xizhi's calligraphy made, and Xingsi was to use these characters in his composition. The seventh generation descendant of Wang Xizhi, Zhiyong, was said to have retired to an inner chamber of the Yongxin monastery and copied out eight hundred copies of this essay in block and cursive scripts, which he then distributed to various temples in Zhedong. In China, an 1109 printing of Zhiyong's "Thousand-Character Essay" by Xue Sichang known as the Guanzhong text exists. In addition, an original of the work was transmitted to Japan. In this version, there are 202 lines with ten characters per line, but one section is missing. The style of copying is identical to the Guangzhong text, and the calligraphic style of both the block and cursive characters is very similar, leading to the conclusion that the Japanese text is also Zhiyong's composition. As far back as the Nara period, a similar "Thousand-Character Essay" is recorded as having been brought to Japan and identified as "a rubbing of the calligraphy of General Wang" in the Todai-ji's catalogue of tribute articles. The "Thousand-Character Essay" in possession of the Ogawa family at present is without a doubt this item, which came into private hands. Though it is identified as "a rubbing of the calligraphy of General Wang," and indeed the "Thousand-Character Essay" was originally Wang's calligraphy, Zhiyong, as his descendant, carried on the tradition of the Wang family calligraphy, so there is no obstacle to prevent us from recognizing this as Zhiyong's work. Since the ancient Six Dynasties-period brush techniques as well as variant characters peculiar to that period appear in many places in this work, it is indeed possible to confirm this as an original of Zhiyong. As an original, the calligraphy far surpasses that of the Guanzhong text and is one of the great works that have been transmitted to Japan.

32. Ding Daohu: "Qifa Temple Stele." Sui dynasty. Ink rubbing. Private Collection.

This stele is the composition of Zhou Biao and the calligraphy of Ding Daohu. It was built in 602 of the Sui dynasty in Xiang District (Hubei Province, Xiangyang). It commemorates the rebuilding of the Qifa Temple in 584 by the people of Xiang. This temple was destroyed during the Northern Zhou. At first it was named the Guangfu Chan Hall by Governor General Wei Shikang, but later the name was changed to Qifa Temple. In the Song dynasty it was changed again to the Longxing Temple. We know little of Ding Daohu beyond that he was from Qiao (Anhui province), served in the College of Xiang, and excelled in block script. We know that two of his works, this "Qifa Temple Stele" and the "Xingguo Temple Stele," existed in Xiangyang. The calligraphy of the "Qifa Temple Stele" was far the better, but this stele perished first, to be followed soon after by the other.

Many Song-period catalogues mention the "Qifa Temple Stele," starting with Ouyang Xiu's *Collected Ancient Catalogues of Postscripts,* but by the time of Wang Xiangzhi of the Song dynasty, it was Ouyang Xiu's citation that was being referred to, suggesting that the original stele was no longer available for inspection or had been destroyed. Fortunately, the only existing copy of a rubbing has been transmitted to Japan, which allows us to actually view the calligraphy in question.

The calligraphy is, together with the "Longcang Monastery Stele," among the most beautiful and graceful of the Sui steles and is one of the sources from which developed the accomplished block script of Ouyang Xun and Chu Suiliang at the beginning of the Tang.

33. Yang Guang: *"Daban Niepan Jing."* Sui dynasty. Ink on paper. Kyoto National Museum.

This sutra (Sanskrit, *Mahāparinirvāna Sutra*) is included in volume twelve of the *Taishō.* Two editions, a forty-volume version translated by Tan Wuchen of Beijing and a thirty-six–volume version translated by the two Liu Song monks

Hui Yan and Hui Guan and revised by Xie Lingyun, exist today. The former is usually called the northern version and the latter the southern version. This manuscript is a single-volume copy of the northern text.

Crown Prince Guang, mentioned in the postscript, is Yang Guang, later Emperor Yang. It is recorded that this scripture was copied for all men as an act of offering. Since the founding of the dynasty, the Sui royal house—both Emperor Wen and his consort Dugu—devoted considerable energy to the copying of the entire Buddhist canon and gave all appearances of being pious Buddhists. The copy of the *Foshuo Yuedeng Sanmei Jing* in the Kyoto National Museum and the *Foshuo Shenshen Dahuixiang Jing* (Stein text no. 2154) in the British Museum, both copied as a result of Dugu's vow to copy the entire canon, are excellent evidence of this devotion. Not to be outdone by his parents, Emperor Yang had the Baotai Scripture Storehouse built in addition to initiating a large-scale scripture-copying project. Shi Falin of the Tang dynasty notes that this project amounted to 903,580 volumes of recopied and newly copied scriptures, stored in 612 storehouses. At any rate, this scripture is very rare as one of the surviving copies made under the Crown Prince's direction. It dates from his thirty-fifth year.

Shi Falin also notes that when Yang ascended to the throne he built the Longsheng Monastery at Gaoyang and had his secretary, Yu Shinan, compose a stele inscription. His calligraphy followed in the orthodox Wang tradition and was studied from Zhiyong. In style, a close association with Yu Shinan, whose calligraphy was so graceful and elegant, is in evidence. When this is considered, the calligraphy of the scripture copies can be seen to be approaching Tang-dynasty block script and together with Zhiyong's "Thousand-Character Essay" forms a single stream of development. This particular example is a masterpiece of Sui-dynasty scripture copying which is clearly leading the way to the development of Tang block script.

34. Anonymous: "Epitaph for Duke Yuan, Officer of the Stables." Sui dynasty. Ink rubbing. Private collection.

This grave inscription was unearthed together with that of Yuan's wife, Ji, in 1815 from Xianning Prefecture in Shanxi Province. In 1818 it came into the possession of Lu Yaoyu, but both stones disappeared during the Taiping Rebellion in 1860. In 1867, Lu Yaoyu's grandson went searching for the stones and finally found them buried in the earth, but more than half of the inscription had been damaged and the remaining twenty-seven lines were of unequal lengths varying from five to twenty characters. The stone fragment was purchased by Yun Yujia of Daxing at a very high price, but its later whereabouts are uncertain. Complete rubbings prior to its damage in 1860 are especially prized.

This grave inscription consisted of thirty-seven lines of thirty-seven characters each engraved in block script. The fact that Yuan's posthumous name, title, date of death, and burial location have been left blank may have been because they were unknown at the time of the composition, or they may have been written in red ink which wore away before the characters could be inscribed.

Yuan was the descendant of the Northern Wei Emperor Zhaocheng, or Shiyijian. He served in the Northern Zhou and Sui courts and was granted the title Master of the Stables in 613. In the same year he followed Emperor Yang on his campaign to Koryŏ and died on the return trip, at sixty-four years of age. In 615 he was buried together with his wife in Daxing Prefecture (Xianning), and the two grave inscriptions were erected. Both are thought to be the work of a single calligrapher.

Lu Yaoyu remarked of this epitaph, "The composition is dignified, the calligraphy is a masterpiece of the northern style. The construction of each character is straight and severe, completely removed from the over-refined tendencies of the northern and southern dynasties, heralding the styles of Ouyang Xun and Yu Shinan." This is a true masterpiece among epitaphs, and Bao Shichen went so far as to affirm that it was the calligraphy of Ouyang Xun.

35. Taizong: "Hot Spring Inscription." Tang dynasty. Ink rubbing. Bibliothèque Nationale, Paris.

This rubbing was discovered at the beginning of this century by Paul Pelliot in the Mogao caves at Dunhuang, and was among the huge number of documents brought back to France. At present it is located in the Bibliothèque Nationale, Paris (P. 4508). It is in the form of a scroll, with the first section missing. Only the last fifty lines are intact. Within the passage, the author refers to himself with the imperial pronoun, and characters usually abbreviated in deference to the emperor appear here in their full form. This, together with the forceful grace of the brushwork, led Luo Zhenyu to identify this as the "Hot Spring Inscription" (*Wenquan Ming*) composed and written by Taizong (598–649). The original stone stele is lost, and no other rubbings have been preserved, but on the new year of 648, Taizong showed his own composition for a "Hot Spring Stele" to his ministers at the Wenquan palace, and ordered that it be inscribed on stone. This rubbing is thought to be from that stele. Wenquan is identified as the Lishan hot spring in Lintong Prefecture of present-day Shaanxi Province. Taizong suffered from paralysis in his later years, and often traveled to hot springs for treatment. This stele speaks of their benefits and scenic beauties.

The stele was constructed with a special pavilion inside at the southern, Zhao-yang Gate of the Wenquan Palace. The stele cap was engraved with the name of the era, Zhenguan, in the mixed scribe script of Taizong. References to this stele are found in Song-dynasty works but no mention is made of it afterwards. The stele itself was probably destroyed immediately after the Song dynasty.

Taizong of the Tang is known as the first to attempt steles in semi-cursive script. This rubbing is unsurpassed in excellence and is extremely valuable because it transmits the actual appearance of Taizong's calligraphy to us today. Borrowing the "backbone strength" of Wang Xizhi, his calligraphy is free and fast-moving, with forceful brushwork that befits the regal character of the emperor.

An ink notation at the end of the rubbing indicates that this came into the possession of Guo Yier from Weigu District on the thirtieth day of the eighth month, the fourth year of Yonghui (653). If this interpretation of the notation, deciphered by Luo Zhenyu, is correct, the rubbing came into the possession of Guo Yier only five years after the completion of the stele itself, making it important as the oldest rubbing from the original. It is in the form of a scroll. Beneath the rubbing, marks indicating numbers can be seen.

36. Huairen, after Wang Xizhi: "*Preface to the Buddhist Canon*, from a Collection of Wang's Calligraphy." Tang dynasty. Ink rubbing. Mitsui Bunko, Tokyo.

This is a rubbing from a stele which was inscribed with the *Preface to the Great Tang Buddhist Canon (Da Tang Sancang Shengjiao Xu)*, using characters assembled from Wang Xizhi's works. The preface was written by Tang Emperor Taizong in August, 648, on the occasion of the new translations of Buddhist scriptures by the Buddhist master Xuanzhuang. The stele was engraved with Taizong's preface and imperial reply, the crown prince Gaozong's composition on the Buddhist canon and his formal reply, as well as approximately five lines of the *Banruo Boluomiduo Xin Jing,* a Buddhist scripture. The monk Huairen of the Hongfu Monastery was ordered by Taizong in the 650s to assemble characters from among the imperial holdings of Wang Xizhi's work, and after twenty years, in 672, he had completed his task. The stele is presently located in the Shaanxi

Provincial Museum in Xi'an. In the upper section of the stele are seven niches with Buddhas carved into them. These have given the name "Seven Buddhas Stele" to this stone.

Most of Wang Xizhi's calligraphy is printed in copybooks, and because the blocks from which they were printed were carved and recarved, the original appearance of Wang's works is none too faithfully reproduced. In contrast, this stele relied on the great quantity of Wang Xizhi originals which were in the imperial possession during the Tang dynasty. Since this stele is made up of a collection of characters from various sources, the preferences of the Tang Chinese are in evidence to a certain degree; there are also occasional ruptures in the continuity of the piece. But even so, it is probably the best work showing the actual appearance of Wang's calligraphy.

37. Ouyang Xun: "Inscription for the Memorial Pagoda of Chan Master Yong" (Huadu Temple Stele). Tang dynasty. Ink rubbing. Ōtani University Library, Kyoto.

This is the inscription at the stupa where the relics of Chan Master Yong of the Huadu Monastery are installed. Master Yong was an eminent monk of the "Three Stage Teaching" (san jie jiao), which had been founded by Chan Master Xinxing of the Sui. The monument was constructed on November 16, 621, after the death of Master Yong, next to the stupa of Master Xinxing at Chiming hill in Nanshan near Changan. The title reads, "The memorial stupa inscription for the late monk, Chan Master Yong of the Huadu Monastery," and is the composition of Li Baiyao of the Tang. The calligraphy is by Ouyang Xun. It is commonly known as the "Huadu Temple Stele" and, together with Ouyang Xun's "Jiuchenggong Palace Spring Inscription," is praised as excellent calligraphy.

The original rubbing was destroyed at an early date in the persecutions of the Three Stage Teaching. We can imagine the original stone by viewing this fragment of a Tang rubbing, which was discovered at Dunhuang. A Song-dynasty copy of the rubbing also circulated, and for a time was confused with the actual rubbings, but once the Tang rubbing was discovered, the true nature of the Song version became clear, and the two were distinguished. Nevertheless, the calligraphy of the Song tracing is not necessarily inferior, and it was in fact very well received from the start. This version is of the lineage of that Song copy. It was in the collection of Weng Fangguang of the Qing dynasty, who kept it constantly at his side and devoted all his energies to its study. Since it was regarded as an incomparable masterpiece, a great number of postscripts written in its praise were included in the same album, many of these by Qing-dynasty personages. They are excellent examples of the subtle art of appreciating stele printings. Within these postscripts, we find much excellent resource material concerning the study and theory of calligraphy, making it more valuable historically than any other rubbing from the same stone.

38. Chu Suiliang: "Yan Pagoda Prefaces to the Buddhist Canon." Tang dynasty. Ink rubbing. Tokyo National Museum.

This is a set of two stones, with Tang Emperor Taizong's *Preface to the Buddhist Canon* (*Sancang Shengjiao Xu*) on one stone and the Crown Prince's (later Emperor Gaozong) *Account of the Composition of the Preface to the Buddhist Canon* (*Shu Sancang Shengjiao Xu Ji*) on the other. The "preface" stone was erected in October of 653 and the "account" in December of the same year. Both are the work of Chu Suiliang (596–658), composed when he was fifty-eight.

Yan Pagoda is the name of the tower that was built to house and protect the stones, and it still stands today within the temple precincts of the Dacien Monastery in the southern part of Xi'an in Shaanxi Province. At first, a stone chamber was built in the upper floor of the tower, and the stones were placed within it, facing south. Later, during the time of Empress Wu, the structure was rebuilt as a seven-story tower, and a niche for the stones was built on the lowest level, again facing south. The "preface" stone was installed on the east and the "account" stone on the west. The "preface" was written right to left, and the "account" left to right, with the lines aligned so that they stood as a complementary pair. The compositions are carved into high-quality black marble and, because they were protected by the tower, remain in excellent condition.

These are regarded as Chu Suiliang's most mature work. In contrast to the other two of the three great Tang masters, Yu Shinan and Ouyang Xun, whose calligraphy remained within the bounds of established techniques, Chu's calligraphy transcended these bounds and showed a great deal of rhythm, movement, and strength of line: in all, a quick and graceful style. The plate shows a Song rubbing. A library stamp of the Xiaopenglai Archives is visible, indicating that this was part of the collection of the famous Qing-dynasty metal and stone inscription scholar, Huang Yi. The first two lines were accidentally reversed when the rubbing was made into a scroll.

39. Anonymous: *"Collected Works of Wang Bo."* Tang dynasty. Ink on paper. Tokyo National Museum.

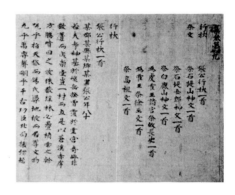

This is an ancient copy of a collection of the work of Wang Bo (647–74), counted as one of the four masters of the early Tang, together with Yang Jiong, Lu Zhaolin, and Luo Binwang. The *Collected Works of Wang Bo (Wang Bo Ji)* was originally thirty volumes in length, but it was soon lost, and only later editions are available to us now. A twenty-volume, Qing-dynasty version was one of the most widely circulated of these. The present copy is not included in the later collections, and it is important as a supplement to them, since it consists of the twenty-ninth and thirtieth volumes bound as one.

With regard to the date of the copy, Konan Naitō suggested that it was copied from 685–89, prior to Empress Wu's creation of the *zetian* characters, because the characters do not appear in the work. In addition, the character for the name of the Empress's grandfather, *hua,* is found in its complete form throughout the text—it was the custom to abbreviate characters of the names of members of the imperial family by omitting the final stroke. The calligraphy carries on the old style inherited from the Sui and northern dynasties. The line is rhythmic, and the characters are written with a slight slant to the right, which imparts a dynamism to the generally stately style.

A seal reading "Treasure of Kōfuku" is stamped on the work, indicating that this piece was brought to the Kōfuku-ji in Japan long ago. The Buddhist scripture on the reverse seems to have been copied at the end of the Heian period.

40. Anonymous: *"Commentary and Notes on the Spring and Autumn Annals."* Tang dynasty. Ink on paper. Fujii Museum, Kyoto.

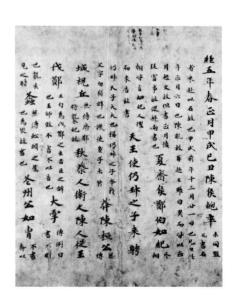

The *Commentary and Notes on the Spring and Autumn Annals (Chunqiu Jing Chuan Jijie)* is the title of a work which includes the *Spring and Autumn Annals*, the *Commentary* of Zuo Qiuming of the Zhou state, and the *Notes* of Du Yu of the Jin. The *Spring and Autumn Annals* is based on a chronological account of the ancient state of Lu. Confucius and his disciples selected a 240-year interval in that history, from the reign of Duke Yin in 722 B.C. to Duke Ai in 481 B.C., and with a few additions, made it into one of the Confucian classics. The *Chuan* of Zuo Qiuming is a commentary on that work and Du Yu's *Jijie* a set of notes on Zuo's work.

This volume is an anonymous Tang copy on seven lengths of yellow linen paper, in approximately 146 lines. It represents the second volume of the work, though some passages are missing. On the reverse, a postscript in vermillion ink relates how, on the 7th of July, 1078, a monk of the Henjō-in copied this from a Song printed text in the Seika-ji Treasury of Emperor Saga. This reveals that this piece was already in Japan during the reign of Emperor Shirakawa in the eleventh century. Later, in the Meiji era, it was in the collection of Tanko Kashiwagi. Yang Shoujing, who was in Japan at that time, saw this piece and mistakenly identified it as the calligraphy of a Northern Qi writer. He finally purchased it and brought it back to China. After his death, the text came into the hands of Li Guo-song of Hefei. In 1929, Konan Naitō heard of this and directed Ota Teizō to purchase the piece, which then returned to Japan for the first time in fifty years.

The style of the calligraphy continues in the tradition that persisted from the Six Dynasties to the Sui. There is a freshness underneath its rather flattened and thickened appearance. The postscripts of Yang Shoujing, Konan Naitō, and Nagao Uzan tell of the strange history of this work and praise the virtues of this copy.

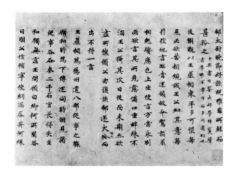

41. Anonymous: *"New Version of the Anecdotes."* Tang dynasty. Ink on paper. Kyoto National Museum.

The composition of Liu Yiqing of the Liu Song, with a commentary by Liu Xiaobiao of Liang, the *New Version of the Anecdotes* was a collection of stories about the aristocracy from the Han and Wei through the Jin to the Song in three volumes and thirty chapters. This is a Tang copy of the work.

This work was discovered during the collation of the ancient writings in the Tō-ji's storehouse that was carried out by Kanebumi Nishimura around 1877. At the end of the scroll is the right half of a stamp reading *Kōhō*, signifying that during the Northern and Southern Courts period of Japanese history it belonged to the scholar monk Kōhō of the Tō-ji Kanchi-in, and after his death, probably reverted to the temple storehouse.

The title, *New Version of the Anecdotes* (*Shishuo Xinyu*), is a general title assigned to this work in the Liu Song. According to the text, it was originally called simply *Anecdotes,* and began as an eight-volume work by Liu Yiqing. Later, a separate edition in ten volumes with Liu Xiaobiao's commentary was produced. By the Tang dynasty, the work was known by the longer title.

There is no date on this copy, but in places in the *Guizhen* chapter, the character *zhi,* which was part of the name of Emperor Gaozong, is replaced with *li.* This indicates that it was copied during the Tang, sometime after the beginning of Gaozong's reign. The calligraphy is forceful and bold and reflects the polished learning of the writer, making it a masterpiece among Tang copies.

42. Anonymous: *"Biography of Yang Xiong, Han Annals."* Tang dynasty. Ink on paper. Private collection.

The *Han Annals* is a record of the historical events of a 230-year period from the time of Gao Liu Bang of the Han to Wang Mang's governance. Ban Gu (32–92) of the Later Han composed it at the request of his father, Ban Biao. This is a Tang copy of that work, beginning in the *Biography of Yang Xiong,* the fifty-seventh of eighty-seven volumes. The first section of the chapter is missing, and the text begins with the character *fan,* continuing to the end of the work.

At the end of this volume is a postscript indicating that it was received from Lord Kazan'in in the spring of 1453, which evidences that this work had been handed down in the Kazan'in family. Later, in the Meiji era, it came into the possession of Seisei Takezoe, and during the early Shōwa era it was to be found in the Ayazo Takei collection. At present it belongs to Jun'ichi Ueno of Hyōgo.

Reading notes in black and red ink, notes in Japanese *kana,* and corrections appear alongside the text. The calligraphy is straightforward and masterful enough, close to Ouyang Xun's style. One stroke of the two characters *yuan* and *min* is omitted, which probably indicates that this is an early Tang work, since those characters appear in Tang emperors' names.

The corrections and notes between the columns are in the same hand as the fifteen characters reading, "On the twenty-first day of the fifth month [of 948] these notes were completed by Fujiwara Yoshihide." Biographical details are unclear, but the date indicates that these are original corrections from more than one thousand years ago. Their value is only increased by the fact that the notes quote many passages from lost works prior to the Six Dynasties, the Sui, and the Tang.

There are four seals at the beginning of the scroll and three at the end.

43. Sun Guoting: *"Treatise on Calligraphy."* Tang dynasty. Ink on paper. Taipei Palace Museum.

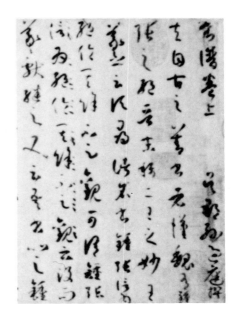

Traditionally, study of *cao* script concentrated on Wang Xizhi, but the *Treatise on Calligraphy (Shu Pu)* of Sun Guoting (648?–703?) was highly regarded as a preparatory step to Wang. This was not simply because it was a cursive work representative of the Tang dynasty, but because it was one of the major works within the cursive tradition of Wang Xizhi.

During the Song this work was in Emperor Huizong's collection and was kept together with Wang Xizhi's "Shiqi Album" (pl. 19). It passed into private hands afterwards, and a traced carving was made of it during the Ming and Qing, from which many printed versions were reproduced. The original came into the possession of Emperor Qianlong of the Qing and remained in the palace collection. It was in two rolls, but during the mid-Ming dynasty it was rebound in one scroll 26.5 centimeters wide and 9 meters long. The original consisted of 3,711 characters, but 196 characters in the middle have been lost, though they can be supplemented from printed versions.

The content of the work is a ranking of calligraphers from the Han and Wei through the Qi and Liang, and a discussion of their works as well as previous theories of calligraphy. The techniques and study of calligraphy are discussed, and a positive theory of calligraphy is propounded. The author regards the applied scripts—block, semi-cursive, and cursive—rather than the decorative scripts as the true bases of calligraphy. From that point of view, the traditional scripts and techniques are summarized. He proceeds to critically assess these, and in general endorses the aesthetic ideals of the Six Dynasties. Nevertheless, he enlarges upon and expands this aesthetic and, as a calligrapher himself, is also able to weave his own experience into his theoretical discussions, resulting in a treatise that is of interest even today.

44. He Zhizhang: *"Classic of Filial Piety* in Cursive Characters." Tang dynasty. Ink on paper. Collection of the Japanese Imperial Household, Tokyo.

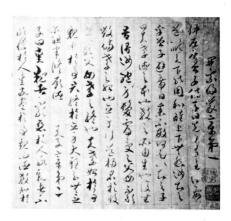

This is a scroll in which the Confucian classic, the *Classic of Filial Piety (Xiao Jing)*, is written entirely in cursive script. At the end of the scroll is the passage, "The Hejian original, with a double-glued cover attached, winter of the second year of Tianlong [961]." This was just two years after Taizu's accession to the Song throne. The passage indicates that when the scroll was rebound at the beginning of the Song, it was already known as the Hejian original. He Zhizhang was active from the second to the fifth decade of the eighth century, during the reign of Tang Emperor Xuanzong. Because he held the post of Director (*jian*) of the Secretariat, he was known as He Jian. In the catalogue of Song Emperor Huizong's prized calligraphy, a *cao* version of the *Classic of Filial Piety* by He Zhizhang is also listed, providing another reason for this attribution. He Zhizhang also enjoyed a reputation as a poet and was known to have associated with Zhang Xu, who was renowned for his wild cursive script. He himself excelled in cursive, and he was said to often write a very extravagant and free cursive script while drunk that was so unique that he could not duplicate it when sober. It is easy to imagine him writing a cursive version of the *Classic of Filial Piety*, usually written in a stately block script. This cursive script shows excellent technique and is justly famous as a representative of the glory of Tang cursive script.

45. Anonymous: "Epitaph Inscription for Princess Yongtai." Tang dynasty. Ink rubbing. Shaanxi Provincial Museum.

This grave inscription was unearthed in September of 1960 from a tomb 2.5 kilometers to the southeast of Gaozong's tomb in Qian Prefecture of Shaanxi Province. Princess Yongtai was the granddaughter of Gaozong and Empress Wu, the sixth daughter of Zhongzong. In 700 she was made the district ruler and

married Wu Yanji. The next year, at seventeen, she died. In 706 she was entombed in the royal tombs with her husband. This epitaph was placed in the grave at that time.

The mother of Zhongzong and Ruizong, Yongtai's grandmother Empress Wu, ascended the throne in 690 and changed the dynasty name from Tang to Zhou. In her later years, especially, she was enamored of the brothers Zhang Yizhi and Zhang Changzong and turned much of the business of government over to them, inviting criticism from all quarters. According to contemporary sources, Yongtai, her husband Wu Yanji, and her brother Li Zhongrun secretly criticized Empress Wu. The Empress learned of this and drove them to their deaths, it is said. In the chronicles, their cause of death is given alternately as suicide, beating, and strangling, but more recent scholarship asserts that no passages in Yongtai's epitaph suggest that she was killed by Empress Wu, but rather that she died due to complications during pregnancy.

There are thirty-two lines to the inscription, with thirty-two characters per line. Tang documents record Xu Yanbo as the author of the passage. He was a well-known literary personage of the time. The calligrapher's name is not mentioned, but the severe and graceful block script is well suited indeed to the tragic Princess's story. The inscription cover contains an inscription in seal script with nine characters arranged in three lines, reading "The epitaph of the late Princess Yongtai of the Tang."

46. Yan Zhenqing: "Eulogy for a Nephew." Tang dynasty. Ink on paper. Taipei Palace Museum.

A *cao*-script composition written by Yan Zhenqing (709–85) eulogizing his cousin Xi Jiming, who was killed in the An Lushan uprising. The work dates from September 758, when Zhenqing was fifty years old. In this rebellion, Yan Zhenqing and his cousin, Yan Gaoqing, the magistrate of Changshan, acted in concert to raise a force and crush the rebels. They captured the leader of the rebels and took several thousand captives. Gaoqing sent his son, Quanming, with this news as a messenger to Chang'an, but when he reached Taiyuan, Chengye, governor of Taiyuan, stopped him and claimed the credit for the victory as his own. When urgent requests for support came from Changshan, he ignored them. As a result, Changshan Castle fell, and Gaoqing was killed along with his young son, Jiming. Quanming escaped and was able to reach Zhenqing, whereupon Zhenqing sent him off with ransom to retrieve the corpses of his father, Gaoqing, and his younger brother Jiming. Gaoqing's corpse was missing one leg, and nothing remained of Jiming but his head. This eulogy, then, was written when Quanming returned with the head.

The original text of the eulogy went through the possession of a great many collectors in the Yuan, Ming, and Qing dynasties, and finally came into the possession of Emperor Qianlong. Besides the original, printed copies appear in several collections.

The calligraphy flows with the passion of grief, and is a powerful embodiment of the horrible turn of events it laments.

47. Huaisu: *"Autobiography."* Tang dynasty. Ink on paper. Taipei Palace Museum.

This is a work written by Huaisu in cursive script, recording the story of his study of calligraphy as well as poems written in his praise by literati of the time. At the end of the scroll, the date of the copy appears: tenth month, winter of 777. Huaisu relates how he lived in Changsha, where he entered Buddhist orders at a young age. With the time that remained after reading the scriptures and practicing meditation, he pursued calligraphy, of which he was inordinately fond. However, he had no opportunity to inspect the calligraphy of the masters, and what models he could find were very rudimentary, so he packed up and headed west for Luoyang, where he gained audiences with high-ranking ministers of the day. While those arrangements were proceeding, he finally encountered fragments of the writings of Zhang Xu and others, and was suddenly enlightened. When the scholars saw him writing on smooth paper and white silk, they thought it nothing strange. Later he made the acquaintance of the Secretary of the Department of Justice, Yan Zhenqing, and since Lu Xiang and Zhang Wei had seen Huaisu's calligraphy previously, praising it in poetry, Huaisu requested a preface from Yan. In response, Yan Zhenqing wrote the *Preface to the Cursive Script Poems of Sage Huaisu* (*Huaisu Shangren Caoshu Ge Xu*). Following this, Huaisu gives poems written after Zhenqing's preface by the leading literati of the day. Passages consisting of a series of poems praising Huaisu's calligraphy actually outnumber passages concerned with autobiographical information.

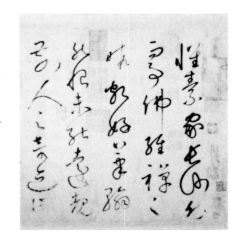

The work consists of fifteen pages and 136 lines. At the start of the work there are five or six characters per line, but toward the end, only one or two large ones. The shapes of the characters follow the writer's emotional flow and abound in many subtle variations, but the fine, polished line is never disrupted. This is a great work that demonstrates the quintessential form of the genre of wild cursive script.

At first this piece was in the collection of the Li family, at the beginning of the Southern Tang. Its transmission before entering the collection of the Qing Emperor Qianlong is recorded in detail in the postscripts.

## 48. Cai Xiang: "Poems in Thanks for an Imperial Gift." Song dynasty. Ink on paper. Museum of Calligraphy, Tokyo.

Cai Xiang (1012–67) was born in Putian, the administrative capital of Xinghuajun (Fujian Prefecture). He passed the imperial examinations in 1030, during the reign of Renzong. He finally became one of the three great ministers responsible for the economy of the Song dynasty.

Though he is numbered as one of the four masters of Song in the phrase "Su, Huang, Mi, Cai," it was originally Cai Jing who was being referred to. In its original form, the phrase was not only chronologically accurate, but proceeded in the established series of tones of the Chinese language. However, people of later times were critical of Cai Jing's character, and he was replaced by Cai Xiang, though the neatness of the phrase suffered consequently. This shows what a high opinion people had of Cai Xiang, not just as a calligrapher, but as a man of strong convictions and integrity.

The "Poems in Thanks for an Imperial Gift" (*Xieci Yushu Shibiao Juan*) were written as a gesture of thanks to Emperor Renzong, who wrote the characters of Cai's personal name, Jun Mo, and presented them to him in 1052. In response to this special favor, Cai wrote a letter of appreciation and a series of seven-character-line poems in an ancient style.

The mention of various official titles and posts current at the time have allowed us to date the work as being from 1052.

Of the four Song masters, Su Shi and Huang Tingjian were of the literati school, while Mi Fu and Cai Xiang excelled at the more orthodox traditions of calligraphy. Cai Xiang was, in fact, twenty-four years older than Su Shi. For that reason, and perhaps also because his teacher Ouyang Xiu thought highly of him, Su Shi praised Cai as "the best in the realm."

He excelled in block, semi-cursive, cursive, and wild-cursive scripts. His large block script was patterned after Yan and his semi-cursive and cursive followed the ancient techniques of Wang Xizhi. As for the individual styles of his calligraphy, Su Shi, influenced by the theories of Ouyang Xiu, ranked his semi-cursive script first, his small block second, and his cursive third, saying, "Cai Xiang's small block gets better and better the smaller it becomes." Su praised him, remarking that "his semi-cursive and cursive are so good because his block script is excellent."

This work is representative of his small block script. According to Chen Jiru (1558–1639) of the Ming, it combines the brushwork of Yan and Qing. In all, three versions of the work exist. In addition to this one, another is to be found at the Taipei Palace Museum and a third in the Tokyo National Museum. The version reproduced here is the original and the other two are tracings.

49. Su Shi: "*Cold Meal in Huangzhou* Poem Scroll." Song dynasty. Ink on paper. Private collection.

There is little more that needs to be said of Su Shi (1036–1101). He is a monumental figure of Chinese art history. Su Shi was the first in history to be punished under the censorship laws. He was sentenced to one hundred days in prison, but was able to avoid the death penalty. Due to the good auspices of Wang Anshi's brother, Anli, and the mercy of the imperial consort he was exiled to Huangzhou (Huanggang in Hubei Province). He arrived there in February of 1080. In a poem written at the start of his third year of exile, 1082, when he was forty-seven, he wrote, "Already three cold meals have passed/Since I have come to Huangzhou." "Cold meals" refers to the prohibition, in honor of the death of Jie Zitui of the Jin, of cooked meals on the day before the spring Qingming festival.

There are many theories regarding the date of this piece. Towards the end of the first stanza, the character *bing* has been stamped in and the character *zi* erased. In the third line of the second stanza, traces of the erased character *yu* are visible. This probably indicates that this was composed in the period of exile, when Su Shi had much free time and was not pressed by his public duties. The fact is that in the extended passages of his works written before his banishment there is not a single erasure or over-writing.

This work, together with the postscript by Huang Tingjian, is a masterpiece of poetry and postscript composition, representing the apex of the literati-school calligraphy. According to Huang Tingjian's postscript, "This poem resembles Li Bo's work, but I'm afraid even Li Bo doesn't compare," and "the calligraphy combines the brushwork of Yan Zhenqing, Yang Ningshi, and Li Jianzhong, and is so wonderful that even its author was hard put to reproduce it." Yan Zhenqing of the Tang and Yang Ningshi of the Five Dynasties were the most highly praised of calligraphers, and Li Jianzhong of the early Song was the most highly regarded calligrapher by the gentry class of the time. To say that Su Shi combined the talents of all three was nothing if not the highest praise.

However, it is hard to identify any definitive influences in this calligraphy. As Su Shi said himself, "My calligraphy follows my feelings. I have no techniques." This is the calligraphy of a free spirit who has transcended the orthodox techniques of old. Some of the scholar class criticized Su Shi because his brushwork was not in accord with those ancient techniques, but Huang Tingjian quoted Du Zhou of the Han, who said, "The features of the calligraphy of the former Wang became the rules, and those of the latter Wang the laws" and argued that originally there were no rules in calligraphy, which pleased Su Shi no end.

Su Shi himself was likely to have said, "I do not regret that my calligraphy lacks the techniques of the two Wangs, but that the Wangs lack my technique." In fact, Su Shi quoted these words of Zhang Rong of the Southern Qi in a preface he composed to a cursive script composition of Huang Tingjian.

Finally, with regard to the history of this work of poetry, Konan Naitō's postscript supplies the details. From the three seals, it is clear that from Qianlong's reign on, this work was kept within the imperial treasury. In 1860, it fell into private hands.

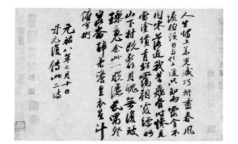

50. Su Shi: "*Hermit Li Taibo* Poem Scroll." Song dynasty. Ink on paper. Osaka Municipal Museum of Fine Art.

In the history of calligraphy, Su Shi's point of departure is Yan Zhenqing and Huaisu, in contrast to the tradition centering around Wang Xizhi. He was the living ideal of the literati group, both as a calligrapher and a man. The "*Hermit Li Taibo* Poem Scroll" (*Li Taibo Xian Shijuan*) here, together with the "*Cold Meal in Huangzhou* Poem Scroll," are the best known and most accomplished of the more than fifty albums of Su's calligraphy remaining today.

This work is a semi-cursive script rendition of two poems attributed to the hermit Dan Yuanzi (Yao Anshi). Yao Anshi associated with Wang Dingguo and Su Shi in the late eleventh century, and Su Shi was enraptured with him, saying, "his style is unique, and his opinions unusual." Whether these two poems, which

Yao recited and attributed to Li Bo, are really the work of Li Bo is unclear. They to not appear in the *Collected Works of Li Taibo*, but in an essay Su Shi quotes two lines and seems to believe that they are without any doubt Li Bo's poetry. In the same essay, he says that he saw these poems written by Yan Zhenqing in Biandu, and "the ink was fresh and vivid, and the paper seemed strong and new." Whether this was really an autograph of Yan Zhenquing remains unproven, but perhaps these were poems that had been transmitted orally from the Tang dynasty. Yet, there are some twenty variations between the versions of the two poems that appear in the essay and those in this original work.

As befits a famous work, there are many seals stamped on it. The stamp of the Yuan master Zhao Mengfu appears at the beginning of the roll, indicating that this was once one of his dearest possessions. Postscripts by the Jin personage Cai Song-nian (1107–59) and Shi Yisheng (died 1160) also appear there, proving to be excellent sources from the Jin period, which are otherwise so scarce. The calligraphy of these two is written in a style informed by Su Shi's work. The Ming scholar Zhang Bi (1425–87) writes in his postsript that this shows that the Jin Chinese revered Su Shi on a par with Confucius, and also that while the study of Cheng Zi was popular in the south, Su Shi was assiduously studied in the north.

There is a long postscript by Gao Shiqi (1645–1704) of the Qing and, finally, a postscript by Chen Deqian (1673–1769).

According to his disciple Huang Tingjian, Su Shi was not good at the technique of writing with a raised elbow. This did not affect his leftward strokes, but his strokes to the right were somewhat cramped, and criticized on those grounds by the scholar-gentry of the time. He rejected the sheep-bristle brush as unsuitable, favoring instead the stiffer, traditional brush. Perhaps for that reason this calligraphy seems a little flattened. Nevertheless, the tips of each stroke are well-defined. The rounded strokes and superior rhythm of Su Shi's calligraphy and his wonderful compositions clearly reflect his wide learning and sophisticated sense of style.

### 51. Huang Tingjian: "Epitaph Drafts for Wang Zhong and Shi Fu." Song dynasty. Ink on paper. Tokyo National Museum.

In addition to these two epitaph inscription texts, we have other works of Huang's, but the epitaph insciptions have a larger number of characters and have been well known for their authenticity since early times. These two texts were composed at different times and are independent works, but they are bound together in a single scroll and have been grouped under a single title. They are drafts for epitaph inscriptions for Wang Zhong and Shi Fu.

According to the inscription, Wang Zhong was a maternal relative of Huang. His mother ordered him to compose the eulogy. According to the second epitaph, the family of Shi Fu had moved to Weishan in Sichuan Province six generations earlier, but from his generation they settled in Luzhou in the same province. Careful examination of the text as given in the *Yu Zhanghuang Xiansheng* (Collected Writings of Dr. Yu Zhanghuang) shows that the missing characters at the bottom of the second line of the epitaph are to be read *Yan cong*. This indicates that Shi Yan, Shi Fu's ancestor eight generations back, was an attendant at the Department of History of the Tang Secretariat. Up to five generations back, his ancestors had served in government posts, but his great-grandfather, Shi Pu, lived in a time of disorder and was unsuccessful, so that form his generation to that of Shi Fu's father, Shi Zongjian, the family was in decline.

Because his family was poor, Shi Fu attempted but failed at the Meizhou and Kaifeng examinations, and made his living as a tutor of the children of the scholar class in Luzhou. He was an unambitious man, and was given the name Shi Lao ("Venerable Poet") because whenever he took to drinking, he wrote poetry that made quite an impression on the other guests. He died in 1096 and was entombed in 1099, corresponding to the time Huang Tingjian was living in exile in Rongzhou. This was probably a composition of that period.

The Wang Zhong epitaph inscription, then, was written in Huang's second period, from 1084 to 96, while the Shi Fu epitaph inscription belongs to the fourth period of his life, 1096-1100. Huang doesn't specifically identify the sources from which he studied block script, but he may have studied an ancient rubbing of Yu Shinan's "Confucius' Tomb Tablet," and he said of Zhong Yao's small block script, "Zhong Yao has many different kinds of calligraphy, but I enjoy his small block script in particular," which provides some hints in this direction.

Of the two grave inscriptions, the Wang Zhong text does not exhibit Huang's special feature, the extended horizontal stroke, and wavering strokes are also rare. In the Shi Fu text, the long strokes characteristic of Huang's work are in evidence, as he is approaching the style of his later years.

In the 1088 postscript, Huang says, "In my youth I gladly wrote in cursive script, but I noticed that there was a certain vulgarity about it, and now I confine myself to block script." He believed that "excelling at block script was the basis for mastery of cursive." Still, the block script of the Song calligraphers was different from that of the Tang, and in general closer to semicursive script.

52. Huang Tingjian: "Li Taibo's *Recalling Past Wanderings* Poem Scroll." Song dynasty. Ink on paper. Fujii Museum, Tokyo.

Not only was Huang Tingjian counted as one of the four great masters of the Song, together with his teacher Su Shi, but he was also the greatest proponent and formulator of the theories of the literati school of calligraphy, which stood in contrast to the more traditional Wang Xizhi style of calligraphy. The general practice and theory of his calligraphic studies is available to us in the *Colophons of Shangu (Shangu Tiba.)* With regard to the development of his own calligraphy, we can delineate five periods: his youth (study of Zhou Yue of the Song); 1086–93 (study of Zhong Yao and Yu Shinan); 1094–97 (study of Huaisu's *Autobiography*); 1098–1100; and 1101–5. Though we can divide his career into these five periods, we can not specify exactly what he studied during all of these periods. We can assume from his praise of Yan Zhenqing, Zhang Xu and Yang Ningshi that he must have studied these works, too. In his theories, Huang valued "free and flowing inspiration," and deemed cursive script most appropriate for this expression.

This "Li Taibo's *Recalling Past Wanderings* Poem Scroll" (*Li Taibo Yi Jiu Yu Shijuan*) was completed in 1094, when he was over fifty years old, and was not discovered until the Yuan dynasty. The first half was lost, and there is no artist's signature, but according to the postscript composed by Zhang Duo of the Yuan dynasty in 1295, this is without a doubt Huang Tingjian's cursive calligraphy, a rendition of a poem by Li Bo recalling his old travels, presented to General Yuan San of Qiao District. Zhang Duo, in his postscript, declares, "I love the calligraphy of Su Shi, Huang Tingjian, and Yuan Zhang and, to a certain extent, can distinguish the genuine from the fake. When I was governor of Zhangyue (Fujian Province), Dong Junxiang brought to me a length of cursive calligraphy that had been buried in the earth, asked my opinion of the work, and then presented it to me. When I brushed off the dust, I was surprised to see what I thought was an original work of Huang Tingjian. I showed it to Li Mingfu, a resident of Min, and he identified it as a poem of Li Bo, the first half of which unfortunately was missing."

Following this postscript by Zhang Duo is another by Shen Zhou (1427–1509) of the Ming, dated 1506. Wang Fenggang (1733–1818) of the Qing dynasty claims that there were also postscripts by Zhu Yunming (1460–1526) and Xiao Haizhuo, but these no longer exist.

The cursive script at which Huang Tingjian was such a master was probably written with a sheep-bristle brush. A selection in the fifth volume of the *Colophons of Shangu* entitled, "Essay Discussing Su Shi's Brush" contains a passage which declares, "Su Shi preferred to use a brush of the *Zhuge* school of Xuancheng. The *zaohe* brush was favored by some in recent times who prized oddities, but Su Shi thought it inappropriate for actual use." However, in another essay, Huang says, "because it responds to a person's feelings," he preferred the "effortless *zaohe* brush." This *zaohe* brush, according to Liang Zhangjin of the Qing, is the present-day sheep-bristle brush, and an inspection of the works of Huang Tingjian supports this conclusion.

53. Huang Tingjian: "*Cold Meal in Huangzhou* Poem Scroll Postscript."
    Song dynasty. Ink on paper. Private collection.

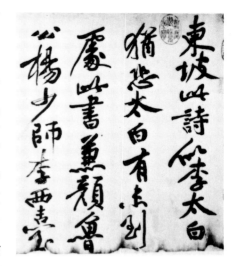

There is no signature on either Su Shi's calligraphy or Huang Tingjian's postscript,
but since ancient times no one has disputed that these were authentic works, so
expert is the brushwork. Huang Tingjian himself was of a different opinion:
"When I was in Qiannan, I did not realize how weak my characters were, but
when I looked at my calligraphy before coming to Rongzhou, only three or four
out of ten seemed at all passable. Only now do I realize that I hardly understand
the ancients' injunction to "gravity and directness (*chenzhao tongkuai*)."

Like Su Shi, Huang Tingjian's calligraphy was based on Yan Zhenqing's style
and was also informed by studies of Zhang Xu, Huaisu, and Yang Ningshi. And
also like Su Shi, he achieved a "technique of no-technique." Huang jokingly
said of Su Shi's calligraphy, "The master's calligraphy is like a crab crawling
along," to which Su Shi replied, "And yours is like a snake wrapped around a
tree." It is truly remarkable how well they put their fingers on the characters of
each other's work. Huang praised his teacher saying, "I studied Su Shi along
with Yan, but Su Shi's ability was a natural gift, and my own hand was clumsy."
In fact, Su Shi was probably not naturally skillful, with his inability to exploit the
soft brush and his weakness in the raised elbow technique of writing. Huang,
on the other hand, was clever with the soft brush, and also had the urgency of
a true seeker in his study of calligraphy. At any rate, those things had little to
do with the finished quality of their work.

In the *Colophons of Shangu* there are almost fifty pieces in which Huang wrote
a postscript to poems by Su Shi, of which this work is a wonderful example.

54. Mi Fu: "Gangxian Poem Scroll." Song dynasty. Ink on paper. Tokyo
    National Museum.

Mi Fu (1051–1107) had a distinctive way of writing the "grass radical" with
alternating horizontal and vertical strokes that is identifiable here even though
this work is unsigned. Mi Fu is one of the four great Song masters and is especially
closely associated with Su Shi and Huang Tingjian. But, in contrast to those two,
who are known for their "no-technique technique" and were proponents of the
literati style of calligraphy, Mi followed the ancient techniques faithfully and
was a specialist in calligraphy and painting. He was born into a landed administrator's family. His mother was wet nurse of Empress Yongzong, and so from
an early age he grew up in aristocratic circles, finally gaining a post in the Revisions
Department of the Secretariat. But, perhaps because he did not sit for the examinations like Su Shi and Huang Tingjian, his highest post was second assistant
of the Board of Rites. A controversy soon arose concerning this appointment,
and he was forced to resign. When Emperor Huizong instituted calligraphic
studies, Mi Fu was given the post of Doctor of Calligraphy and Painting (in 1104,
at age fifty-four), and he had the opportunity to study many ancient works that
were in the imperial collection. He was particularly well versed in the authenti-
fication of ancient works and copies, and there are many anecdotes about his
work in this capacity. According to his own account, he studied the calligraphy
of Yan Zhenqing, Liu Gongquan, Ouyang Xun, and Chu Suiliang, gradually
approaching the quiet simplicity of the Wei and Jin calligraphy. Of the two
Wangs, he studied Wang Xianzhi in particular, and devoted himself also to the
techniques of other Jin-period calligraphers, which distinguished him from others
of the orthodox school of calligraphy.

This work, the "Gangxian Poem Scroll" (*Gangxian Shijuan*), dates from Mi
Fu's later years, 1102–10, according to Dr. Yasushi Nishikawa. There is no
signature, but a red stamp of the two characters, *Mi Fu*, is stamped nine times
on the seam of the paper. The style of the character *fu* in seal script is called
"two bows back to back." This piece is different from Mi Fu's others, with their
strong forward movement and firm brush tip. Instead, there are great variations
of dark and light, wet and dry. It may be because the characters are large, or due to
the nature of the white cotton paper, as the calligraphers of ancient times believed.

Seals in old Song and Yuan styles appear on the work, including the seals of such well-known calligraphers as Cao Rong and Wang Hongku of the Qing, telling of the ancient transmission of the work.

Many have declared Mi's calligraphy to be "crisp, masterfully rhythmical brushwork," and regarded his large characters as the best. That Wu Sheng regarded his calligraphy as superior to that of Jin and Tang masters deserves note.

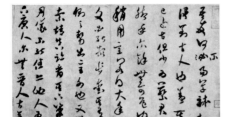

## 55. Mi Fu: "Four Cursive Albums." Song dynasty. Ink on paper. Osaka Municipal Museum of Fine Art.

These four albums of cursive script were in the imperial collection of calligraphy during the reign of Gaozong of the Southern Song which was originally known as "the nine cursive script albums," because it contained a series of nine works bound together. This is confirmed by the authenticity of the postscript of Mi Fu's son, Mi Youren which reads: "The nine cursive script works above," with the official stamp of the imperial government on it. Of the four (actually five) albums in the Osaka Municipal Museum of Fine Art—the "New Year's Album" (*Yuan Ri Tie*), the "Wu You Album" (*Wu You Tie*), the "Mid-Autumn Poem Album and Mu Qiong Album" (*Zhong Qiu Shi Tie, Mu Qiong Tie,* two albums bound as one), and the "Hai Dai Album" (*Hai Dai Tie*) the "Wu You Album" comes closest to the style of the Jin calligraphy that was Mi Fu's model. This letter to a friend says, "The form of your cursive script is close to that of the ancients, but it's a shame that it remains influenced by Cai Xiang. It will probably improve if you can get a hold of Da Nian's "Thousand-Character Essay." I enjoy the liveliness of the side elements of the characters in that work because they surpass the calligraphy of the two Wangs. The originals of Suo Qing of the Jin no longer exist. The "Yue Ying Album" is probably the work of Tang writers, for it lacks the ancient feeling of the Jin calligraphers."

According to these statements, Mi Fu was in search of the "classic elevation" of the Jin calligraphers, and was not interested in comparing his work to the Tang artists. In particular, from Mi Fu's standpoint, with his regard for ancient techniques, the masters of wild cursive such as Zhang Xu wrote "vulgar characters that distorted the ancient techniques. They may attract attention, but to educated people like myself, they are nothing but common calligraphers." And, "Huaisu strove to add some quiet simplicity to his calligraphy, but due to the fashions of his time, he fell short of classic grace." Thus, even the work of the likes of Zhang Xu and Huaisu, which was so highly regarded by those of the literati school such as Su Shi and Huang Tingjian, was completely beyond the pale when considered from a standpoint which placed the greatest value on classical techniques. This can best be demonstrated by directly comparing Mi Fu's "Wu You Album" with Wang Xizhi's cursive script albums, and those of Zhang Xu and Huaisu. If we suspend all preconceptions and compare them objectively, we will find that Mi Fu's observations were not mere puffery. In spite of the fact that his calligraphy is from a later period, the resemblance to Jin calligraphy is striking. His calligraphy actually did attain the classic elevation of the Jin. It was a combination of natural talent and a near mania for collecting ancient calligraphy that carried him that far. Ironically, it was Su Shi who first instructed Mi Fu to study the Jin works.

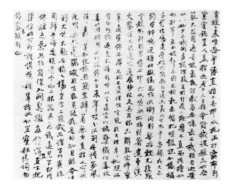

## 56. Yuanwu Keqin: "Diploma." Song dynasty. Ink on paper. Tokyo National Museum.

The lay name of Yuanwu Keqin was Luo, and he was from Chongning in Pengzhou (Sichuan Province). He entered religious orders as a youth, and after studying under Chan masters in several places, received the teaching of Wuzu Fayan of the Yanqi sect of Linji Chan. He resided first in local temples in Sichuan, the Liuzu Monastery and the Zhaojie Monastery. Later he met Zhang Shangying, the Prime Minister towards the end of the Northern Song. At his invitation, he moved to the Lingqian Hall in Hunan Province. There he composed a critique and commentary, the ten-volume *Blue Cliff Record,* regarded as the premier classic of the Chan school. Keqin's reputation reached as far as the imperial court, and he was granted the title, Foguo (Enlightened One) by Emperor Huizong, and was ordered to take up residence in the Tianningwanshou Monastery in the capital, Kaifeng. When the Northern Song fell before the invading armies of Jin, he escaped to the south and took up residence in the Jinshan Monastery, where he was granted the name Yuanwu by Gaozong.

This sermon is the first half of a work entitled *Instructions to Long Zhicang* (*Shi Long Zhicang*), included in volume forty of the *Record of the Sermons of Chan Master Yuanwu Foguo* (*Yuanwu Foguo Chan Shi Wulu*), edited by Keqin's disciple Huqiu Zhaolong. In the text included in volume forty-seven of the *Taishō*, the work is dated, "1124, by the elderly monk Foguo." This would make Keqin sixty-two, and in residence at the Tianningwanshou Monastery at the time of its composition. Originally, some thirteen postscripts by Yuan-dynasty monks were appended to the work. Today, only three survive—by Dongyan Jingri and others, from 1308. These are, then, post-Yuan compositions that were written after the work arrived in Japan. This is one of the oldest surviving Chan documents of the Song and Yuan, and is especially prized.

57. Gaozong: *"Preface to the Collected Writings of Huizong."* Song dynasty. Ink on paper. Private collection.

Gaozong (1107–87) of the Southern Song was the ninth son of the remarkably talented Huizong (1082–1135). After his father's fall from power, he fled to the south and, after arriving in Jiankang, moved from place to place, only firmly establishing himself in control of the Southern Song in 1141. Even during this political turmoil, he himself claims that he never set aside his brush for a single day, so interested was this emperor in the art of calligraphy.

Gaozong studied Huang Tingjian, then Mi Fu, and finally moved on to the two Wangs. Comparing the writings of his twenties, his thirties, and his forties, the development of his style becomes abundantly clear. The Emperor's study of calligraphy did not stop at the standard education thought necessary for a ruler. He composed a specialist work on calligraphy, the *Brush and Ink Treatise* (*Hanmo Zhi*), and in the preface boldly claimed, "There are no calligraphic techniques from the Wei and Jin through the Six Dynasties that I have not practiced."

This *Preface to the Collected Writings of Huizong* (*Huizong Wenji Xu*) was written in 1154, when Gaozong was forty-eight. A hundred-volume collection of Huizong's works had been completed in September of that year, sponsored by Qin Kuai, who has a bad reputation for his advocacy of peace negotiations with the Jin armies. Gaozong received this at the Chuigong Palace and immediately composed a preface to it. The collection was installed in the Tianzhang Pavilion.

Unfortunately, the first half of this preface has been lost. Still, the graceful, imperial calligraphic style is evident. It is especially carefully written, perhaps, because it was to crown a collection of his father's writings. This style of block script that Gaozong practiced and perfected all his life, the highly refined, dignified block script of the southern dynasties, is of a kind with the *Yushu Shijing*. When we consider that one is an original and the other a stone carving, we appreciate just what Gaozong had achieved in this work.

As printing technology improved from the Song dynasty on, those who excelled at this dignified block script declined in number. In addition, from the viewpoint of those such as Huang Tingjian and Su Shi of the literati school, this professional excellence was not highly regarded. That Gaozong could perfect his truly excellent block script against this background speaks for his outstanding ability, and probably also indicates a special interest in block script on his part. In the *Brush and Ink Treatise* he expounds the importance of excelling at both block and cursive. His personal style in calligraphy no doubt owed something to his study of the block script of Zhiyong's "Thousand-Character Essay in Block and Cursive Scripts" which he himself owned.

Just as Huizong favored Mi Fu, Gaozong called his son, Mi Youren, to his own side and had him write authentifying postscripts for Mi Fu's works and those of others.

58. Gaozong: "Volume of Proclamations Granted to Liang Rujia." Song dynasty. Ink on paper. Tokyo National Museum.

This proclamation was made in 1135 by Gaozong to announce his intention to reward his important minister, Liang Rujia, on his birthday. Gaozong awarded four proclamations to Liang, bound together in one scroll. This is the first of them, written when Gaozong was twenty-nine. The second was written in 1136, the third in 1141, and the fourth in 1143. It is extremely interesting to observe the progress of Gaozong's study of calligraphy through these successive works. The first proclamation shown here still exhibits the influences of Huang Tingjian, but it is a little too free, and towards the end borders on the showy. Huang said to those who studied his calligraphy, "It is no use studying my calligraphy. Those who do will weaken their own calligraphy and lose all vigor." Gaozong, with his gifts, avoided this weakness, but was too strident and exhibits the vulgarity that Huang Tingjian's friends pointed out in his calligraphy. Fortunately, in the second proclamation, though there is no change in the style, a quiet assurance has been achieved. The third, the 1141 proclamation, clearly shows a transition to Mi Fu's style of writing. The fourth, written when Gaozong was thirty-seven, is completely under the sway of Mi Fu and clearly shows the results of his long studies—a freedom from all traces of vulgarity.

This is not to say that Huang Tingjian's calligraphy is in any way vulgar, but that Gaozong, through his unceasing efforts, was able to reach a new level of achievement in his writing. In his forties, as can be seen in the *Preface to the Collected Writings of Huizong,* he managed to transcend even the superlative work of Mi and evolve a graceful style of calligraphy, exhibiting a perserverance that is rare even in a professional calligrapher. The words, "no ancient technique have I not practiced," in the *Brush and Ink Treatise* are not empty boasting.

This proclamation is written on "phoenix stationary" appropriate to an imperial message, and a seal with an extended passage is stamped on it.

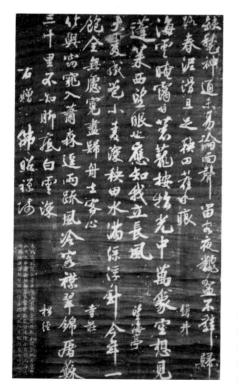

59. Fan Chengda: "Memorial Poem for Chan Master Fo Zhao." Song dynasty. Ink rubbing. Imperial Household Agency, Archives and Mausolea Department, Tokyo.

Many original works of post-Song–dynasty calligraphy exist, and there is little need to resort to rubbings. As a result, printings from steles and copybooks have come to be regarded rather lightly. Nevertheless, in any discussion of the work of Fan Chengda (1126–93), this stele is always referred to because it is a faultless Song rubbing whose transmission through the ages is fully documented.

The founder of the Tōfuku-ji, National Teacher Shōichi, brought back many calligraphic works and rubbings at the end of his six-year period of study in China, and this work, together with Su Shi's "Chenkui Pavilion Stele" (*Chenkui Ge Bei*), was among them. This was in 1241. The rubbing remained with the Tōfuku-ji until the end of the Edo period, when it was finally purchased by the government. In 1891, it came into the ownership of the imperial library, where it remains today. The poem, by Fan Chengda, who was one of the great poets of the Southern Song, is a series of four quatrains in seven-character lines, together with some calligraphy in small characters in the lower left by Chan Master Fo Zhao, or Zhuoan Deguang. The quatrains are written in two lines each, with the title of each poem written below the work. To the lower left is engraved Deguang's remarks, recording how Fan Chengda, in 1181, at the age of fifty-six, was transferred to Jinling and visited Ayuwangshan. He composed a poem and presented it to Deguang, but it was so marvelous that he couldn't bear to keep it to himself and had it engraved in stone so many could enjoy it.

This anecdote can be taken as an example of the refined intercourse that took place between local administrators and the clergy in their territory, or from another viewpoint, the flattery that was directed to the ruling elite.

The original stone no longer exists, and the work is known to us solely through this single rubbing. Compared to other engravings from the period, it is extremely well done, and when we compare it with a preface written by Fan four year later, we can't but be impressed with the faithfulness of the inscription to Fan's art.

Fan is thought to have studied the calligraphy of Su Shi, Huang Tingjian, and Mi Fu. The manner in which he flattens out the upper elements of the characters, such as the rain radical, is thought to be taken from Su Shi. The long, wavering extension of the leftward strokes, such as in the first two characters in the sixth line, is recognized as Huang's influence, and the general strength of the brushwork, Mi's. A traditional criticism of the work has been "though lacking somewhat in gracefulness, there is a noticeable vigor." Still, there are many characters that surpass Mi Fu's, who was said to have "reached the limit in the force and liveliness of his brushwork." This is not the calligraphy of a specialist who studied all of the ancient techniques, but should be regarded as the writing of a poet giving free reign to his innermost feelings.

60. Zhu Xi: "Cursive Draft of the Collected Notes on the *Analects*." Song dynasty. Ink on paper. Kyoto National Museum.

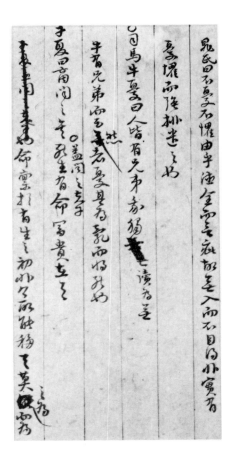

Zhu Xi's greatest work in his philosophical studies was to assemble and compose commentaries on four Confucian classics—the *Analects* (*Lun Wu*), *Mencius* (*Mengzi*), the *Great Learning* (*Da Xue*), and the *Doctrine of the Mean* (*Zhong Yong*). The "Cursive Draft of the Collected Notes on the *Analects*" (*Lun Wu Zizhu Cao Gao*) featured here is thought to be a composition of Zhu Xi's forty-eighth year, when the commentary was completed, in 1177.

Zhuzi (Zhu Xi, 1130-1200) is such an important philosopher that his calligraphy was likely to be preserved on that score alone. However, when we pick out those works related to calligraphy from among his enormous oeuvre, we find that he did not neglect the art by any means. Zhuzi's father was fond of Wang Anshi's calligraphy, owned several of his works, and was said to be able to determine authentic works from forgeries. Zhuzi no doubt was influenced by his father from a young age. Further, he mentions that he studied the "Cao Cao Album" (*Cao Cao Tie*), and the techniques of the "Yue Yi Treatise." This distinguished him from most of the scholar-gentry of the Southern Song, who were largely interested in following Huang Tingjian and Mi Fu's styles; instead, he aimed at perfecting the ancient techniques of the Wei and Jin.

However, he himself admitted, "I suffer from weak brushwork, do not properly support the brush, and don't have a natural gift for calligraphy, making it impossible for me to manage the soft-tipped rabbit's-hair brush." Still, though he was a Confucian scholar, and as such believed calligraphy to be a frivolous pursuit, he also felt it reflected the character of men, and thus partook of some importance. As his calligraphy shows, he wrote rather quickly, as did Wang Anshi, and the hurried nature of his characters show a person who was a quick thinker. With regard to his own fault, he commented, "Once Zhang Chi said of Wang Anshi's calligraphy, 'Why is he in such a hurry?'; and of Han Qi, upon observing that not a single stroke had lapsed from block into semi-cursive script, 'He must be at peace with himself.' I am forced by this anecdote to consider my own faults." This confession is what we might expect from a staunch Confucian.

At present, three works by Zhu Xi are available: one each in block, semi-cursive, and cursive scripts. In comparing these three works in three styles, we can see that all are written with a well-pointed brush of a combination of animal hairs. Though all exhibit considerable speed in writing, the cursive work ranks first in expertise, followed by the semi-cursive, and finally the block. The semi-cursive script letter written by Zhu Xi to a friend resembles Wang Anshi's letters remarkably. His calligraphy never reached the level of "classic elevation" that is to be found in the Wei and Jin work, but his cursive technique was correct, and in an age when proper technique was on the decline, he was able not only to sustain but surpass the minimum standard. Though his calligraphy does not really deserve study as such, his writings on calligraphy are certainly worth perusing.

61. Zhang Jizhi: *"Jingang Banruoboluomi Jing."* Song dynasty. Ink on paper. Chishaku-in Storehouse, Kyoto.

Zhang Jizhi (1186–1266) was from Liyang in Anhui Province. He was the nephew of Zhang Xiaoxiang, who was regarded at the time as a literary talent, and his father was Zhang Xiaobo, who held an important cabinet post.

Zhang passed the imperial examinations and took a post in the government, but he did not meet with great success, and when he retired as an old man he had received nothing more than honorary secretariat rank. Still, perhaps because he lived to be eighty-one years old, and no other calligraphers worthy of mention lived during the Southern Song, he has a reputation as a calligrapher. In the 445th volume of the *History of the Song (Song Shi)* he is referred to as "famous throughout the land for his calligraphy; his writings were the most prized of all by the Jin Chinese."

Like all other Southern Song calligraphers, he studied Mi Fu of the Northern Song, and Ouyang Xun and Chu Suiliang of the Tang, but his works that remain exhibit a real uniqueness. Jizhi had very close relationships with Chan monks, rejected all orthodoxy, and concentrated on discovering his self-nature, which accounts for the distinctive Chan flavor to his work. This rather radical calligraphy naturally received mixed appraisals in China, a land with a long and carefully guarded tradition. Reaction ranged from the highest praise—of, for example, Dong Qichang of the Ming dynasty, who regarded the creativity of Chan calligraphy as the outflowing of the innermost self extending to engulf the universe—to those who decried it as perverse. In general, Zhang Jizhi was thought to excel at large characters and to be able to write them with as much control as if they were the smallest block script. Even in his small block script his creativity shines through. His large characters, probably written with one great burst of energy, are written with a "no-technique technique" that had a greater effect on Chan calligraphy than the world of calligraphy at large. In Japan, however, which was largely free from those traditional restraints, his calligraphy was better received. This is particularly interesting when considered in conjunction with the record in the *History of the Song* telling of the popularity of his work among the Jin people.

This *Jingang Jing* was written in 1253 when Zhang was sixty-eight. In a later catalogue, there are two entries for this scripture by Zhang, one at age sixty-eight and another at seventy-eight. We know that Zhang was an ardent believer in Buddhism, and copied these works time and time again. Remarking on the *Jingang Jing,* Liang Wenshan of the Qing dynasty says that "it derives from Ouyang and is based on Chu Suiliang," declaring that Zhang's calligraphy was clever and that of a great master, but not quite reaching the level of true genius. This rather circuitous comment is not inappropriate.

Of course, we cannot be sure that Zhang's *Jingang Jing* discussed by Liang is the same version seen here, but no doubt it resembled it enough for his remarks to apply.

62. Cai Songnian: "Postscript to Su Shi's *Hermit Li Taibo* Poem Scroll.' " Jin dynasty. Ink on paper. Osaka Municipal Museum of Fine Art.

Cai Songnian (1107–59) was from Zhending in Hebei. He served the Jin in a succession of high posts, was also trusted by Prince Hai Ling, and was representative of the active role of the Han Chinese in the administration of the early Jin. He was an excellent writer who excelled at lyric poetry, and was on a par with his contemporary Wu Ji (Mi Fu's son-in-law), earning the description of his work as "Wu-Cai style."

The Jin invaded Dubian (Kaifeng), the Song capital, in the Jingkang Disturbance of 1126, and a massive amount of cultural treasures was carried off. For that reason, perhaps, when the Song occupied north China, they soon became sinicized themselves. However, very few writings or paintings have come down to us, and only a very few calligraphers, such as Ren Xun, Zhao Feng, Wang Tingyun, and Zhao Bingwen, are known to us. All of them probably studied

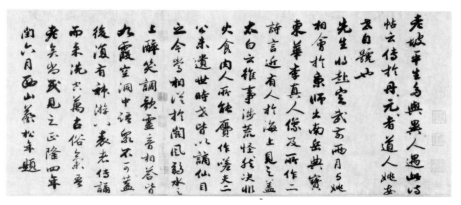

mainly Su Shi, Huang Tingjian, and Mi Fu of the Northern Song. The "Postscript to Su Shi's '*Hermit Li Taibo* Poem Scroll'" (*Su Shi Li Taibo Xian Shijuan Ba*) was written when Cai Songnian was fifty-three, just before his death. The influence of Su Shi is clearly recognizable.

63. Wang Tingyun: "Postscript to Painting of Bamboo." Jin dynasty. Ink on paper. Fujii Museum, Kyoto.

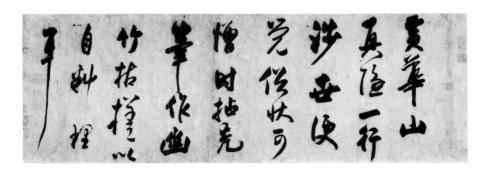

Wang Tingyun (1151–1202) was from Liaodong, Chenzhou. He passed the examinations in 1176. For a long time he studied at a temple in Huanghuashan in Zhangde, and he styled himself Master of Huanghuashan. During the reign of Zhangzong he became an associate of the Hanlin Academy and, together with the Secretariat official Zhang Rufang, gathered and collated an enormous number of works of painting and calligraphy into 550 volumes. He also compiled a collection of original works and copybooks of the ancients and published them in the ten volumes of the "Xuexi Hall Album" (*Xuexi Tang Tie*).

In the *History of the Jin* (*Jin Shi*), Wang is said to have studied Mi Yuanzhang, and to have been regarded with Zhao Feng and Zhao Jingwen as a great calligrapher. Wang Shizen of the Ming comments in more detail: "Tingyun lived in Jin and was a contemporary of Huai Yong and Zhao Feng, with whom he shared a reputation as a great calligrapher. His semi-cursive script was remarkably similar to that of Mi Fu and Mi Youren. His block script was a little stiff, with plenty of 'backbone,' but definitely inferior in appearance." He was also a masterful painter and excelled in painting mountain, water, and bamboo scenes. This is abundantly clear if we examine the painting that precedes this work. The fact that he was favorably compared to Mi Fu and Mi Youren indicates that he also had considerable talent for calligraphy.

64. Mi'an Xianjie: "Sermon." Song dynasty. Ink on figured silk. Ryūkō-in Storehouse, Kyoto.

Mi'an Xianjie, whose lay name was Zheng, was from Fuqingxian in Fuzhou (modern Fujian Province). He selected the name Mi'an for himself. He studied under Ying'an Tanhua, who was in the lineage of Yuanwu Keqin. He was made the head monk of Jingshan Wanshou Monastery in Linan (Hangzhou) by im-

perial decree in 1177. Even after transferring to the Lingyin Monastery in 1180, he continued to enjoy Xiaozong's support. In 1183, he moved to Tiantangshan in Ximing (Zhejiang Province).

This sermon, as indicated in the postscrit, was written in the Budong Quarters of the Jingshan Wanshou Monastery, in August of 1179, in response to a request by Chan Practitioner Zhang. At that time Xianjie was sixty-two, and his mature style is reflected in this work. The sermon teaches that Chan followers should not be dependent on anything and, in every circumstance, persevere in their practice without lapsing. This sermon is not included in the two volumes of his recorded teachings.

Xianjie's followeres numbered almost one hundred, and among them Songyuan Chongyue (1132–1202), Caoyuan Daosheng, and Poan Zuxian (1136–1211) each founded their own schools, which were transmitted to Japan and were the source of the twenty-four schools of Zen that arose there. In other words, Xianjie is the partiarch of all these schools, and as a result, this work is valued very highly by Zen and tea ceremony schools and their followers in Japan. In fact, special Mi'an alcoves were built just to hang this piece. This is the only example of an extant writing by Mi'an, and it is also extraordinary because it is written on brocade paper with a design of plum blossoms.

65. Wuzhun Shifan: "Diploma." Song dynasty. Ink on paper. Tōfuku-ji Storehouse, Kyoto.

This is a sermon given by Wuzhun Shifan (1177–1249) to the Japanese monk Enji (1202–80) who went to Song China to study Buddhism. It is also included in the *Record of the Sermons of Shifan* (*Shifan Yulu, Zokuzōkyō*, 2–26–5). The lay name of Shifan was Yong, and he was from Zitong (Sichuan). After receiving the precepts at eighteen, he left Sichuan for Jiangnan and studied with many Chan masters from different places, finally arriving in Jingshan where he became a disciple of Poan Zuxian. Traveling to various temples, beginning with the Qingjing Monastery in Mingzhou (Zhejiang Province), he was installed as the head monk of the Jingshan Wanshou Monastery in 1232 by imperial decree. The following year the main temple burned down, and he turned his energies to its reconstruction. It was then that he received the title Chan Master Fojian from Emperor Lizong, gaining at the same time the funds for rebuilding. When Enji arrived at Jingshan in 1236, the project had just been completed. This "Diploma" (*Yinkezhuang*) was written by Shifan the next year, 1237, at age sixty-one. One year after Enji had returned to Japan, in 1242, the temple buildings of the Jingshan were again destroyed by fire. Enji sent one thousand boards to Shifan at that time as a donation for the reconstruction. A letter of thanks from Shifan also exists. It is quite important in the tradition of Japanese calligraphy, where it is known as the *Hashiwatashi no Bokuseki*. In addition to this "Diploma," Enji also brought back the *Diagram of the Schools of the Buddha's Lineage* (*Fozu Zongpai Tu*), Shifan's autographed portrait, and other materials. Shifan continued to send plaques for Zen halls and letters to Enji, with the result that Shifan's calligraphy makes up a considerable portion of the Chan writings which have been transmitted to Japan.

Shifan resided at Jingshan for twenty years and contributed greatly to the rise of his sect of Chan. Many masters came forth from among the ranks of his disciples, among them Wuxue Zuyuan and Wuan Puning, who came to Japan. Many Japanese monks in addition to Enji also traveled to Jingshan to study.

66. Xianyu Shu: "Du Fu's *Thatch Roof Destroyed by the Autumn Wind.*" Yuan dynasty. Ink on paper. Fujii Museum, Kyoto.

Xianyu Shu (1257–1302) was from Yuyang, or Beijing. Xianyu is a name of the Beidi tribe. During his lifetime he rivaled Zhao Mengfu in fame and was also closely linked with Deng Wenyuan of the Shu Kingdom. In fact, however, neither could compare with Zhao Mengfu. Xianyu never held high rank and ended as a minor official of the Taichang Monastery. For that reason, he is not very highly regarded in the *Outline of the History of Calligraphy* and other works. Perhaps because he was a petty official, in his youth he was unable to escape tired conventions in his calligraphy, which remained somewhat vulgar. Still, Zhao Mengfu praised his work very highly and said of his cursive script, "Xianyu far surpasses the others, and none can compare with him in force." According to a popular story, Zhao Mengfu was so jealous of Shu's fame that he exchanged three of his own works for one of Shu's, which he burned afterwards. This is the reason so few of Shu's works have come down to us—so the story goes, though of course there is little to substantiate it.

Xianyu Shu studied the calligraphy of Zhang Tianxi. Once while the two of them were in the countryside they saw two men pulling a cart through the mud, and were enlightened as to the essence of calligraphic technique. Perhaps it was the continuous marshalling of the flow of energy necessary for that muddy task that impressed them.

Xianyu's personality is strongly reflected in his calligraphy. He was strong-willed and sometimes arrogant, often argued with his superiors, and if he was dissatisfied, immediately abandoned his post. When he composed poems and wrote characters under the influence of wine, he produced fantastic creations. This work is a version of the great poet Du Fu's famous *Thatch Roof Destroyed by the Autumn Wind* (*Maowu Wei Qiufeng Suobo Hua*), and Xianyu's free brushwork is much in evidence.

67. Zhao Mengfu: "Epistle to Zhongfeng Mingben." Yuan dynasty. Ink on paper. Seikadō Bunko, Tokyo.

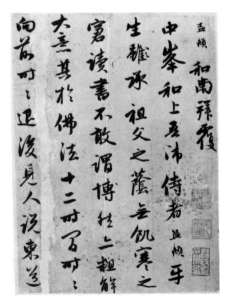

Zhao Mengfu (1254–1322) was also known as Zi'ang, Hermit Songxue, and Oubo, and was a member of the Song imperial family from Wuxing (Huzhou Zhejiang Province). He was invited to serve by Shizu of the Yuan, and continued to hold posts under five emperors, finally becoming one of the leading scholars of the Hanlin Academy. He was, however, subject to criticism during his lifetime because he served in a "barbarian" dynasty though he was of the Song imperial house. Still, he was a representative member of the cultural elite of the Yuan dynasty and, in addition to being a scholar, was an excellent painter and calligrapher. The role he played in preserving and developing traditional Chinese culture during the Yuan dynasty was extremely valuable. His influence in painting and calligraphy was felt with particular strength in the Ming dynasty. He was regarded as having penetrated the most profound teachings of both Buddhism and Taoism; in particular, he studied under the Buddhist monk Zhongfeng Mingben (1263–1323). According to Mingben, they met in 1304, when Zhao invited Mingben to his offices. They met three more times and exchanged letters with great frequency. Whenever Zhao received a letter from Mingben, he burned incense and bowed before it, and he always referred to himself as "disciple" in his replies. More than a dozen such replies to Mingben appear in later copybooks. The contents of this letter reveal that it was written soon after Zhao met Mingben. "I have heard that you are to take up your staff and head for the mountains," (lines fourteen to fifteen), reads the letter, suggesting that it was written in 1305, when Mingben returned to Tianmushan.

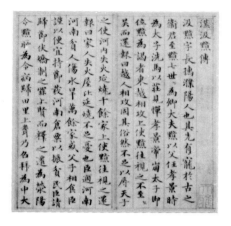

68. Zhao Mengfu: *"Biography of Han Ji'an."* Yuan dynasty. Ink on paper. Eisei Bunko Foundation, Tokyo.

Zhao Mengfu is also known by his posthumous name, Wen Min. He was a great genius, often said to have been unsurpassed for 500 years before or after, and 10,000 leagues in any direction. He was accomplished in poetry, literature, painting, calligraphy, and all of the arts.

His calligraphy was so well known outside of China that it is said an Indian monk came to purchase his works. His influence was strongly felt in both Korea and Japan. In China, later generations have been very cool towards Zhao because, though a descendant of the Song, he served a barbarian dynasty. But if it had not been for him, it is extremely doubtful whether the cultural tradition of Tang and Song would have been transmitted to the Yuan and Ming dynasties. This critisism of his politics cannot outweigh the merits of his revival of the classical tradition.

Zhao Mengfu was also active in government and was intimate with the Yuan emperors, though of course there was a natural limit to how far he could advance among the conservative Mongols, with their distaste for the "southerners." However, his reputation at court expedited his artistic activities and was an aid in the spread of his influence.

This *"Biography of Han Ji'an"* (*Han Ji'an Chuan*) is written in a handsome small block script and is a work of his sixty-seventh year. It is thought to resemble, in brushwork, Ouyang Xun's "Wen Yanbo Stele," and is a very appropriate style for copying the life of the indominitable minister Ji'an, who managed to intimidate even Emperor Wu. Unmarred by any gratuitous pomposity, it is a masterpiece with a vigorous and beautiful style.

69. Feng Zizhen: "Words Presented to Muin Genkai." Yuan dynasty. Ink on paper. Gotō Art Museum, Tokyo.

Feng Zizhen (1257–1327?) was also known as Hermit Guaiguai, and was from Youzhou (Hunan Province). He specialized in classics, was reputed to have read every book there was, and shook a generation with his writings. We know little of his professional career. He was intimate with Zhao Mengfu, who introduced him to Zhongfeng Mingben. At first, Feng looked down on Mingben, but after Mingben replied in rhyming verse to Feng's *Hundred Verses on the Plum Blossoms* poem, and after Feng saw and was impressed by Mingben's nine-character poem on the same subject, they became fast friends. Because of the friendship of these two, many Japanese monks who went to China to study with Mingben brought back Feng's works. Muin Genkai (died 1358) entered China in 1308 and studied under Zhongfeng Mingben until 1326, when he returned to Japan with Qingzhuo Zhangcheng. This work was given by Feng Zizhen to Genkai when they met at Wumen in Sizhou. The signature indicates that Feng had already retired from his post. Feng Zizhen's style belongs to the Northern Song Mi Fu tradition, and also exhibits tendencies resembling Zhang Jizhi of the Southern Song. Though he was not a Chan monk, his writings are treated in the same category, and in early Japanese tea-ceremony records are dubbed *Fukaisoku bokuseki*.

70. Kangli Kuikui: "Li Bo's *Ancient Wind* Poem." Yuan dynasty. Ink on paper. Tokyo National Museum.

The personal name of Kuikui (1295–1345) was Zishan. He was from Kangli in the western regions and was the son of Fu Mumu, a trusted retainer of Shizu. He and his older brother Huihui were known as the "two jewels." He studied classics and history and served in a variety of posts in the imperial archieves. He claimed to be much favored by the emperor, and received satisfaction from being able to speak out before him. He also devoted himself to the care of the collections of imperial treasures of antiques and works of art, the Kuizhang Archives and the Xuanwen Archives. He undertook many projects in both the cultural and the political realms, including reinstituting the examination system and initiating the compilation of histories of the Liao, Jin, and Song.

Kuikui was fond of scholars and men of learning, and advocated the Chinese culture among the Yuan nobility, who disliked the Chinese. His support for this position frequently brought him into conflict with conservative elements at court, but he was respected by the Yuan emperors due to his uprightness and loyalty.

He is said to have practiced 30,000 characters each day, mastered Jin brushwork, and been clever at block, semi-cursive, and cursive scripts. People were reputed to fight for scraps of his correspondence. Although very few of his original works have been preserved, the 1935 Jun Haneda mission discovered three of his steles at Niaodancheng in Rehe and brought back rubbings of them to Japan. These consisted of some eighteen stanzas of the famous poet Li Bo's *Ancient Wind Poem* (*Gu Feng Shi*) in fifty-nine verses. The movement of the brushwork is certainly worth looking at, but two verses in the middle are missing.

71. Yang Weizhen: "Draft for Zhang Clan Memorial Stele." Yuan dynasty. Ink on paper. Private collection.

Yang Weizhen (1296–1370) was from Shaoxing in Zhejiang. He passed the imperial examinations in 1327. Prior to that, his father had erected the Wanjuan Tower in the wilderness of Tieyashan and forced Yang to seclude himself there for five years of intensive study. He was never allowed to leave, and even food was supplied to him with a basket and a pulley. Yang later held various lower-ranking posts, and in these capacities he strove to lessen the burden of the people's sufferings. His stubborn nature, though, was an obstacle to success in the bureaucracy. He abandoned his official post at the time of the military uprisings towards the end of the Yuan dynasty and, after wandering through the mountains of Zhexi, moved to Songjiang Huating and devoted his life to the arts.

He presided over the cultural scene of the last thirty years of the Yuan, lost himself in poetry and wine, and earned himself the name "bewitched scholar" for his eccentric behavior. At the beginning of the Ming he was invited to serve at court as one of the surviving elders by Emperor Tazu, but he refused, saying that it was not proper for an old woman with one foot in the grave to go off again as a young bride. However, to help decide on the proper form for a new edition of the classics about to be published by the new dynasty, he set out for Nanjing and served for a short time, after which he immediately retired again. The remark of Wenhao Songlian, "Refusing the imperial proclamation of the Lord, he left in the plain robe he was summoned in," was a well-known tribute to Yang's uprightness. He was once said to have proposed a toast with a serving maid's shoe, which he then passed around to the other guests. This disregard for public opinion was no doubt a form of personal protest against the domination of the Mongols.

The "Draft for Zhang Clan Memorial Stele" was a composition for the stele of the Zhang clan of Huating. This composition of his seventieth year exhibits Yang's calligraphic style, which was said to be "pure and vigorous, even though his cursive and semi-cursive don't pass muster."

199

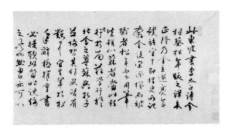

72. Zhang Bi: "Postscript to Su Shi's '*Hermit Li Taibo* Poem Scroll.'" Ming dynasty. Ink on paper. Osaka Municipal Museum of Fine Art.

Zhang Bi (1425–87) was from Huating in Jiangsu Province. He passed the examinations in 1466, and was appointed governor of Nan'an. He is famous for his excellent cursive script, but his wild cursive was particularly masterful, and Wang Ao commented, "people came from foreign lands to purchase his wild-cursive works." Zhang Bi is quoted in volume four of Wang's *Collected Works of Zhong Donghai* (*Zhong Donghai Quan Ji*): "I do not seek to write clever poetry or eccentric characters, but take the fullness of heaven's truth as my master," a statement which indicates the goal he was pursuing in his work. Dong Qichang, from the same village, respected these words and regarded them as the essence of calligraphy.

This work is a postscript to Su Shi's rendition of the "*Hermit Li Taibo* Poem Scroll" (*Li Taibo Xian Shijuan*). According to the postscript, this is a composition of 1483, on the occasion of a visit by Zhang's son, Hongzhi, and Liang Kezai of Nanhai to Zhang, who was governor of Nan'an at the time. They brought with them this work of Su Shi and showed it to Zhang, requesting a postscript. The calligraphy is not wild cursive but a mix of semi-cursive and cursive. There are previous postscripts by Cai Songnian of Jin, Shi Yisheng, Liu Yi, and Gao Kan, as well as a semi-cursive postscript by Cai Gui. Though Zhang's work resembles these earlier postscripts to a certain extent, the calm form of the "fullness of the heavens" is also apparent. At the end are three seal impressions in vermillion, identifying the author.

73. Chen Xianzhang: "Poem Scroll." Ming dynasty. Ink on paper. Eisei Bunko Foundation, Tokyo.

Chen Xianzhang (1428–1500) was from Bosha village in Xinhui of Guangdong Province—hence the origin of one of his titles, Master of Bosha. He was a candidate for the national examinations in 1447. When he was twenty-seven, he studied with Wu Kangzhai, a master of Zhuzi's teachings, and read extensively the books of ancient wisdom. Still, he felt he had not gained anything and returned to his village to continue his study and search for the way, even forgetting to eat and sleep. He could not accept Zhuzi's principle of mind. He abandoned his studies and sat quietly, whereupon he discovered the truth that "the principle of heaven can be experienced anywhere." His thought was to later influence Wang Yangming's study of the mind.

This volume of poems contains verses in seven-character lines (*lu*) which appear in the *Collected Works of Chen Bosha* (*Chen Bosha Quanji*). Concerning Chen's calligraphy, Zhang Xu remarked in his preface, "He made a brush out of reeds bound together. This practice was much imitated, and the results known as 'reed brush characters.'" This work is in the reed brush style, and does not fit any normal standard. It is closely related to the calligraphy of the Chan monks. In this piece we can see the free expression of the rarified, elevated state he attained through the experience of "heaven's principle everywhere," and which was also the goal of his scholarly studies.

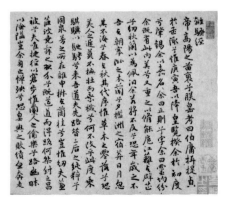

74. Zhu Yunming: "*Li Sao Classic* Scroll." Ming dynasty. Ink on paper. Chōkaidō Bunko, Yokkaichi.

Zhu Yunming (1460–1526) had an extra finger on his right hand and was called "Extra Finger Sheng" and "Branch Mountain." He was from Changzhou in Jiangsu, and stood as a candidate for the imperial examinations in 1492. At the early age of five, he was writing characters over one foot high, and at nine, composing poetry. As he grew up he read widely and wrote very well. He did not enter directly into the bureaucracy but was promoted from a candidate to governor of Guangdong in Xingning Prefecture, later becoming the magistrate of Yingtian (the capital) in 1522. Soon afterwards, he retired and returned to his village. He was fond of wine and despised all vulgarity, living a life free from the restrictions of the etiquette of the bureaucrats. He composed the "Huaixing Hall Collection" (*Huaixing Tang Ji*) and compiled the *Records of Xingning Prefecture* (*Xingning Xian Zhi*), the draft of which still exists. He was numbered together with Tang Yin, Wen Huiming, and Xu Zhenqing as one of the "four geniuses of Wu." Calligraphy was his forte. He studied block script from his father-in-law Li Yingzhen and semi-cursive and cursive from his maternal grandfather Xu Youzhen.

This "*Li Sao Classic* Scroll" is a version of the *Li Sao* of the *Odes of Chu* (*Chu Ci*). According to the postscript, it was written when Zhu was thirty-one, in 1490. The calligraphy is mainly block, with semi-cursive and cursive mixed in, and the brushwork is free and relaxed. He was famous for his wild cursive, but he also studied the small block script of Wei and Jin from an early age, was expert at its tracing, and already had an established reputation at that time for his graceful, antique style. A red ink seal, "Wuxia Aming," is stamped after the postscript, and at the beginning of the scroll are three stamps that indicate this work was in the collection of one You Tong, of that village.

75. Zhu Yunming: "*Red Cliffs Ode.*" Ming dynasty. Ink on paper. Tokyo National Museum.

This work is a version of Su Shi's "Former and Latter *Red Cliffs Ode*" (*Qian Hou Chi Bi Fu*) in cursive script on paper with columns and a floral pattern. There are many Ming versions of the *Red Cliffs Ode*, and Zhu Yunming himself produced several of these, revealing just how fond he was of both Su Shi and his work. Zhu's cursive script can be divided into three types—a wild cursive with a definitely classical, antique flavor; a very graceful, connected cursive; and a vertically extended, eccentric wild cursive. This work falls into the second category, and it compares favorably with Wen Zhengming in both the surety of its techniques and its purity of feeling. According to the signature, it was completed in Zhu's sixty-second year, in 1521. Below the final signature, a square, negative seal of Zhu Yunming is stamped, and at the beginning of the scroll are another negative-impression square seal reading "Changzhou" and a red seal saying, "Qishan," both place names in Suzhou.

Zhu Yunming's study of cursive script under his grandfather, Xu Youzhen, included the work of Zhang Xu and Huaisu. In his later years he made a great impression with his wild cursive, which unfortunately invited many forgeries. Still, his thoughts on calligraphy were based on the theories of the traditionalists, and he insisted that calligraphy should carry on the patterns of the ancients and criticized self-indulgent eccentricities. The belief that copying the works of the ancients is derivative must be abandoned, he declared. This makes an understanding of his own wild cursive somewhat problematical, but as we can see from the seals at the ends of this work and the "*Li Sao Classic* Scroll," he loved Suzhou and was very proud of his homeland. His wild cursive is probably best understood as a product of the Suzhou style and grace, which allowed a freedom of feeling that outweighed the demands of more orthodox traditions.

76. Wen Zhengming: "Twelve Verses from Tao Yuanming's Drinking Poem." Ming dynasty. Ink on silk. Kyoto National Museum.

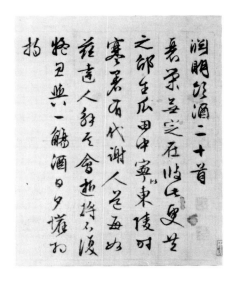

Wen Zhengming (1470–1559) was from Changzhou in Jiangsu province. Since his ancestors were from Hengshan in Hunan, he was also called Hengshan. His father Lin was a member of the bureaucracy and, as governor of Wenzhou, known for his unwavering integrity. Wen himself finally became a successful candidate in 1522, after sitting for the examinations repeatedly, but did not find a post. In his biography it is said that "he was not bright as a child." Still, he studied the classics with his father's friend, Wu Kuan, painting with Shen Zhou, and calligraphy with Li Yingzhen, cultivating the talents which finally earned him a post in the Hanlin Academy in 1523. He retired after only three years, unable to endure the enmity of his colleagues, and from then on devoted himself to the three arts of poetry, painting and calligraphy. He was much admired and respected for his integrity and stood at the head of the cultural community in Suzhou. A collection of his poems survives, the *Fujian Collection* (*Fujian Ji*), and his poetry was regarded as graceful and refined. He is also known for publishing the "Tingyun Hall Album" (*Tingyun Guan Tie*).

This work is a rendition of Tao Yuanming's drinking poem on silk paper with black thread columns, written in semi-cursive and cursive scripts. The signature identifies it as a work of Wen's eighty-fifth year, 1554. His son, Wen Jia, said of his calligraphy that he was unskilled in his youth but often copied engraved characters, starting with the Song and Yuan masters, until he was enlightened as to the secrets of good brushwork. Afterwords, he concentrated exclusively on Jin and Tang techniques. One story has it that the subject matter of this early copying was ten books of thousand-character essays. His teacher, Li Yingzhen, did transmit the ancient techniques, but he also valued variations and looked for this from Wen. In short, his calligraphy was a combination of unceasing practice following old models and creative variation—the beautiful result of which is clearly demonstrated in this work. Even in his old age, not one stroke is slack or amiss, and each retains its clear purity. A square, negative-impression seal with Wen Huiming's name, and another square, red seal with "Hengshan" are impressed at the end of the work. At the beginning of the scroll, a rectangular, negative-impression seal with the characters "Tingyun" and another, square, reading "Hui Zhongfu," are to be found.

77. Wang Shouren: "Helou Pavilion Poem Scroll." Ming dynasty. Ink on paper. Tokyo National Museum.

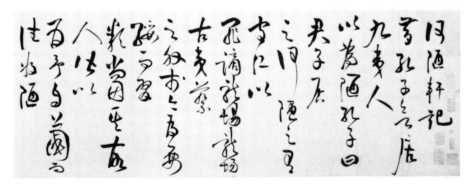

Wang Shouren (1472–1528) was from Xuyao in Zhejiang, but lived for most of his life in Shaoxing. He excelled in both military and civil arts and is well known as the founder of the Yangming school of philosophy. According to the genealogy compiled by his disciple Jian Dehong, he was descended from Wang Xizhi, but this is unsubstantiated. He joined the bureaucracy in 1499. When Prime Minister Wei Zhongxian took power and began to pressure his opponents, Wang presented a memorial to the emperor (1506), incurring the wrath of Wei. He was thrown into prison and beaten as a result. Later, he was demoted to post station commander at Longchang in Guizhou, in the distant southwestern corner of China. After great hardship, he left to take up his post (1508) and came to realize "my nature is insufficient for the path of the saints. It was a mistake to look for truth in worldly phenomena." This was the foundation of his later position, equating mind with absolute truth.

This work is a record of his stay at the Helou Pavilion in Longchang, which was sent to one Shun Gong. It is also included in the *Collected Works of Duke Wang Wencheng* (*Wang Wencheng Gong Quanshu*), volume twenty-three. When he arrived at Longchang he lived in a cave and like the common people planted fields, occasionally gathering herbs to make his living. When he taught the natives, who also lived in caves, how to build houses, they built one for him in return. This was the Helou Pavilion, the name taken from a chapter of the *Analects*. His calligraphy was graceful and full of movement, and traces of Huaisu's influence can be observed. In his autobiography, he writes, "I first studied calligraphy by copying the old copybooks and learning to imitate them. Later, writing lightly without missing a stroke, firmly concentrating my efforts, and only after long study did I master the techniques." Thus we can say that his calligraphy started with the imitation of ancient works and moved on to follow his own feelings. That tendency is apparent even in his writings during his experience at Longchang. At the end, a square, red seal with his name, and a half-red, half-negative–impression seal reading "Yangming Shanren" are stamped.

78. Dong Qichang: "Semi-cursive and Cursive Calligraphy Scroll." Ming dynasty. Ink on paper. Tokyo National Museum.

Dong Qichang (1555–1636) was from Songjiang in Jiangsu, and entered the bureaucracy in 1589. He was in the National University, but retired from his post, only to be called to serve again, as the secretary of the Nanjing Board of Rites. He devoted himself to poetry, painting, and calligraphy and had especially great influence in the appreciation and criticism of the last two. He was the formulator of the theory of the reform movement in calligraphy, idealized the "richness of the heavens," and aimed for a simple, natural expression. His theories can be followed in his works, the *Illustrated Essays from a Chan Cell* (*Hua Chan Si Suibi*) and the *Ceremonial Terrace Collection* (*Rong Tai Bieji*). When he was censured for neglecting his duties in favor of his artistic activities, he declared that love of calligraphy and painting was the true mark of a gentleman and defiantly called the criticism his "greatest good fortune." Both his words and actions showed a strong-headed selfishness, greed, and lack of concern for others. With usurious interest rates he collected on loans he avidly set about collecting works of painting and calligraphy, so angering his fellow citizens that he was attacked on several occasions. His era was one in which it was fashionable to indulge oneself in the arts and other leisure activities. In the world of thought, Wang Yangming marked the beginning of a free exchange of ideas, and Li Zhuoyu was also living at the time. He taught freedom from all conventions and the cultivation of the pure, true mind of a child. The condemnation of ambition and profit, to him, was mere hypocrisy. Dong absorbed these currents of thought and, combining them with certain Chan principles, made them the basis for his aesthetic. His own selfishness, greed, and unconcern for any compunction, he regarded as his spontaneous, natural self.

Here we have a section of the postscript to his "Semi-cursive and Cursive Calligraphy Scroll" (*Xing Cao Shu Juan*). According to the postscript, three friends came to visit him while he was shut up in the Yunyinshan residence in Suzhou due to heavy rains. He prepared some *huyue* tea, ground some Korean ink, and wrote various things at random. This explains the lack of any particular order to the sections of this work. It contains verses in praise of the first patriarch; poems to two monks; verses on the joys of Chan meditation; a comparison of the poetry of Li Bo and Du Fu; and a discussion of the calligraphy of Su Shi and Zhao Mengfu, with appended notes on calligraphic theory. He promotes Chan teachings in calligraphy and even applies them to his discussions of poetry. The work begins in semi-cursive script and, as it builds, moves to cursive, culminating in a wild-cursive postscript. Though this work is said to be modeled after Huaisu, it is neither eccentric nor extravagant, but quietly sophisticated in its brushwork, offering a good contrast with Huaisu's works. At the end, two negative-impression seals are stamped, with a red seal impressed at the beginning of the scroll.

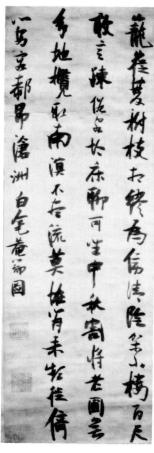

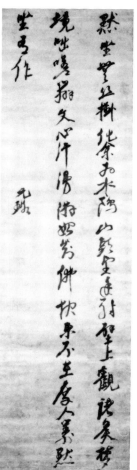

79. Zhang Ruitu: *"Building a Small Pagoda Between the Sala Trees* Poem Scroll." Ming dynasty. Ink on silk. Kyoto National Museum.

Zhang Ruitu (1570–1641) was from Jinjiang in Fujian Province. He entered the bureaucracy in 1607. He began at the Hanlin Academy, but transferred from the post of Secretary of the Board of Rites to Secretariat of the Board of Annals (1626). In the next year, he was accused of offenses by Wei Zhongxian and, together with Shi Fenglai, left his post (1628). The next year, charges were filed, one of which was that previously, when Wei Zhongxian had erected a shrine in Xihuapan, Shi Fenglai had composed a memorial to the throne and Zhang had written it out. After retiring from office, he returned to his village with only the clothes on his back, became interested in Chan, and gave expression to his cultivated nature in poetry, painting, and calligraphy. His connected cursive is well known for its sudden twists and turns, resembling dancing willow leaves as they fall. His work is simple and pure, warm and full of religious succor. There are many theories concerning his creation of this style, which suggests a transcendence of all bonds and a striving for independence and freedom. During his life, Zhang was as highly regarded as Xing Tong, Mi Wanzhong, and Dong Qichang. In the Qing dynasty, however, due perhaps to Zhang's failure as an official, as well as the great interest in copybook studies, he was neglected. From an early period, though, his works were brought to Japan by Zen monks of the Huangbo sect.

This *lu*-style poem in seven-character lines is included in the miscellaneous chapter of the *Collected Works of Bo Haoan (Bo Haoan Ji)*. The poem describes the pleasures of living in his hut in isolation from the rest of the world. It probably dates from after his retirement. His usually extravagant brushwork is much subdued here, and a profound emotionalism flows from the warm, relaxed brushwork. Two seals are stamped at the end of the work.

80. Ni Yuanlu: *"Seated in Silence* Poem." Ming dynasty. Ink on polished silk. Chōkaidō Bunko, Yokkaichi.

Ni Yuanlu (1593–1644) was from Shangyu in Zhejiang. In 1622 he joined the bureaucracy. In the 1630s, he wrangled with remainders of Wei Zhongxian's faction and learned of their strength. He advanced to the post of scholar of the Hanlin Academy and Minister of the Census Department, but soon Beijing was attacked by Li Zicheng. Emperor Zhuanglie committed suicide, and the Ming came to an end (1644). Upon hearing of this, Ni arranged his robes, made obeisance to the imperial palace, and strangled himself with a length of cloth. During the reign of Fu Wang he was granted the posthumous title Wenzheng, and during the Qing, Wenzhen. He is mainly known, together with Huang Daozhou, as one of the fiercely loyal ministers at the end of the Ming, but he was also an excellent poet, painter, and calligrapher. We have two collections of his work, the *Collected Words of Duke Ni Wenzhen (Ni Wenzheng Gong Wenji)* and his *Collected Poems (Shiji)*. There were many calligraphers of exemplary character at the end of the Ming, but he was superlative in the strength of his integrity and the degree of his refinement.

This work is a *li*-style poem in five-character lines, completed at one sitting. The clever use of brush and paper and the sharp turns and twists of the strokes are his special characteristic, along with the large empty space reserved at the end and used for his signature. Below the signature is a square, red seal with his name and a square, negative-impression seal reading "Taishi Shi."

According to the genealogy composed by his son, Huiding, he constructed a house for himself in his later years in the southern corner of Shaoxing, designing the windows, lintels, and other fittings himself, and making quite a job for the carpenters with his detailed requests. This feeling for design is also apparent in his calligraphy. Also, according to his son's work, he was suffering from eye problems at the time, and plastered scraps of works by Cheng Junfang and Fang Yulu on the walls, in front of which he often sat silently. The work featured here dates from this period.

81. Huang Daozhou: "Reply to Sun Boguan's Poem." Ming dynasty. Ink on polished silk. Chōkaidō Bunko, Yokkaichi.

Huang Daozhou (1585–1646) was from Zhangpu in Fujian Province. He entered the bureaucracy in 1622, the same year as Ni Yuanlu. In the 1630s he became a lesser administrator of the imperial household, but he attacked Yang Sichang and others who had been made imperial scholars and was exiled to Jiangxi (1638). Once again, he angered the emperor and was imprisoned and exiled to Guangxi (1641), but he was restored to his post in one year and began serving immediately. The Ming were destroyed in Beijing (1644) by the warlord Li Zicheng, and Fu Wang established himself in Nanjing. Huang immediately went into his service as Minister of the Board of Rites. When the government of Fu Wang was eventually conquered by the Qing, he joined the Tang Wang government that had been set up in Fujian, his native province. There he became a scholar of the Wuying Palace, but when forcing a march of troops with Hui Fu of the Ming, he was captured by the Qing armies and killed outside the gates of Nanjing. He is well-remembered as a faithful minister who gave his life for his country and in defense of his honor, but he was also a learned scholar who had mastered divination, astronomy, and calendrical calculations, in addition to excelling in literature, calligraphy, and painting.

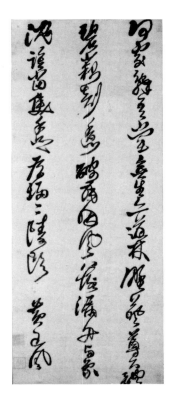

The poem in five-character lines appears in the forty-second volume of *Huang's Zhang River Collection* (*Huang Zhangpu Ji*). There are some variations. Huang studied Zhong Yao and mastered Qin seal and Han scribe scripts as well as others, but he was particularly accomplished in semi-cursive and cursive. This work is a classical-style cursive script which still manages to preserve a pure, fresh spirit. At the end, a negative-impression, square seal and a square, red seal bear his name and title, and a rectangular, red seal is stamped at the beginning.

82. Wang Duo: "*Xiangshan* Poem." Qing dynasty. Ink on polished silk. Fujii Museum, Kyoto.

Wang Duo (1592–1652) excelled at poetry, literature, calligraphy, and painting, but was a particularly accomplished calligrapher. He is often ranked with Dong Qichang, and in Japan, especially of late, has been highly esteemed.

The *Wusheng Shi Shi* (*History of Painting*) claims that he "followed the two Wangs in his semi-cursive and cursive script, and his block derives from Zhong Yao. While he does model his work after the masters, he also vividly expresses his own feelings." Thus, though he did devote himself to the copying of ancient copybooks, his originality can be seen in the way he brands these classical models with his own individuality. He himself remarked, "it is difficult to copy the copybooks exactly, just as it is difficult to surpass them." All his life, even after he made a name for himself as a calligrapher, he continued the daily practice of copying from the copybooks one day and producing his own works upon request the next. His purpose in applying himself to the copybooks was to master the most basic techniques of the old works, not merely to reproduce the minor elaborations. Occasionally he used these ancient works simply as a framework to express his own feelings, and he went so far as the change lines and phrases when the spirit moved him. His sustained and free connected cursive script is unique, and his block script combines the elegance of Zhong Yao and the "backbone" techniques of Yan Zhenqing and Liu Gongquan with a vigor that he "sought just as the ancient masters sought."

This work is a poem written upon visiting the Xiangshan Monastery in Luoyang, which was presented to a relative, Ying Wu. It was composed at the age of forty-nine. As a work of his most mature period, the lightness and heaviness are well-balanced, and a unified rhythm persists throughout, though it is written in independent units rather than one continuous line.

83. Fu Shan: "*Wandering Hermits* Poem in Twelve Scrolls." Ming dynasty. Ink on polished silk. Chōkaidō Bunko, Yokkaichi.

Fu Shan (1607–84) was from Taiyuan in Shanxi. Studying at home, he explored the classics and the writings of the philosophers and went on to study Taoism and medicine. At the age of thirty-eight (1644), he became entangled in the confusion that accompanied the fall of the Ming and wandered in various areas with his son, Bi, selling medicines and describing his sorrow for his lost country in poetry. In his later years, he was put forward for a scholar's post, but he adamantly refused and would not even enter the gates of the capital. He returned to his home and died soon after. He was a person of the first rank in both learning and character, accomplished in calligraphy and painting, and possessed a highly developed intelligence. In volume four of his *Shuanghong Altar Collection* (*Shuanghong Kan Ji*), the "Teaching Calligraphy To My Descendants" chapter, he relates how he studied the block-script techniques of Jin and Tang from his twenties, on to Zhao Mengfu of the Yuan, Dong Qichang of the Ming, then back again to Yan Zhenqing of the Tang dynasty. He remarks, "Though my work might have been rough, it was never clever; though ugly, never coquettish; though disjointed, never facile; though blunt, never common." He makes no allowances for orthodoxy here, but strives only for utterly truthful expression, and describes a style that values uniqueness more than mere beauty.

This "*Wandering Hermits* Poem in Twelve Scrolls" (*You Xian Shi Shier Ping*) is an extended work describing the supernatural hermits of Taoist lore. It is written in semi-cursive, cursive, ancient scripts, and seal scripts, changing and developing in a most ingenious manner. He was able to express without reservation his most elevated ideals in this work. It is important to note that he was the first to incorporate the style of metal-engraved characters into his brushwork. The twelve verses are included in volume thirteen of the *Shuanghong Altar Collection,* with slight variations in phrasing between the two editions. Here we see the first, fourth, eighth, and twelfth verses, and following the last, a postscript which does not appear in the collected version. Below the signature is a square, red seal reading "Fu Shan" and a negative-impression seal.

84. Jiang Chenying: "Poem." Qing dynasty. Ink on polished silk. Kyoto National Museum.

Jiang Chenying (1628–99) made a name for himself as a poet from an early age. He was known, together with Zhu Yizun and Yan Shengsun, as one of the "Three Lay Masters of Jiangnan"—even to Emperor Kangxi. He joined the bureaucracy when he was seventy, but the Emperor so loved his writings that he was immediately promoted to the third rank in the Hanlin Academy.

He was said to be most accomplished in small block script, which he modeled after Zhong Yao and Wang Xizhi. But, since he had studied Mi Fu and Dong Qichang in his youth, it was the influence of Dong's style that was strongest, even on into his old age. He was the most refined and elegant of the early Qing calligraphers. A copybook of his work, the "Laoyi Archives Copybook" (*Laoyi Zhai Fashu*), exists. He was also a discriminating critic, and he composed a study of stele printings.

85. Zhang Zhao: "Ancient Poem by Du Fu." Qing dynasty. Ink on polished silk. Tokyo National Museum.

Zhang Zhao (1691–1745) studied law, music, and was also well known for his plum-blossom paintings—a man of many talents. He was particularly highly regarded in the world of the arts for his calligraphy and favored by three emperors, Kangxi, Yongzheng, and Qianlong.

His study of calligraphy began with Dong Qichang, going on to Yan Zhenqing and Mi Fu. He was able to combine their styles, and create a "grand and graceful" style of his own. Ruan Yuan said of him, "Zhang Zhao was one of the great masters of the Qing, whose work showed a certain virility, Of the several hundreds of works in the imperial possession, his copies have the most vigorous brushwork of them all." Critics have, however, often pointed out a tendency toward vulgarity in his work. Qing Yong's comment is typical: "Both his large and small characters are good, but why is it that when one tries to imitate them, one falls into vulgarity? It is because he has copied Mi Fu's techniques *too* closely." There is a degree of truth in this remark. Still, perhaps in part because he was a high official of the time, his calligraphy met with favor from his contemporaries, and many albums of his work were printed. He also published two volumes of critical writings on calligraphy.

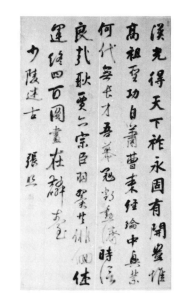

## 86. Zheng Xie: "In Praise of Ink Painting of Bamboos." Qing dynasty. Tokyo National Museum.

Zheng Xie (1693-1765) devoted his career to paintings of orchids, bamboos, and stones. His painting style is prized for its freshness. Among the "Eight Eccentrics" of Yangzhou, his was the least eccentric of painting styles. Of the three arts at which he was regarded a master, his calligraphy showed the greatest individuality. This painting of bamboo on a four-paneled screen, for example, employs calligraphic strokes in the picture itself.

His calligraphy was a unique combination of scribe script, block, and semi-cursive, a kind of miscellaneous script of his own design. Still, it exhibits an unmistakable block-script flavor. Actually, he himself spoke of his calligraphy as "six-and-one-half calligraphy, the extreme of a hard, square style." "Six-and-one-half" is a reference to the relationship of his calligraphy to *bafen* ("eight parts") scribe-style script, meaning that his aim was to approximate that style, and express the feeling inherent in the stone- and metal-inscription characters. However, in his brushwork on the strokes projecting to the left and right and the hesitation shown in the longer strokes, he admitted owing a great deal to the influence of Huang Tingjian.

Yang Shoujing noted that scholars referred to the cursive and semi-cursive of Zheng, together with the scribe script of Jin Nong, as having "fallen into a demon's way," and though he recognized their originality, he thought it an unfit model of calligraphic technique.

These remarks concerning the painting are written from left to right, an unconventional format. But the use of calligraphic techniques in the painting and painting strokes in the calligraphy, as well as careful consideration in unifying the entire surface, are much in evidence.

## 87. Jin Nong: "Poem." Qing dynasty. Ink on paper. Chōkaidō Bunko, Yokkaichi.

Jin Nong (1687-1763) was elevated from commoner status to doctor of literature in 1736, but he could not find an appropriate office, and though he often suffered poverty, he managed to devote his life to poetry, literature, painting, and calligraphy. The solitary life of the literati was the dominant theme of his existence. He was a literate critic of ancient works, and under the influence of the scholarly work of He Zhuo he also produced fruitful results in the collection of metal- and stone-inscription albums. Today he is best known for his calligraphy and painting.

He is said to have begun painting at the late age of fifty and was most skilled at renditions of bamboos, plums, and horses. His method was to depict the familiar and near at hand from a personal and rather stylized viewpoint, with a lively spirit and feeling.

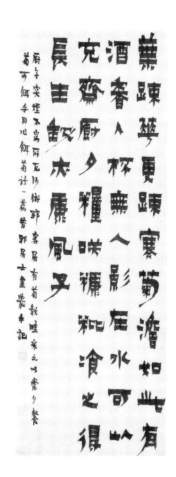

He created a distinct style of block and scribe script. His style, even in semi-cursive and cursive, bore little resemblance to the then popular Zhao and Dong. His work transcended traditional bounds. His block script was an elongated, "gothic" creation, as if put together from strips of paper, and in his later years, he attained a trimly elegant style with a bright, fresh look, "reaching the ancient ideal, somewhere between block and scribe script." His scribe script, too, changed several times, but the style of this poem, written in his sixties, is his most glorious. Taking two steles as his models, he carefully prepared the tip of the brush in order to achieve this effect when he wrote large characters. This unique style, in which he also made the start of the strokes heavy, the endings light, and the long leftward extensions sharp, was called "lacquer-script style." The basis of this seemingly strange style was the metal and stone inscriptions and their startling combination of abstract line and emotional expression.

88. Wang Wenzhi: "Bound Volume of Copies of Jin Calligraphy." Qing dynasty. Ink on colored paper. Tokyo National Museum.

Wang Wenzhi (1730–1802) was well-known during his lifetime as a poet and, together with Yuan Mei, founded a school of his own. We have his *Menglou Poems* (*Menglou Shiji*). He was also recognized as a calligrapher from a relatively early time. At the age of twenty-six, he accompanied an ambassador to the Ryū-kyūs, where the local people greatly admired his calligraphy and collected it as a treasure.

He excelled, in particular, at block and semi-cursive scripts. Block he studied from Chu Suiliang, and semi-cursive from the "Orchid Pavilion Preface" and the "Preface to the Buddhist Canon," but the real base of his style was the work of Zhao Mengfu and Dong Qichang. Qian Yong notes that in his later years he studied Zhang Jizhi of the Song, and his influence can be seen in works that exhibit especially sharp "dot" strokes.

He was recognized by his contemporaries as one of the founders of the copybook school, and he composed postscripts for many famous works. All of them are in a richly elegant style, just as is this "Bound Volume of Copies of Jin Calligraphy" (*Lin Jin Shu Ce*). Yang Shoujing appraised his work, remarking, "his technique was elegant and natural, but he was criticized for being over-refined," and to be sure, his semi-cursive and cursive script does give that impression. His graceful, sensual calligraphy has had its admirers as well as detractors.

89. Liu Yong: "Copybook of Calligraphic Techniques." Qing dynasty. Ink on metallic paper. Private collection.

In his long life and career, Liu Shian (1719–1804) adopted a great variety of models for his calligraphy. He was said to have stuided Zhao Mengfu in his youth. In his middle age, he tested his mettle against Dong Qichang and then moved toward Su Shi. In his later years, he concentrated his energies on Zhong and Wang, finally arriving at the study of the stele inscriptions of the northern dynasties. However, it is difficult to trace each of these influences in his works, particularly those prior to his middle years. From the works that are now in existence, it appears that he devoted his greatest energies to the study of Zhong Yao, at least from his middle age on.

He favored dark ink, and did not connect his rounded characters. His special trait was the way he enlarged the white spaces and developed this into a kind of abstract technique for distributing space. His calligraphy was criticized by some as "ink pigs" (referring to his ample use of ink and the dull heaviness of the strokes) and "rabbit droppings." But there were many who appreciated the fullness and strength of his work, saying its "appearance was rich, and spirit heavy with nuance." Though he did use ample ink on the brush, he avoided the appearance of heaviness. He aimed for a simplified expression, and had a unique, extended rhythm. In his final years, he produced work of a beauty becoming to the great formulator of copybook studies, rich with hidden implications and calm restraint. This is a work of his sixty-fifth year, when his work had already reached its final style, fully exploiting a subtle and varied technique. He uses here a gorgeous type of gold-flecked paper, indicating that he was concerned with the decorative effect that this showy material would provide.

90. Liang Tongshu: "Two Poems in Seven Stanzas by Lu You." Qing dynasty. Ink on polished silk. Tokyo National Museum.

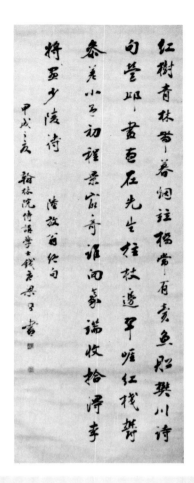

Liang Shizheng, the father of Liang Tongshu (1723–1815), compiled the *Shiqu Baoji* together with Zhang Zhao and other high-ranking scholars, as well as assisting in editing the *Ancient Seals of the Western Qing (Xi Qing Gu Jian)*. Most of the important documents of the imperial court were in his hand, since he was a famous calligrapher of the period. Tongshu, as an aristocratic child, was tutored at home and acclaimed as a calligraphy genius from his youth. By the age of twelve he excelled at writing large characters, and when his father did not have time to write things requested of him, Tongshu wrote in his stead.

At first he followed Yan Zhenqing and Liu Gongquan, employing Mi Fu's techniques in his middle years and finally reaching a degree of freedom towards the end of his career. Even in old age, he excelled in the so-called "fly's head" slim *kai,* and left behind powerful works in large characters. "He bore the burden of fame for sixty years. His stele printings spread throughout China. He was lionized together with Liu Yong and Wang Wenzhi, in the formula, 'Liu, Liang and Wang.' " There were so many who sought his works that he could not allow his brush to dry out, and he devised a special brushcover, according to one story. Even after ninety he never relaxed his efforts, writing the countless drafts for stele inscriptions that were requested of him.

This work is from his ninety-second year, one year before his death. It is in semi-cursive script and seems a little lacking in spirit.

We have several albums of his works. He was also an insightful critic and left works in this vein. He was learned in the theories of calligraphy and composed the *Pinluo Hermitage Discussion of Calligraphy (Pinluo An Lunshu)*, which dealt in detail with the techniques for holding a brush of the softest long sheep bristles.

91. Deng Shiru: "Four Styles Album." Qing dynasty. Ink on paper. Tokyo National Museum.

Deng (1743–1805) devoted his entire life to calligraphy. He specialized in it and brought a new spirit to all the different forms. The sources of his block script are disputed. The gentle, flattened style of his early period gradually evolved into a sharper, more rigid style. From the first, he directed his attention to printed editions of the Six Dynasties steles, and in his later years, evidenced the "clear depth" cited by Bao Shichen. In his semi-cursive and cursive, the vertical strokes are extended with great determination, with strong beginnings, and in a tenacious manner. His seal script evolved from a Li Yangfeng style in the first period to a Qin-Han style and finally to a hybrid style that included even elements of the stone-drum and funerary-relic scripts, so broad was his learning. He did not, as had been done up until then, singe or cut off the brush tip to sharpen it, but introduced a new style with a soft-tipped brush. His scribe script, also the result of extensive study of Han and Wei inscriptions, changed three times during his career. In the first period, it was flattened and richly rounded. In the middle period, he evolved a stroke rhythm distinct from Zheng Fu and Gui Fu. Finally, in his later years, his calligraphy increased in solemnity and came to have heavier, more sombre reverberations.

The work under consideration here is the scribe-script section of a work in the four styles of seal, scribe, block, and cursive scripts and was probably a work of his fifty-fifth year. Overtones of the Wei scribe-script style are still strong, expressing the process of his work's evolution from his middle to old age. The strength of the brushwork results in the highest degree of freshness in this work. His famous remark, "The open spaces should permit a horse to gallop through; the written areas should be dense enough to block the wind. If one always calculates the white space and then allocates the black, rare results will be achieved," is demonstrated in this work.

92. He Shaoji: "In Praise of Horse Paintings." Qing dynasty. Ink on paper. Private collection.

This is a poem in seven-character lines discussing paintings of horses. It is written on four lengths of paper. The year of its composition is unclear, but Yang Shoujing described it as "heavenly flowers scattering and falling," and the determination evident in its brilliant and large revolutions probably places it within the calligraphic style of He Shaoji's mature period or even later.

The basis of the style of He Shaoji (1799–1873) was the Yan techniques that he followed up to his middle years. When he was young, he knew of Bao Shichen and his "concealed beginning and smooth ending" technique. He was instructed in the importance of the northern steles by his teacher Ruan Yuan, but he did not succumb entirely to their influence. He devoted great energy to the study of seal and scribe scripts after the age of fifty, and gave the greatest polish to his scribe-script calligraphy. "After waking, I always practiced several sheets of scribe script," he said, remarking on his daily regimen, and this devoted practice continued into his last years. His remarkable commitment to calligraphy helped him to create a unique semi-cursive and cursive that combined the best features of all forms. Though of course he also had natural talent, he struggled with great determination to purify and distill the techniques of his art.

The expansive scale and strong determination of his work, in which not even the smallest stroke shows any lapse or indecision, was due to his unique method of moving the brush—he preserved a firm pressure with the tip of the brush while moving it slowly across the paper. His control was precise and delicate, for the slightest bit of excess pressure on the long-tipped brush he favored would have resulted in the collapse of the tip. Because he used the method of Li Guang of the Han dynasty known as "drawing the bow with monkey arms," in his later years he dubbed himself "Old Man Monkey" or "Old Monkey-arms." The technique was to use an extremely soft brush tip and write with an outstretched, elevated arm. He instructed, "You must hold your elbow quite high and apply the strength of your entire body. Before you're half-finished, you should be dripping with perspiration and your clothes soaked." The concentrated strength of the elevated arm technique produced a tension that stopped just short of destroying the characters altogether.

93. Zhao Zhiqian: "Four Scrolls." Qing dynasty. Ink on speckled paper. Tokyo National Museum.

Zhao Ziqian (1829–84) was a man of strong political convictions, though unfortunately he never attained a passport into the central bureaucracy. Because of his frank and unbending character he did not fit in very well, and he also encountered much personal misfortune. In his works of later years, we can see the strong feeling that was the result of his public and private sufferings.

In his thirties, he went to the capital several times in response to examination announcements. On the first occasion he became friends with Chen Shuyong and Wei Xiceng, and his diligent studies of metal and stone inscriptions later added a polish to his calligraphy and seal carving. Before the age of thirty he had already created a distinctive seal-carving style, and after these studies, his accomplishments showed a sudden advance. The style he later proclaimed as "Northern Wei Calligraphy" was also based on these studies and seems to have evolved from his work with seals. We see it first in his calligraphy from his middle thirties. Further expanding Bao Shichen's "concealed beginning and smooth ending" technique, he devised a new style. From his middle forties this evolved into an effortless technique, and in his later years he advanced even further to a dignified style with considerable gravity and density. By the end of his life, as can be seen in this "Four Scrolls" he had attained a new freedom with vigor penetrating every stroke, discarded the fixed notion of a "Northern Wei Style," and fully exploited space in an uncramped, full, and expressive manner. Here he has blended various forms of script in a style that at a glance appears to be effortless, but actually required the most profound and careful preparation and polishing. He excelled at scribe script due to his work with seals, of course, and his true masterpieces were to be found in this style rather than block or semi-cursive calligraphy.

94. Kang Youwei: "Five-Character Couplet." Qing dynasty. Ink on paper. Tokyo National Museum.

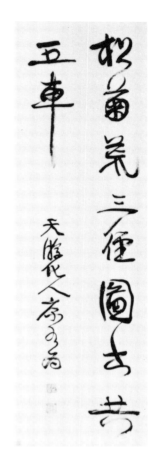

Kang Youwei (1858-1927) lamented the chaos China found herself in, was greatly concerned with saving his country, and was in favor of a republican form of government with a constitutional monarchy. While he was being persecuted by the conservative factions, the Xinghai Revolt occurred, and he joined forces with the movement to restore Emperor Guangxu to his throne.

Kang's reputation as a politician, thinker, and educator varies. He was an impassioned advocate, and this trait is evident in his theories of calligraphy, too. His *Guang Yi Zhou Shuang Ji* (Two Oars of the Great Ship of the Arts), a work of his thirty-second year, is a continuation of the stele studies that had dominated since Ruan Yuan and Bao Shichen, which suppplements and expands their researches. However, Kang did not sharply distinguish northern and southern traditions, but rather upheld the majestic, vigorous style of calligraphy that continued from the Han and Wei into the Northern and Southern Dynasties period. Of the Qing calligraphers, he especially admired the work of Deng Shiru and Zhang Yuzhao, and sought a style of brushwork combining both angular and rounded strokes and a beauty rich in meaning, with universal appeal.

As he himself said, "I have a god in my eye and a demon in my arm, but I have never been able to achieve the profound dignity of the ancients." In the calligraphy of his later works, an ambitious attempt to incorporate the brushwork of Deng Shiru's scribe, crusive, and semi-cursive scripts is apparent, but it lacks cohesion, and his calligraphy never reached the standards he set in his theoretical works.

95. Yang Shoujing: "Description of Peach Blossoms and Spring." Qing Dynasty. Ink on paper. Tokyo National Museum.

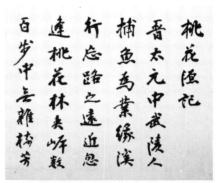

Yang Shoujing (1839-1915) came to Japan in 1880 as ambassador and resided there for four years. During that time he associated with politicians and scholars and introduced them to and promoted studies of the steles of the Six Dynasties.

He was originally a geographer, but was also known for his scholarly work in the study of metal and stone inscriptions and his works concerning calligraphy. These works considered the printed versions of stele rubbings from the point of view of the evolution of calligraphic techniques, in contrast to the historical researches of other scholars. In this regard, he attempted to confirm and correct the theories of both Ruan Yuan and Bao Shichen, and he is more widely followed in Japan than he is in his native China.

He practiced seal, scribe, block, semi-cursive, and cursive scripts, but was most accomplished in semi-cursive and cursive. His manner of holding the brush followed Zhang Zhao's copybook school tradition, but his calligraphic style was a synthesis of the two traditions. "Yang Shoujing followed the methods of Ouyang Xun. His semi-cursive script was done with a brush held perpendicular to the paper, and is better than Weng Fanggang's, but his small block script cannot compare." As this evaluation indicates, his calligraphy was not of exemplary quality.

# CHRONOLOGY OF CALLIGRAPHERS
## AND THEIR WORKS

| DATE | DYNASTY | EVENTS | CALLIGRAPHERS | WORKS |
|---|---|---|---|---|
| B.C. 1400? | Shang Dynasty | | | Bone and tortoiseshell inscriptions |
| 1100? | Zhou Dynasty | End of the Shang dynasty, establishment of the Zhou, with its capital at Hao | | |
| 770 | Eastern Zhou | Ping Wang Dong Qian transfers capital to Luoyang. Spring and Autumn Annals period (722–440) | | |
| 494 | | Wu Wang Fu Cha defeats Yue Wang Gou Jian | | B.C. 494   Gou Jian, Prince of Yue's sword inscription (pl. 3) |
| 403–256 | | Warring States Period | | 422?   Stone-drum inscriptions<br><br>313   Divinatory script of Chu<br><br>300?   Chu characters on silk (pl. 2)<br>Zhongshan bronze inscriptions (pls. 4, 5) |
| 256 | | Zhou defeated by the Qin | | |
| 249 | | Shi Huang of the Qin ascends the throne | | |
| 221 | Qin Dynasty | The empire is unified, divided into districts and prefectures; weights, measures, and writing standardized | | |
| | | | Meng Tian (died 210)<br><br>Li Si (died 208) | |
| 219 | | Shi Huang makes journeys to various locations and leaves stone inscriptions | Cheng Miao | 219   Taishan, Langye Terrace stone inscriptions (pl. 7) |
| 202 | Former Han Dynasty | Liu Bang founds the Han dynasty | | 194   Mawangdui Tomb bamboo tablets, *Laozi* on silk (pl. 6)<br><br>149   Lu Lingguan Palace stone inscription |
| 136 | | Confucianism made the official religion of the realm | | 131   Qunchen Shangchou stone inscription |

| DATE | DYNASTY | EVENTS | CALLIGRAPHERS | WORKS |
|---|---|---|---|---|
| | (Former Han) | | | 102 B.C.–68 A.D. Bamboo tablets of the Han dynasty |
| 91 | | Sima Qian's *History* (*Shi Ji*) | | |
| | | | | 56 B.C. Lu Xiaowang Stone inscription |
| 48 | | Cursive script (*caoshu*) created by Shi You | Shi You | |
| 1 A.D. | | | | |
| 8 A.D. | | Wang Mang assumes the throne, end of the Former Han dynasty | | |
| 25 | Later Han | Guangwu founds the Later Han | | 66 A.D. Stone Inscription Commemorating the Opening of the Baoxie Road (fig.16) |
| 100 | | Xu Shen's *Dictionary of Characters and Phrases* | Xu Shen | |
| | | | Cao Xi | |
| | | | Du Du | 137 Stele Recording the Virtues of Pei Cen (fig. 19) |
| | | | Cui Yuan (77–142) | 148 Stone Gate Verses (fig. 17) |
| | | | | 153 Yi Ying Stele (fig. 11) |
| | | | | 156 *Liqi* Stele (pl. 9) |
| | | | | 159 Zhang Jing Stele (fig. 18) |
| | | | | 164 Kong Zhou Stele (fig. 12) |
| | | | | 165 Tomb Steles of the Western Peaks of Mt. Hua (fig. 13) |
| | | | | 169 Shichen Stele (fig. 14) |
| | | | | 175–83 Xiping Stone Classic (fig. 15) |
| | | | | 185 Cao Quan Stele (pl. 10) |
| | | | | 186 Zhang Qian Stele (pl. 11) |
| 190 | | Capital transferred to Chang'an | | |
| | | | Cai Yong (132–92) | |
| | | | Zhang Zhi | |
| | | | Liu Desheng | |
| | | | Shi Xuanguan | |
| 205 | | Cao Cao prohibits burial steles | | |

| DATE | DYNASTY | EVENTS | CALLIGRAPHERS | WORKS |
|---|---|---|---|---|
| | (Later Han) | | Zhang Chang (died 206) | |
| | | | Handan Chun | |
| | | | Liang Hu | |
| | | | Wei Ji | |
| 220 | Three Kingdoms Period: Wei | Fall of the Later Han, establishment of the Wei, and the beginning of the Three Kingdoms Period (Wei, Wu, and Shu) | | |
| | | | Zhong Yao (151–230) | Xuanshi Memorial (fig. 21), Memorial awarding an Honorary Name to Gong Qing (220, fig. 20), Imperial Accession Memorial |
| | | | Hu Zhao (162–250) | |
| | | | Wei Dan (179–253) | |
| | | | Huang Xiang | Jijiu Zhang, Wenwu Album |
| 263 | | Fall of the Shu | Zhong Hui (225–64) | 240–48  Stone Classic in Three Styles |
| 265 | Western Jin | Fall of the Wei, founding of the Jin | | 276  Divine Omen Stele (pl. 12) |
| 280 | | | | 278  Imperial Academy Stele (fig. 31) |
| | | | Wei Heng (252–91) | 296  Zhufo Yaoji Jing (fig. 38) |
| | | Defeat of the Wu by the Jin | Su Jing (239–303) | Yueyi Album |
| | | | Lu Ji (261–303) | Pingfu Album (pl. 13) |
| 311 | | Yongjia Revolt | | |
| 316 | | Fall of the Western Jin, beginning of the Five Barbarians and Sixteen Kingdoms Period (316–439) | | |
| 317 | Eastern Jin | Yuan Di founds the Eastern Jin | | |
| | | | | Li Bo's Draft of a Letter (328, pl. 14) |
| | | | Chi Jian (269–339) | |
| | | | Wang Dao (276–339) | |

| DATE | DYNASTY | | | EVENTS | CALLIGRAPHERS | WORKS |
|------|---------|---|---|--------|---------------|-------|
| | (Eastern Jin) | | | | Wei Shuo (272–349) | |
| | | | | | Wang Xia (323–58) | Epitaph for Liu Ke (357) |
| | | | | | Wang Xizhi (303?–61?) | Yue Yi Treatise (fig. 22), Orchid Pavilion Preface (fig. 25), Paean to Dong Fangshuo (fig. 24), Imperial Court Classic (fig. 23), Wang Lüe Album, Sang Luan Album (pl. 16), Kong Shizong Album (pl. 17), Feng Ju Album (pl. 18), Shiqi Album (pl. 19) |
| | | | | | Huan Wen (312–73) | |
| | | | | | Chi Yin (313–84) | |
| | | | | | Xie An (330–85) | Fifth Day of the Eighth Month Album |
| 386 | Northern Wei | | | Northern Wei is founded by Tuoba | | |
| | | | | | Wang Huizhi (died 388?) | |
| | | | | | Wang Xianzhi (344–88) | Di Huang Tang Epistle (pl. 20), Ode to Luo Shen (fig. 28), Jinbao Muzhi |
| | | | | | Wang Ningzhi (died 399) | |
| | | | | | Wang Xun (349–400) | |
| | | | | | Huan Xuan (369–404) | |
| 420 | | Song Dynasty | | Collapse of the Eastern Jin, founding of the Song | | |
| | | | | | Kong Linzhi (369–423) | |
| 439 | | | | The north is unified under the Northern Wei, and the Northern and Southern Dynasties Period begins | | |
| | | | | | Yang Xin (370–442) | |
| | | | | | Kou Qianzhi (365?–448) | |
| | | | | | Cui Hao (died 450) | |
| | | | | | Xiao Sihua (406–55) | |

| DATE | DYNASTY | | | EVENTS | CALLIGRAPHERS | WORKS |
|------|---------|--|--|--------|---------------|-------|
| | (Northern Wei) | | | | Bo Shaozhi | |
| 479 | | Qi Dynasty | | Collapse of the Song, founding of the Qi | | |
| | | | | | Wang Sengqian (426–85) | |
| | | | | | | 492 *Dafangdeng Daiji Jing* (pl. 27) |
| 494 | | | | Northern Wei capital transferred to Luoyang | | |
| 495 | | | | Excavations begin at Longmen | | |
| | | | | | | 496 Epitaph for Yuan Zhen (pl. 22) |
| | | | | | | 498 Title Inscription for Buddhist Image Constructed by Duke Shiping (pl. 23) |
| 502 | | Liang Dynasty | | Qi is defeated by the Liang | | |
| 505 | | | | Longmen Binyang cave construction begins | | 505 *Daban Niepan Jing* (fig. 40) |
| | | | | | | 510 *Dazhidulun Jing* (fig. 42) |
| | | | | | | 513 *Huayan Jing* (pl. 29) |
| | | | | | | 514 Yi He Inscription (pl. 25) |
| | | | | | Zheng Daozhao (died 516) | Zheng Xi Steles (fig. 30), Confucian Didactic Verses (511, pl. 24) |
| | | | | | Jiang Shi | |
| | | | | | Bei Yiyuan | Stele for Zhongwu Xiao Dan, Prince of Shixing (pl. 26) |
| | | | | | | 520 Epitaph for Sima Bing |
| | | | | | | 522 Zhang Meng Long Stele (fig. 33) |
| | | | | | | 523 Gao Zhen Stele. (pl. 21), *Vinaya* Preface (pl. 28) |
| 534 | W. Wei | E. Wei | | North splits into Eastern and Western Wei. Yungang cave construction ends | | |
| | | | | | Tao Hongjing (456–536) | |
| | | | | | Xiao Ziyun (487–549) | |
| | | | | | Ruan Yan | |
| 550 | | N. Qi | | Collapse of the Eastern Wei, founding of the Northern Qi | Yu Jianwu (died 550) | 550 *Pusa Chutai Jing* (pl. 30) |

| DATE | DYNASTY | | | EVENTS | CALLIGRAPHERS | WORKS |
|---|---|---|---|---|---|---|
| 557 | N. Zhou | (N. Qi) | Chen | Collapse of the Liang, establishment of the Chen. Collapse of the Western Wei, founding of the Northern Zhou | | |
| | | | | | Zhao Wenyuan | Tomb Steles of the Western Peaks of Mt. Hua (567) |
| 574 | | | | Northern Zhou prohibition of Buddhism and Taoism, return of all monks to lay status | | |
| 577 | | | | Wu Di of the Northern Zhou defeats the Northern Qi | | |
| 580 | | | | Northern Zhou revival of Taoism and Buddhism | | |
| 581 | Sui Dynasty | | | Collapse of the Northern Zhou | | |
| 589 | | | | Sui defeats the Chen, unifies the land | | |
| | | | | | Fang Yanqian (547–615) | 597 Epitaph for Dong Meiren (fig. 46) |
| | | | | | Hu Chuo | |
| | | | | | Shi Ling | |
| | | | | | Ding Daohu | Qifa Temple Stele (602, pl. 32) |
| | | | | | | 615 Epitaph for Duke Yuan, Office of the Stables (pl. 34) |
| | | | | | | Longcangsi Monastery Stele (fig. 45) |
| | | | | | | Epitaph for Li Jingxun |
| | | | | | | Tomb Stele of Xiu, Head of the Chen Clan |
| | | | | | | Tomb Stele of Cao Zhi |
| | | | | | | Statue Inscription of Du Qianzu and Others |
| | | | | | Zhao Xiaoyi | |
| | | | | | Zhiyong | Thousand-Character Essay (pl. 31), Postscript to Feng Ju Epistles |
| | | | | | Zhiguo | |
| 618 | Tang Dynasty | | | Sui emperor killed. Tang established by Li Yu | | |
| 627 | | | | Establishment of the Hong Wen Department, with Yu Shinan and Ouyang Xun | | |
| | | | | | Yu Shinan (558–638) | Memorial Stele at Confucius' Tomb (627), Epitaph for Lord Runan, Jishi Album (636) |

| DATE | DYNASTY | EVENTS | CALLIGRAPHERS | WORKS |
|---|---|---|---|---|
| 639 | (Tang) | Taizong presents rubbings of Wang Xizhi's works to his ministers. Chu Suiliang's rubbing of the Yue Yi Treatise completed | | |
| | | | Ouyang Xun (557–641) | Huang Fudan Stele (627), Fang Yanqian Stele, Huadu Temple Stele (631, pl. 37), Jiucheng Palace Spring Inscription (632, fig. 47), Wen Yanfu Stele (637) |
| | | | Taizong (598–649) | Jin Ci Inscription (646), Hot Spring Inscription (648 pl. 35) |
| | | | Huairen | *Preface to the Buddhist Canon* after Wang Xizhi (672, pl. 36) |
| | | | Chu Suiliang (596–658) | Yique Buddhist Image-niche Stele (641, fig. 48) Dharma Master Meng's Stele (642), Fang Xuanling Stele (630), Yan Pagoda Prefaces (653, pl. 38) |
| | | | Ouyang Tong (died 691) | Master Daoyin Stele (663), Epitaph for Quan Nansheng (679) |
| 684 | | Empress Wu comes to power | Sun Guoting (648?–703) | Treatise on Calligraphy (687, pl. 43) |
| 697 | | Wang Fangqing presents the Wang-family copies of Wang Xizhi's calligraphy to the throne | Empress Wu (623–705) | Stele for Crown Prince Sheng-xian (699) |
| | | | | 706  Epitaph Inscription for Princess Yongtai (pl. 45) |
| | | | | 708  Epitaph for Wei Jiong |
| | | | Xue Ji (649–713) | Chan Master Xin Xing Stele |
| | | | | 718  Epitaph for Wei Xu |
| 727 | | Zhang Huaikuan's Critique of Calligraphy (*Shu Duan*) | | |
| | | | | 740  Epitaph for Zhang Jiuling |
| | | | He Zhizhang (659–744) | *Classic of Filial Piety* in Cursive Characters (740, pl. 44) |
| | | | Li Yong (678–747) | Li Sixun Stele (739), Lushansi Monastery Stele (730, fig. 50) |
| | | | Emperor Xuan-zong (685–762) | Taishan Inscription, Stone Terrace *Classic of Filial Piety* |
| | | | Zhang Xu | Autobiographical Album (714) |
| | | | Shi Weize | Chan Master Dazhi Stele |
| | | | Li Yangbing | Title Inscription of the Banruo Terrace (772) |

| DATE | DYNASTY | EVENTS | CALLIGRAPHERS | WORKS |
|---|---|---|---|---|
| | (Tang) | | Han Zemu | Epitaph for the Lord of Nanchuan Xian (752) |
| | | | Xu Hao (703–82) | Epitaph for Zhang Tinggui (746), Stele for Amoghavajra (781) |
| | | | Yan Zhenqing (709–85) | Eulogy for a Nephew (758, pl. 46), Contest for Rank (764), Datang Zhongxing Verses (771), Stele for the Yan Clan Tomb (780), Eulogy for Bo Fu, Poem of Parting for General Pei |
| | | | Huaisu (born 725) | *Autobiography* (777, pl. 47) |
| | | | Chen Chuanshi (769–827) | 810 Epitaph for Prince Hui |
| | | | Liu Gongquan (778–865) | 848 Epitaph for Zheng Derou<br>*Jingang Banruo Jing* (824), Xuanbi Pagoda Stele (841) |
| 907 | Five Dynasties, Later Liang | Collapse of the Tang, founding of the Later Liang, and the beginning of the Five Dynasties period | | |
| | | | | 918 Lament for Wang Jian Tablet (fig. 53) |
| 923 | Later Tang | Collapse of the Later Liang, founding of the Later Tang | | |
| 934 | Later Jin | Collapse of the Later Tang, founding of the Later Jin | | |
| | | Dengxin Hall Album | | |
| | | Sheng Yuan Album | | |
| 937 | | Dynasty name changed to Liao | | |
| | | | | 943 Lament for Li Pian Tablet |
| 947 | Later Han | Later Han founded | | |
| 951 | Later Zhou | Later Zhou founded | | |
| | | | Yang Ningshi (873–954) | Luhong Caotang Shizhi Postscript (947) |
| 960 | Northern Song | Collapse of the Later Zhou, founding of the Song | | |
| | | | Xu Jie (921–75) | |

| DATE | DYNASTY | | EVENTS | CALLIGRAPHERS | WORKS |
|---|---|---|---|---|---|
| | (Northern Song) | | | Nantang Houzhu (937–78) | |
| 979 | | | Later Han defeated by the Song, empire unified | | |
| 992 | | | Printing of the Chunhua Pavilion Album | | |
| 1004 | | | Peace treaty with Liao | | |
| | | | | Cai Xiang (1012–67) | Poems in Thanks for an Imperial Gift (1052 pl. 48), *Four Sages and One Scoundrel,* Tao Sheng Album |
| | | | | Ouyang Xiu (1007–72) | *Collected Ancient Catalogues of Postscripts* (1063) |
| | | | | Su Shi (1036–1101) | *Cold Meal in Huangzhou* Poem Scroll (1082, pl. 49), *Hermit Li Taibo* Poem Scroll (1093, pl. 50) |
| | | | | Huang Tingjian (1045–1105) | Li Taibo's *Recalling Past Wanderings* Poem Scroll (pl. 52), Epitaph drafts for Wang Zhong and Shi Fu (pl. 51), *Cold Meal in Huangzhou* Poem Scroll Postscript (pl. 53) |
| | | | Mi Fu's *History of Calligraphy, Catalogue of Masterpieces* | Mi Fu (1051–1107) | Gangxian Poem Scroll, (pl. 54), Four Cursive Albums (pl. 55), Three Semi-Cursive Albums, Thousand-Character Essay in Small Block Characters, Eulogy for Empress Dowager Taxing |
| 1115 | Jin | | Establishment of the Jin | | |
| 1126 | | | Jin armies capture the capital of the Song | Cai Jing (1047–1126) | |
| 1127 | | Southern Song | | Wu Shuo | |
| | | | | Yuanwu Keqin (1063–1135) | Yuanwu Keqin's Diploma (pl. 56) |
| | | | | Huizong (1082–1135) | Thousand-Character Essay (fig. 59) |
| 1144 | | | *Albums of Ancient Inscriptions on Bronze Ding and Yi Vessels* completed | | |
| 1147 | | | Huang Bosi's *Study on the Chunhua Pavilion Album* | | |
| | | | | Mi Youren (1072–1151) | |
| | | | | Wang Sheng (1076–1150?) | |

| DATE | DYNASTY | | EVENTS | CALLIGRAPHERS | WORKS |
|---|---|---|---|---|---|
| | (Jin) | (Southern Song) | | Cai Songnian (1107–59) | Postscript to Su Shi's *Hermit Li Taibo* Poem Scroll (1159, pl. 62) |
| 1168 | | | Hong Kuo's *Scribe and Li Script Dictionaries* | | |
| | | | | Zhang Xiaoxiang (1133–70) | |
| 1185 | | | Junxibi Pavilion Copybook | | |
| | | | Gaozong's *Brush and Ink Treatise* | Mi'an Xianjie (1118–86) | Sermon (pl. 64) |
| | | | | Gaozong (1107–87) | *Preface to the Collected Writings of Huizong* (1154, pl. 57), Volume of Proclamations Granted to Liang Rujia (pl. 58) |
| | | | | Fan Chengda (1126–93) | *Memorial Poem for Chan Master Fo Zhao* (1181, pl. 59) |
| 1195 | | | Qunyu Hall Album | | |
| | | | | Zhu Xi (1130–1200) | Cursive Draft of the Collected Notes on the *Analects* (pl. 60) |
| | | | | Wang Tingyun (1151–1202) | Postscript to Painting of Bamboo (pl. 63) |
| 1203 | | | Jiang Kui's Jiangping Album | | |
| 1206 | | | Chinggis Khan comes to power | Yang Wanli (1124–1206) | |
| | | | | Wu Jie | |
| 1208 | | | Jiang Kui's *Continued History of Calligraphy* | Lu You (1125–1210) | |
| 1224 | | | Sang Shichang's *Consideration of the Orchid Pavilion* | | |
| | | | | Jiang Kui (1155–1231) | |
| 1234 | | | Collapse of the Jin | | |
| 1242 | | | Yu Song's *Further Consideration of the Orchid Pavilion Preface* | | |
| | | | | Wuzhun Shifan (1177–1249) | Diploma (1237, pl. 65) |
| 1260 | Yuan Dynasty | | Khubilai Khan ascends the throne, Yuan dynasty | | |
| | | | | Zhang Jizhi (1186–1266) | |
| | | | | Yu Yunwen | |
| | | | | Zhao Mengjian (1199–1264) | |

| DATE | DYNASTY | | EVENTS | CALLIGRAPHERS | WORKS |
|---|---|---|---|---|---|
| 1268 | (Yuan) | (Southern Song) | Cao Zhige's *Jewels of the Jin Archives Album* | | |
| 1271 | | | Dynasty name changed to Yuan | | |
| 1276 | | | Song capital captured, and emperor put to death | | |
| 1279 | | | Fall of the Southern Song and unification of China under the Yuan | | |
| | | | | Xianyu Shu (1257–1302) | Du Fu's *Thatch Roof Destroyed by the Autumn Wind* (1298, pl. 66) |
| 1322 | | | Zheng Yun's *Yan Ji* completed | Zhao Mengfu (1254–1322) | Three Gates Record (1302–9), Miaoyan Temple Record (1309–10), Thirteen Postscripts to the Orchid Pavilion (1310), Dan Ba Stele, Epistle to Zhongfeng Mingben (pl. 67), *Biography of Han Ji'an* (1320, pl. 68) |
| | | | | Feng Zizhen (1257–1327?) | Words Presented to Muin Genkai (pl. 69) |
| | | | | Deng Wenyuan (1259–1329) | |
| | | | | Wu Qiuyan | *Xue Gu Bian* |
| 1342 | | | Chen Yiceng's *Secret Teaching of the Hanlin Academy* | | |
| | | | | Ke Jiusi (1290–1343) | Postscript to the Orchid Pavilion Preface (1336) |
| | | | | Kangli Kuikui (1295–1345) | Three Verses Scroll (1336), Li Bo's *Ancient Wind* Poem (pl. 70) |
| | | | | Yu Ji (1272–1348) | |
| | | | | Wang Meng | |
| | | | | Zhang Yu (1277–1348) | |
| | | | | Rao Jie (died 1367) | |
| 1368 | Ming Dynasty | | Founding of the Ming | Zhou Boqi (1298–1369) | |
| | | | | Yang Weizhen (1296–1370) | Draft for Zhang Clan Memorial Stele (1365, pl. 71) |
| | | | | Ni Zan (1301–74) | |
| 1376 | | | Tao Zongyi's *Brief Introduction to the History of Calligraphy* | | |

| DATE | DYNASTY | EVENTS | CALLIGRAPHERS | WORKS |
|---|---|---|---|---|
| | (Ming) | | Song Lian (1310–81) | |
| | | | Song Ke (1327–87) | |
| | | | Jie Jin (1369–1415) | |
| | | | Shen Du (1357–1434) | |
| | | | Shen Can (1377–1453) | |
| | | | Jiang Ligang | |
| | | | Zhang Bi (1425–87) | Postscript to Su Shi's *Hermit Li Taibo* Poem Scroll (1483, pl. 72) |
| 1489 | | Jin Jingwang's Baoxian Hall Album | | |
| | | | Xu Youzhen | |
| | | | Li Yingzhen (1431–93) | |
| | | | Chen Xianzhang (1428–1500) | Poem Scroll (pl. 73) |
| | | | Wu Xuan (1435–1504) | |
| | | | Shen Zhou (1427–1509) | |
| | | | Li Dongyang (1477–1516) | |
| | | | Zhu Yunming (1460–1526) | *Li Sao Classic* Scroll (1490, pl. 74), *Red Cliffs Ode* (1508, pl. 75) |
| | | | Wang Chong (1494–1533) | |
| | | | Li Shen (1477–1544) | |
| | | | Wang Shouren (1472–1528) | Helou Pavilion Poem Scroll (1508, pl. 77) |
| | | | Chen Shun (1483–1544) | |
| | | | Wen Zhengming (1470–1559) | Twelve Verses from Tao Yuanming's Drinking Poem (1554, pl. 76) |
| | | | Wen Peng (1498–1573) | Eulogy for Duke Xu |

| DATE | DYNASTY | EVENTS | CALLIGRAPHERS | WORKS |
|---|---|---|---|---|
| | (Ming) | | Guang Jishui (1509–74) | |
| | | | Feng Fang (died 1576?) | |
| | | | Wen Jia (1501–83) | |
| | | | Zhou Tianqiu (1514–95) | |
| 1604 | | Dong Qichang's Huhong Hall Album | | |
| | | | Wang Zhideng (1535–1612) | |
| | | | Xing Tong (1551–1612) | |
| | | | Mo Shilong | |
| | | | Mi Wanzhong | |
| 1616 | | Nurhachi assumes power, changes the dynasty name to Later Jin | | |
| 1636 | | Dynasty name of Later Jin changed to Qing | Dong Qichang (1555–1636) | Semi-Cursive and Cursive Calligraphy Scroll (1603, pl. 78) |
| | | | Chen Jiru (1558–1639) | |
| | | | Zhang Ruitu (1570–1641) | *Building a Small Pagoda Between the Sala Trees* (pl. 79) |
| 1644 | Qing Dynasty | Ming emperor commits suicide. Qing capital transferred to Yanqing | Ni Yuanlu (1593–1644) | *Seated in Silence* Poem (pl. 80) |
| | | | Huang Daozhou (1585–1646) | Reply to Sun Boguan's Poem (pl. 81) |
| | | | Wang Duo (1592–1652) | *Xiangshan* Poem (pl. 82) |
| | | | Gu Yanwu (1613–82) | |
| | | | Chen Quan (1624–82) | |
| | | | Fu Shan (1607–84) | *Wandering Hermits* Poem in Twelve Scrolls (pl. 83) |
| | | | Zheng Fu (1622–93) | |
| | | | Jiang Chenying (1628–99) | Poem (pl. 84) |

| DATE | DYNASTY | EVENTS | CALLIGRAPHERS | WORKS |
|------|---------|--------|---------------|-------|
| | (Qing) | | Zhu Yizun (1629–1709) | |
| | | | Chen Yixi (1648–1709) | |
| 1716 | | Kangxi Encyclopedia completed | | |
| | | | Cha Sheng (1650–1722) | |
| | | | Yang Bin (1650?–1722?) | |
| | | | He Zhuo (1661–1722) | |
| | | | Wang Shu (1668–1739) | |
| 1744 | | *Shi Qu Bao Ji* compiled | | |
| | | | Zhang Zhao (1691–1745) | Ancient Poem by Du Fu (pl. 85) |
| 1750 | | Three Treasures Hall Album | | |
| | | | Jin Nong (1687–1763) | Poem (pl. 87) |
| | | | Zheng Xie (1693–1765) | In Praise of Ink Painting of Bamboo (1753, pl. 86) |
| | | | Ding Jing (1695–1765) | |
| 1767 | | Wang Shu's *Bamboo and Clouds Postscript* | | |
| 1778 | | Reprint of the Chunhua Pavilion Copybook | | |
| | | | Jiang Ren (1743–95) | |
| | | | Huang Yi (1744–95) | |
| 1798 | | Wang Fanggang's *Metal and Stone Inscriptions of the Han Dynasties* | | |
| | | | Wang Wenzhi (1730–1802) | Bound Volume of Copies of Jin Calligraphy (pl. 88) |
| | | | Huang Yi (1744–1802) | |
| 1803 | | Wang Fenggang's *Su-Mi Library Orchid Pavilion Manuscript* | Xi Gang (1746–1803) | |
| | | | Liu Yong (1719–1804) | Copybook of Calligraphic Techniques (pl. 89) |

| DATE | DYNASTY | EVENTS | CALLIGRAPHERS | WORKS |
|------|---------|--------|---------------|-------|
| | (Qing) | | Qian Daxin (1728–1804) | |
| 1805 | | Wang Chang's *Volume of Jin Stone Inscriptions* | Gui Fu (1736–1805) | |
| | | | Deng Shiru (1743–1805) | Four Styles Album (pl. 91) |
| | | | Qian Dian (1741–1806) | |
| 1808 | | Duan Yucai's *Annotated Dictionary of Characters and Phrases* | | |
| | | | Qian Bojiong (1738–1812) | |
| 1814 | | Cheng Xinwang's Jin Archives Copybook | Zhang Wentao (1763–1814) | |
| | | | Liang Tongshu (1723–1815) | Two Poems in Seven Stanzas by Lu You (pl. 90) |
| | | | Yao Nai (1731–1815) | |
| | | | Yi Bingshou (1754–1815) | |
| | | | Liang Yan | |
| | | | Sun Huangyan (1753–1818) | |
| | | | Wang Fanggang (1733–1818) | |
| | | | Chen Hongshou (1768–1822) | |
| | | | Chen Xiwang (1752–1823) | |
| | | | Wu Yingguang (1773–1843) | |
| | | | Ruan Yuan (1764–1849) | |
| | | | Bao Shichen (1775–1885) | |
| | | | Wu Xizai (1799–1870) | |
| | | | He Shaoji (1799–1873) | In Praise of Horse Paintings (pl. 92) |
| | | | Yang Yisun (1813–81) | |
| | | | Zhao Ziqian (1829–84) | Four Scrolls (pl. 93) |

| DATE | DYNASTY | EVENTS | CALLIGRAPHERS | WORKS |
|---|---|---|---|---|
| | (Qing) | | Xu Sangeng (1826–90) | |
| | | | Yang Xian (1819–96) | |
| | | | Wu Dacheng (1835–1905) | |
| | | | Yang Shoujing (1839–1915) | Description of Peach Blossoms and Spring (pl. 95) |
| | | | Wu Changshi (1844–1927) | |
| | | | Kang Youwei (1858–1927) | Five-Character Couplet (pl. 94) |

# Index

*Account of the Composition of the Preface to the Buddhist Canon,*
  Gaozong, 180–81
"Ai Huo Epistle," 169
albums. *See* copybooks
*Albums of Ancient Inscriptions on Bronze Ding and Yi Vessels,*
  Bi Shanggong, 135
Analects, 107, 193
"Ancient Poem by Du Fu," Zhang Zhao, 206–207; Pl. 85
*Ancient Seals of the Western Qing,* Liang Shizheng, 209
*Annals of the Three Kingdoms,* 167, 168
Arthur M. Sackler Collection, New York, 162; Pl. 2
"Autobiography," Huaisu, 130, 184–85; Pl. 47

Bada Shanren, 151
*bafen,* 113, 121, 166, 171; Deng Xie, 207; Gui Fu, 154; transi-
  tion to block script, 122; Zhong Yao's work, 115
bamboo tablets, 107, 164, 165
*Banruo Boluomiduo Xin Jing,* 179
Bao Shichen, 156, 173, 178; "concealed beginning and smooth
  ending technique," 157, 210; theories, 120; Fig. 96
Bei Yiyuan, 174; Pl. 26
Beijing National Palace Museum, 167; Pl. 13
"bent seal" characters, 114
Bi Shanggong, 135
Bibliothèque Nationale, Paris, 179; Pl. 35
"Biography of Han Ji'an," Zhao Mengfu, 143, 198; Pl. 68;
  in Japan, 14
"Biography of Yang Xiong, Han Annals," 13, 182; Pl. 42
"Biography of Yu Fan," 168
bird (–seal) script, 162–63
block script: Bei Yiyuan, 174; as bureaucratic qualification,
  128; Cai Xiang, 185; difference between Sui and Tang,
  128; epitaphs, 122, 171, 178; evolution of, 121–22; first used,
  110; Gaozong, 191; Huang Tingjian, 187–88; jade tablets,
  131; origin, 11; steles, 170; Tang, 13, 115, 126, 173; Yang
  Weizhen, 199; Yu Shinan and Ouyang Xun, 131; Zhang
  Jizhi, 194; Zhao Mengfu, 198; Zhu Yunming, 201; Pls.
  21–23, 28–30, 32–34, 37, 38, 40, 41, 45, 48, 51, 57, 61, 68,
  71, 74, 88

*Bo Haoan Ji,* Zhang Ruitu, 204
*bokuseki,* 137, 196, 198; Figs. 64–70; Pls. 65, 69. *See also* Chan
  calligraphy; *moji*
bone and tortoiseshell inscriptions. *See* oracle-bone inscriptions
*Book of Changes,* 107
"Bound Volume of Copies of Jin Calligraphy," Wang Wenzhi, 208; Pl. 88
*bozhe. See* breaking-wave stroke
breaking-wave stroke, 112, 114, 164, 167, 168, 176
*Brief Introduction to the History of Calligraphy,* Tao Zongyi, 144,
  145
British Museum, 178
bronzes and bronze inscriptions, 11, 150, 163–64; Figs. 2–5;
  Pls. 4, 5
*Brush and Ink Treatise,* Gaozong, 191, 192
brushes, 10, 187, 188, 189, 210; soft-tipped brush, 193, 209;
  sutra copies, 125, 175, 176; reed brush, 146, 200
Buddhist manuscripts, 123–26, 174–75, 177–78; Figs. 37–47,
  Pls. 27–30, 33, 61. *See also* Chan calligraphy; listings under
  specific texts and calligraphers
"*Building a Small Pagoda Between the Sala Trees* Poem Scroll,"
  Zhang Ruitu, 204;

Cai Jing, 132–33
Cai Songnian, 187, 194–95; Pl. 62
Cai Xiang, 14, 132, 133, 185; Fig. 55, Pl. 48
Cai Yong, 113
"Cao Cao Album," 193
"Cao Quan Memorial Stele," 113, 121, 166; Pl. 10
Cao Shiwan, 135
*Catalogue of Masterpieces,* Mi Fu, 134
*Catalogue of Metal and Stone Inscriptions,* Zhao Mingcheng, 173
*Catalogue of Paintings and Calligraphy of the Peiwen Archives,* 151
catalogues of calligraphic works, 134, 151, 152, 153–54, 169,
  173, 183
cave sculpture and inscriptions. *See* Longmen caves
*Ceng Jia Zha Jing,* Fig. 43
censorship laws, 154, 186
*Ceremonial Terrace Collection,* Dong Qichang, 204

*Ceremonies and Rituals,* 109

Cha Sheng, 151

Chan calligraphy, 137–40; Chen Xianzhang, 200; Dong Qichang, 203; Feng Zizhen, 198; Japan, 15–16, 140; Mi'an Xianjie, 195–96; Song and Yuan dynasties, 137–40; Yuanwu Keqin, 190–91; Zhang Jizhi, 136, 194; Zhang Ruitu, 204; Zhao Mengfu, 197; Figs. 64–70; Pls. 56, 61, 64, 73, 79. *See also* Buddhist manuscripts

"Chan Master Dazhi Stele," Shi Weize, 130

Chan sect: clerical organization, 139; literature, 139–40; history and teachings, 137–38; sectarian divisions, 196; sermons, 140. *See also* Chan calligraphy

Chen Deqian, 187

Chen Hongshou, 154, 155; Fig. 93

Chen Jiru, 185

Chen Shou, 168

Chen Xianzhang, 146, 200; Fig. 79; Pl. 73

Chen Xinwang, 152

Chen Yiceng, 145

Chen Yixi, 151

Cheng Zi, 187

"Chenkui Pavilion Stele," Su Shi, 192

Chion-in Treasure House, Kyoto, 123, 176; Pl. 30

Chishaku-in Storehouse, Kyoto, 194; Pl. 61

Chōkaidō Bunko, Yokkaichi, 200, 204, 205, 206, 207; Pls. 74, 80, 81, 83, 87

"chopped-off brushwork," 166, 167

"Chou Yanzhong Stele," 142

Chu characters, 110, 162; Pl. 2

Chu Gen Wang, 143

Chu Suiliang, 134, 152, 166, 177; 180–81, catalogue, 169; Taizong's collection, 128; works in Japan, 15; Fig. 48; Pl. 38

"Chunhua Pavilion Copybook," 118, 127, 132, 170; influence in Song, 135; research on, 150, 152

Chushi Fanqi, example of work, Fig. 70

"*Classic of Filial Piety* in Cursive Characters," He Zhizhang, 14, 183; Pl. 44

cliff inscriptions, 113, 120, 173–74; Pls. 24, 25

cohesion, of characters, 106

"Cold Meal in *Huangzhou* Poem Scroll," Su Shi, 133, 186; in Japan, 14; Pl. 49

"Cold Meal in *Huangzhou* Poem Scroll Postscript," Huang Tingjian, 134, 189; Pl. 53

*Collected Ancient Catalogues of Postscripts,* Ouyang Xiu, 132

*Collected Poems,* Ni Yuanlu, 204

*Collected Works of Bo Haoan,* Zhang Ruitu, 204

*Collected Works of Duke Ni Wenzhen,* Ni Yuanlu, 204

*Collected Works of Duke Wang Wencheng,* 204

*Collected Works of Li Taibo,* 187

*Collected Works of the Four Treasuries,* 154

"*Collected Works of Wang Bo,*" 181; Pl. 39

*Collection of Old and New Documents,* 153–54

"Colophon to Lu Hong's *Caotang Shizhi Du,*" Yang Ningshi, 131; Fig. 52

"Colophon to the Orchid Pavilion Preface," Jiang Kui, Fig. 60

*Colophons of Shangu,* Huang Tingjian, 159, 188

"*Commentary and Notes on the Spring and Autumn Annals,*" 13, 181; Pl. 40

*Commentary on the Dictionary of Characters and Phrases,* Gui Fu, 154

*Commentary on the Historical Records,* in Japan, 13

"concealed beginning and smooth ending technique," 157, 210

Confucian classics, 109, 113, 166, 173, 181, 183, 193; in Japan, 13, 14; Pls. 9, 24, 40, 44, 60

"Confucian Didactic Verses at Yunfengshan," Zheng Daozhao, 120, 173; Pl. 24

"Confucius' Tomb Stele," Yu Shinan, 129, 188

*Consideration of the Orchid Pavilion,* San Sicheng, 135

"*Contest for Rank Draft,*" Yan Zhenqing, 130

"Copybook of Calligraphic Techniques," Liu Yong, 208; Pl. 89

copybook school, 11–12, 150–51, 152, 156

copybooks (albums), 14, 132, 134, 135, 203; Mi Fu, 190; Ming dynasty, 148; Qing dynasty, 150–53; Ruan Yuan, 156; Wang Xizhi, 12, 167–169, 170, 180; Wang Xianzhi, 70; Pls. 13, 16–20, 55

copying methods, 118, 169. *See also* copybooks; ink rubbings

criticism. *See* theories and theoretical writings on calligraphy

*Critique of Calligraphy,* 129

"Cursive Draft of the Collected Notes on the *Analects,*" Zhu Xi, 14, 193; Pl. 60

cursive script, 11, 14, 124, 149; Cai Songnian, 194–95; Chen Xianzhang, 200; Dong Qichang, 149, 203; Fu Shan, 206; He Zhizhang, 183; Huaisu, 184; Huang Daozu, 205; Huang Tingjian, 134, 188, 189; Jiang Chenying, 206; Kangli Kuikui, 199; Li Yingzhen, 144; Mi Fu, 190; Su Shi, 186; Sun Guoting, 183; Wang Xianzhi, 118, 170; Wang Xizhi, 170; Wen Zhengming, 201–2; Zhang Bi, 200; Zhao Mengfu, 142; Zhiyong, 176–77; Zhu Xi, 193; Zhu Yunming, 146–47, 201; Figs. 26, 27, 29, 52, 58, 61, 68, 76, 79, 82, 83; Pls. 19, 20, 31, 43, 44, 46, 47, 49, 52, 53, 55, 60, 72, 75, 76, 78, 81, 83, 84

*Da Lou Tan Jing,* 123; Fig. 37

*Daban Niepan Jing,* Yang Guang, 177–78; Fig. 40; Pl. 33

*Dafangdeng Daiji Jing,* 174–75; Pl. 27

Dahui Zonggao, example of work, Fig. 65

"Dan Ba Stele," Zhao Mengfu, 142

*Dazhidulun Jing,* Fig. 42

Deng Shiru, 154–55, 156, 209, 211; Fig. 91; Pl. 91

Deng Wenyuan, 143, 144, 197; Fig. 74

"Description of Peach Blossoms and Spring," Yang Shoujing, 211; Pl. 95

"Dharma Master Meng's Stele," Chu Suiliang, 15, 129

"Di Huang Tang Epistle," Wang Xianzhi, 14, 118, 120; Pl. 20

Ding Daohu, 15, 177

Ding Jing, 153

"Diploma," Wuzhun Shifan, 196; Pl. 65

"Diploma," Yuanwu Keqin, 190; Pl. 56

divination, with oracle bones and tortoiseshells, 162

"Divine Omen Stele," 122, 167; Pl. 12

Dong Qichang, 149, 203; copybook school, 150, 151; and other calligraphers, 133, 152, 206; and Zhao Mengfu, 142, 143–44; Fig. 83; Pl. 78

"Dong Wuhou Wang Stele," 121; Fig. 32

"Draft for Zhang Clan Memorial Stele," Yang Weizhen, 199; Pl. 71

"Draft of a Letter," Li Bo, 168; Pl. 14

"Du Fu's *Thatch Roof Destroyed by the Autumn Wind,*" Xianyu Shu, 197; Pl. 66

Du Yu, 181

Duan Yucai, 154

Dugu, Empress, 178

"Duke Shiping Monument Inscription," 120, 172; Pl. 23

Dunhuang: copying bureau, 176; Buddhist manuscripts, 16–17, 123; rubbings discovered, 179, 180; Fig. 9

early copybook school, 150, 151

Early Zhou divinatory script, 161

Eight Eccentrics of Yangzhou, 153, 207

Eight Masters of Xiling, 156

Eisei Bunko Foundation, Tokyo, 198, 200; Pls. 68, 73

"Epistle to Zhongfeng Mingben," Zhao Mengfu, 197; Pl. 67
epistles, as calligraphic genre, 118
"Epitaph Drafts for Wang Zhong and Shi Fu," Huang Tingjian, 187–88; Pl. 51
"Epitaph for Dong Meiren," 128; Fig. 46
"Epitaph for Duke Yuan, Officer of the Stables," 178; Pl. 34
"Epitaph for Li Jingxun," 128
"Epitaph for Liu Ke," 122
"Epitaph for Quan Nansheng," Ouyang Tong, 129
"Epitaph for Princess Runan," Yu Shinan, 129
"Epitaph for Princess Yongtai," 130, 183–84; Pl. 45
"Epitaph for Sima Bing," 115
"Epitaph for the Lord of Nanchuan Xian," Han Zemu, 130
"Epitaph for Wang, Wife of Yuan Yang," 122; Fig. 34
"Epitaph for Wang Xingzhi," 122; Fig. 35
"Epitaph for Yuan Zhen," 121, 171–72; Pl. 22
"Epitaph for Zuo Fen," 121
epitaphs, 115, 121, 129, 130, 171; Figs. 34, 35, 46, 81. *See also* listings of specific titles
essay cursive, 114, 141, 168; Pl. 13
"Eulogy for a Nephew," Yan Zhenqing, 130, 184; Pl. 46
"Eulogy for Bo Fu," Yan Zhenqing, 130
"Eulogy for the Empress Dowager Taxing," Mi Fu, 135
extended-meaning characters, 105

Fan Chengda, 13, 135, 192; Pl. 59
"Fang Xuanling Stele," Chu Suiliang, 129
Fang Yanqian, 127
"Fang Yanqian Stele," Ouyang Xun, 129
"Feng Ju Album," Wang Xizhi, 118, 127, 169; Pl. 18
Feng Zizhen, 137, 198
fire caves, 162
Five Dynasties period, 131
Five Tribes and Sixteen Kingdoms, 119–120
"Five-Character Couplet," Kang Youwei, 211; Pl. 94
"flying white" script, 117, 129
forgeries, 148
formats, of calligraphic works, 148
*Foshuo Huan Pujian Jing*, Fig. 39
*Foshuo Pusa Cang Jing*, Fig. 41
"Four Cursive Albums," Mi Fu, 14, 190; Pl. 55
Four Masters of Xiling, 153
"Four Sages and One Scoundrel," Cai Xiang, 133
"Four Scrolls," Zhao Zhiqian, 210–11; Pl. 93
"Four Styles Album," Deng Shiru, 209; Pl. 91
"Fourteen Jinxian Albums," 167–68
Foyin Liaoyuan, 139
Fu Shan, 142, 149, 150–51, 206; Pl. 83
Fuhao, 103
*Fujian Collection*, Wen Zhengming, 202
Fujii Museum, Kyoto, 174, 181, 188, 195, 197, 205; Pls. 40, 52, 63, 66, 82
*Fukaisoku bokuseki*, 198; Pl. 69
funerary testaments, 110

"Gangxian Poem Scroll," Mi Fu, 14, 189–90; Pl. 54
Gansu Provincial Museum, 195; Pl. 8
Gao Shiqi, 187
Gao Xiang, 153
"Gao Zhen Stele," 121, 125, 174; Pl. 21
Gao-clan steles, 170–71
Gaozong, Emperor, 135, 141, 179–81, 182, 191–92; works in Japan, 13, 14; Pls. 57, 58
Gōtō Art Museum, Tokyo, 198; Pl. 69
"Gou Jian, Prince of Yue's Sword Inscription," 162–63; Pl. 3
Gu Yanwu, 154

*Guang Yi Zhou Shuang Ji*, Kang Youwei, 211
Gui Fu, 154
Gulin Qingmao, sample of his work, Fig. 67
Guyang cave, 172

"Hai Dai Album," Mi Fu, 190
*Han Annals*, 182
"Han Chi Stele," 166
*Han Feizi*, 164
Han Zemu, 130
Han-dynasty scribe script, 165, 166
Han-dynasty steles, 19, 112–13, 154, 174; Figs. 11–19; Pls. 9–11
*Hashiwatari no bokuseki*, 196; Pl. 65
"He Ru Epistle," 169
He Shaoji, 156, 157, 210; Pl. 92
He Zhizhang, 14, 183; Pl. 44
He Zhuo, 151, 207
"Helou Pavilion Poem Scroll," Wang Shouren, 202; Pl. 77
"*Hermit Li Taibo* Poem Scroll," Su Shi, 14, 133; Pl. 50
*History of Calligraphy*, Mi Fu, 134, 168, 169
*History of Metal and Stone Inscriptions*, Zhao Mingcheng, 135
*History of Painting*, 205
Hong Kuo, 135
"Hot Spring Inscription," Taizong, 129, 179; Pl. 35
*Hou Ma Treaty*, 162
Hua Xia, 148
"Huadu Temple Stele," Ouyang Xun, 129, 180; in Japan, 15; Pl. 37
Huai Yong, 195
Huairen, 179–80; Pl. 36
Huaisu, 130, 135, 184–85, 186, 188, 190; Pl. 47
*Huan Yu Catalogue of Steles*, 142
Huang, Emperor of Qin, 165
Huang Bosi, 135
Huang Daozhou, 149, 205; Pl. 81
Huang Tingjian, 133–34, 139, 185, 186, 187–88, 189; influence on others, 141, 146, 153, 207; theories of calligraphy, 133, 173, 187; works in Japan, 14; Fig. 57; Pls. 51–53
Huang Yi, 154, 156, 181; Fig. 88
"Huangfu Dan Stele," Ouyang Xun, 129
*Huang's Zhang River Collection*, Huang Daozhu, 205
*Huayan Jing*, Zhang Xianchang, 175, 176; Pl. 29
Huizong, 135, 169, 183, 189, 191; Fig. 59
hybrid scripts, 112, 113–14, 167, 168, 207, 209

ideographs, 9, 105
*Illustrated Essays from a Chan Cell*, Dong Qichang, 203
"Imperial Academy Stele," 121; Fig. 31
"Imperial Accession Memorial," Zhong Yao, 115, 121
imperial collections. *See* individual rulers' names
"Imperial Court Classic," Wang Xizhi, 177; Fig. 23
Imperial Household Agency, Archives and Mausolea Department, Tokyo, 192; Pl. 59
imperial publishing projects, 153–54
"In Praise of Horse Paintings," He Shaoji, 210; Pl. 92
"In Praise of Ink Painting of Bamboos," Deng Xie, 207; Pl. 86
ink: aesthetic appeal, 10; etymology, 10; varieties, 131, 148
ink rubbings, 12; Figs. 2–5, 10–24, 28, 30–36, 45–51, 53; Pls. 3, 4, 7, 9–12, 19, 21–26, 32, 34–38, 45, 59. *See also* commentaries on individual plates listed above
"Inscription Commemorating the Opening of the Baoxie Road," 113; Fig. 16
"Inscription for the Memorial Pagoda of Chan Master Yong (Huadu Temple Stele)," Ouyang Xun, 15, 129, 180; Pl. 37
inscriptions. *See* oracle-bone inscriptions; epitaphs; metal

inscriptions; steles; stone inscriptions; stone-drum inscriptions

Japan, influence of Chinese calligraphy on, 12–17, 137, 140, 143, 152, 157
Japanese Imperial Household Collection, 168, 183; Pls. 16, 44
Jiang Chenying, 151, 206; Pl. 83
Jiang Kui, 135; Fig. 60
Jiang Ren, 153
Jiangnan, during Jin dynasty, 116
Jiangsu, as cultural center, 147
Jiangxi Poetry School, 135
Jiangye steles, 122
Jie Jin, 143
"Jin Ci Inscription," Taizong, 129
Jin Nong, 153, 207; Pl. 87
Jin-dynasty calligraphers, 195. See also Wang Xianzhi; Wang Xizhi.
Jing Ke, 129
"Jingang Banruoboluomi Jing," Zhang Jizhi, 194; Pl. 61
Jingang (Banruo) Jing, Liu Gongquan, 130; Fig. 51
"Jishi Album," Yu Shinan, 129
"Jiu Hua Album," Yang Ningshi, 131
"Jiucheng Palace Spring Inscription," Ouyang Xun, 129, 180; Fig. 47
"Jiuyue Shipiri Epistle," Wang Xizhi, 169
Jun Haneda mission, 199
Juyan tablets, 107–9, 165; Fig. 7; Pl. 8

Kang Youwei, 120, 172–3, 174, 211; Pl. 94
Kangli Kuikui, 14, 144, 199; Fig. 76; Pl. 70
Kangxi, Emperor, 151
karayō (Chinese-style) calligraphy, in Japan, 12
Ke Jiusi, 144
Kharosti writing, 110
Kōfuku-ji, 181; Pl. 39
Konan Naitō, 13, 181, 182, 186
"Kong Shizong Album," Wang Xizhi, 118, 169; Pl. 17
"Kong Zhou Stele," 113; Fig. 12
Kuizhang Archives, 143, 144, 199
Kūkai, works brought from China, 13
Kyoto National Museum, 170, 177, 178, 182, 193, 201, 204, 206; Pls. 27, 33, 41, 60, 76, 79, 84

lacquer-style script, 208
"Lament for Li Pian," 131
"Lament for Wang Jian Tablet," 131; Fig. 53
Langye Terrace inscription, 164; Pl. 7
Lao Gan, 107–8
"Laoyi Archives Copybook," Jiang Chenying, 206
Laozi, 112, 162, 164; Pl. 6
later copybook school, 150–51
Later Works of Calligraphy, Li Sizhen, 129
ledger labels, 108; Fig. 7
Li Bo, 168, 186, 187, 188; Pl. 14
"Li Bo's Ancient Wind Poem," Kangli Kuikui, 199; Pl. 70
Li Guang, 210
Li Jianzhong, 186
"Li Sao Classic Scroll," Zhu Yunming, 200–201; Pl. 74
li shu. See scribe script
"Li Sixun Stele," Li Yong, 130
"Li Taibo's Recalling Past Wanderings Poem Scroll," Huang Tingjian, 134, 188; Pl. 52
Li Tinggui ink, 131
Li Wei, 134, 169
Li Yangbing, 130

Li Yingzhen, 146, 201, 202
Li Yong, 13, 130, 133, 141, 142, 143; Fig. 50
Li Zhuowu, 149
Liang Guozhi, 152
Liang Hu, 141
Liang imperial tomb steles, 122
Liang Shizheng, 209
"Liang Stele for Zhongwu Xiao Dan, Prince of Shixing," Bei Yiyuan, 174; Pl. 26
Liang Tongshu, 152, 153, 209; Pl. 90
Liang Yan, 152
"Liqi Stele at Confucius' Tomb," 113, 166; Pl. 9
literati, 132, 147, 148; school, 185, 188
Liu Chengxuan, 142
Liu Cizhong, 135
Liu Gongquan, 130, 189; Fig. 51
Liu Guyan, 169
liu shu, 9, 104
Liu Yiqing, 182; Pl. 41
Liu Yong, 152, 153, 208; Pl. 89
Liu Youding, 145
"Longcang Monastery Stele," 128, 177; Fig. 45
Longmen caves, 120, 172–73; Fig. 47
Loulan, seal-label from, Fig. 8
Loutan Jing, 176
"Lower Zheng Xi Stele," Fig. 30
Lu Ji, 167–68; Pl. 13
Lu Lingguang Palace inscription, 112
Lu Xioawang stone carving, 112
Lu You, 135; Fig. 61
Lu Zhaolin, 181
Luo Binwang, 181
Luo Zhenyu, 179
Luoyang, 172–73
"Lushan Monastery Stele," Li Yong, 130; Fig. 50

Ma Heng, 107–8
Maeda Ikutokukai, Tokyo, 169; Pl. 17
"Master Daoyin Stele," Ouyang Tong, 129
Master Dongpo. See Su Shi
"Master Mengfa Stele," Chu Suiliang, 129
Mawangdui, 162, 164, 165
"Memorial Awarding an Honorary Name to Gong Qing," 115, 120; Fig. 20
"Memorial Poem for Chan Master Fo Zhao," Fan Chengda, 13, 192–93; Pl. 59
"Memorial Stele for Gao Zhen," 121, 170–71; Pl. 21
Menglou Poems, Wang Wenzhi, 208
"Mengmo Tower Album," Chen Yixi, 151
metal- and stone-inscription studies, 152, 154, 157, 172, 207, 208, 210
Mi Fu, 134–35, 168, 185, 189–90; influence on Ming, 146, 149; influence on Qing, 150, 152; influence on Yuan, 198; and Su Shi, 133; and Wangs, 132, 169; works in Japan, 14; Fig. 58; Pls. 54, 55
Mi Wanzhong, 149
Mi Youren, 135, 190, 191; Fig. 30
Mi'an Xianjie, 140, 195–96; Pl. 64
Miaofa Lienhua Jing, Fig. 44
"Miaoyan Temple Record," Zhao Mengfu, 142
"Mid-Autumn Poem Album and Mu Qiong Album," Mi Fu, 190
military strategy, works of, 110
Ming-dynasty calligraphers, 146–49; 200–205; Figs. 78–83; Pls. 72–81
Mitsui Bunko, 166, 170, 173, 174, 179; Pls. 10, 11, 21, 24, 26, 36

Mogao caves, 179
*moji*, 137
monument inscriptions, 120, 172–73; Pl. 23
*moyai*, 113, 120, 173–74; Pls. 24, 25
Muin Genkai, 198; Pl. 69
Museum of Calligraphy, Tokyo, 164, 168, 170, 175, 180;
    Pls. 7, 15, 20, 48

Neiraku Art Museum, Nara, 167; Pl. 12
"New Version of the Anecdotes," 182; Pl. 41
"New Year's Album," Mi Fu, 190
Ni Yuanlu, 149, 204; Pl. 80
Ni Zan, 143, 144; Fig. 77
northern and southern dynasties, 119–126; Buddhist manu-
    scripts, 125–26; epitaphs, 121–22; influence on Sui, 127–28;
    mutual influences, 175

"Ode to Luo Shen," Wang Xianzhi, 118; Fig. 28
"Ode to the Spirit of Luo River," Zhao Mengfu, 143
Ogawa family collection, 177
oracle-bone inscriptions, 11, 104, 106, 161–62; Pl. 1; Fig. 1
"Orchid Pavilion Preface," Wang Xizhi, 118, 128, 133, 135,
    142; in Japan, 15; research on, 152–53; Fig. 24.
orthodox calligraphy. See Wang-style calligraphy
*Orthodox Tradition of Calligraphy*, Feng Wu, 152
Osaka Municipal Museum of Fine Art, 171, 172, 186, 190,
    194, 200; Pls. 22, 23, 50, 55, 62, 72
Ōtani expedition, 16–17, 168
Ōtani University Library, Kyoto, 175, 176; Pl. 29
*Outline of the History of Calligraphy*. See *Brief Introduction to the
    History of Calligraphy*
Ouyang Tong, 129
Ouyang Xiu, 132, 133, 185; Fig. 54
Ouyang Xun, 128, 129, 180, 182, 194, 198; and steles, 173,
    174, 177, 178; works in Japan, 13, 15; Fig. 47; Pl. 37

"Paean to Dong Fangshuo," Wang Xizhi, 117–18; Fig. 24
"Paean to Dong Fangshuo," Yan Zhenqing, Fig. 49
*Parting Verses*, Yuejiang Zhengyin, Fig. 69
Pelliot, Paul, expeditions, 16, 179
phonetic borrowing, 105
phonetic-semantic compounds, 105
pictographs, 9, 104–5
"Ping An Epistle," 169
"Ping Fu Album," Lu Ji, 167–68; Pl. 13
*Pinluo Hermitage Discussion of Calligraphy*, Liang Tongshu, 209
"Poem," Jiang Chenying, 206; Pl. 84
"Poem," Jin Nong, 207; Pl. 87
*"Poem of Parting for General Pei,"* Yan Zhenqing, 130
"Poem Scroll," Chen Xianzhang, 200; Pl. 73
"Postscript to Painting of Bamboo," Wang Tingyun, 195;
    Pl. 63
"Postscript to Su Shi's *Hermit Li Taibo* Poem Scroll," Cai
    Songnian, 194–95; Pl. 62
"Postscript to Su Shi's *Hermit Li Taibo* Poem Scroll," Zhang
    Bi, 200; Pl. 72
"Postscript to the Album of Huaisu's Writings," Zhao Meng-
    fu, 142–43
*Preface to the Buddhist Conon*, Taizong, 180–81
"Preface to the Buddhist Canon from a Collection of Wang's
    Calligraphy," Huairen, 179–80; Pl. 36
"Preface to the Collected Writings of Huizong," Gaozong,
    14, 191–92; Pl. 57
*Preface to the Cursive-Script Poems of Sage Huaisu*, 185
*Preface to the Great Tang Buddhist Canon*, 15
"Prefect Jiu Zhen Gulang Stele," 122, Fig. 36

Princess Yongtai, 183–4
*"Pusa Chutai Jing,"* 123, 176; Pl. 30

Qian Bojiong, 152
Qian Daxin, 154, 156
Qian Dian, 154; Fig. 90
Qianlong, Emperor, 153, 183; imperial collection, 184, 185,
    186
*Qianyin Hall Metal- and Stone-Postscript Inscriptions*, Qian
    Daxin, 154
"Qifa Temple Stele," Ding Daohu, 15, 128, 177; Pl. 32
Qin Codes, 110
Qin-dynasty seal script, 164
Qin-dynasty stone inscriptions, 112
Qin-dynasty tablets, 165
Qin-dynasty writing, 111
Qing Yong, 207
Qing-dynasty calligraphy, 150–57, 205–11; Figs. 84–98; Pls.
    82–95
Qunchen Shangchou stone carving, 112

*Record of Visits to the Huanyu Steles*, Xing Peng, 154
*"Red Cliffs Ode,"* Wen Zhengming, Fig. 80
*"Red Cliffs Ode,"* Zhu Yunming, 201; Pl. 75
reed brush, 146
Ren Xun, 195
Renzong, 185
"Replay to Sun Boguan's Poem," Huang Daozhu, 205; Pl. 81
"round brush" style, 173, 174
Ruan Yuan, 156, 157, 164, 173; and He Shaoji, 210; and Zhang
    Zhao, 206; theories, 120–21, 175; Fig. 95
Ryūkō-in Storehouse, Kyoto, 195; Pl. 64
Ryūkoku University Library, Kyoto, 168; Pl. 14

sacred writing, 103–4
Saichō, works brought from China, 13
"Sang Luan Album," Wang Xizhi, 118, 168–69; Pl. 16
Sang Sichang, 135
Scientific Expedition to the Northwestern Provinces of
    China, 107
scribe script, 111; Deng Shiru, 155, 209; He Shaoji, 210;
    Qing-dynasty research, 154, 155, 157; silk writings, 162;
    Song-dynasty research, 135; steles, 122, 166, 167, 168; sutras,
    126, 176; tablets, 110, 165; Tang-dynasty works, 130; Zhao
    Zhiqian, 211; Zheng Fu, 154; Figs. 7, 86, 88, 89, 91, 93,
    97; Pls. 8–11, 15, 91
*Scribe-Script Dictionaries*, Hong Kuo, 135
seal script, 110, 111, 130, 135, 150, 171; Figs. 84, 90, 94
seal-carving, 144, 148, 153, 155, 157, 210; Fig. 81
seal-labels, 108; Fig. 8
seals, 114, 148, 154
seal-scribe script, 141
"Seated in Silence Poem," Ni Yuanlu, 204; Pl. 80
*Secret Teachings of the Hanlin Academy*, Chen Yiceng, 145
*Sei-iki Kōko Zufu*, p. 16
Seikadō Bunko, Tokyo, 197; Pl. 67
"Semi-cursive and Cursive Calligraphy Scroll," Dong Qi-
    chang, 203; Pl. 78
semi-cursive script, 11, 176–77, 179, 186–88, 200–201, 203,
    206; of Qing dynasty, 152, 153, 157; of Song dynasty, 14,
    135; of Tang dynasty, 129, 130; of Wang Xizhi, 117, 128;
    Figs. 25, 85, 87, 92, 96; Pls. 31, 35, 50, 51, 72, 74, 78, 83
"Sermon," Mi'an Xianjie, 195–96; Pl. 64
serpent (–seal) script, 162–63
Shaanxi Provincial Museum, 180, 183; Pl. 45
"Shancai Temple Stele," 15

sheep-bristle brush, 134, 187, 188, 201
Shen Can, 143
Shen Du, 143, 151
Shen Quan, 151
Shen Zhou, 146, 147, 188
"Sheng Yuan Album," 131
Shi Ling, 127, 129
*Shi Qu Bao Ji,* 151–52, 209
Shi Weize, 130
Shi Yisheng, 187
"Shichen Stele," 113, 166; Fig. 14
"Shiqi Album," Wang Xizhi, 118, 142, 170, 183; in Japan, 15; Pl. 19
Shōmu, Emperor, 168, 169
*shu* style, of Korean calligraphy, 143
*Shuanghong Altar Collection,* Fu Shan, 206
Shuhuidi, 165
Shun, Emperor, 143
silk writings, 107, 110, 162, 164; Pls. 2, 6
Six Dynasties: aesthetic ideals, 183; historical summary, 119; calligraphy, 156, 209; tombs, 174
Song Ke, 143
Song Lian, 141
Song-dynasty calligraphy, 132–36, 185–94; Figs. 54–61; Pls. 48–61
southern dynasties, 125, 127–28
*Spring and Autumn Annals,* 181–82; Pl. 40
"Statue Inscription of Du Qianxu and Others," 128
Stein, Aurel, 16, 107, 110
"Stele for Crown Prince Shengxian," Empress Wu, 129
"Stele for Gu Liang, Prefect of Jiu Zhen," Fig. 36
"Stele Recording the Virtues of Pei Cen," Fig. 19
stele school, 11–12, 152, 153–57. *See also* steles
steles, 11–12; Han dynasty, 112–13; individual works, 166, 167, 174, 177, 180, 191; Qing dynasty, 154–56; Six Dynasties period, 120–22; southern dynasties, 125; Sui dynasty, 125; Tang dynasty, 129, 130; Zhao Mengfu, 142–43; Figs. 11–14, 18, 19, 30–36, 45, 48, 50, 86; Pls. 9–12, 21, 26, 32, 71
"Stone Gate Verses," 113; Fig. 17
"Stone Inscription Commemorating the Opening of the Baoxie Road," 113; Fig. 16
stone inscriptions, 11–12; individual works, 164–65, 172–74, 179–81; Northern Song, 135; Qin and Han dynasties, 112–15; Qing dynasty, 154–56; Six Dynasties, 119–122; Tang dynasty, 129, 130; Figs. 10, 15–17, 20, 21, 47; Pls. 7, 23–25, 35–38. *See also* epitaphs; steles
"Stone Terrace *Classic of Filial Piety,*" Emperor Xuanzong, 130
stone-drum script, 157, 209; Fig. 98
*Strategies of the Warring States,* 162, 164
*Study of the Su-Mi Library Orchid Pavilion Manuscript,* Weng Fenggang, 152–53
Su Shi, 131–33, 185, 186–88, 192, 195; and Chan clergy, 139; influence on Ming calligraphers, 146; and later copybook school, 151; works in Japan, 13, 14; Fig. 56; Pls. 48, 49
Sui sutras, 13, 17, 126, 177–78; Pl. 33
Sui-dynasty calligraphy, 127–28
Sun Guoting, 130, 156, 183; Pl. 43
Sun Xingyan, 154, 156
sutra-copying, 123
sutras. *See* Buddhist manuscripts
Suzhou, as cultural center, 147
*Systematic Record of Copybooks,* Cao Shiwan, 135

tablets: wooden, 108, 110, 165; jade, 131; Figs. 6, 7; Pl. 8.
  *See also* Juyan tablets
Taipei National Palace Museum, 169, 185; Pl. 18

Taishan stone inscription: Qin dynasty, 112, 164–65, Fig. 10; Tang dynasty, 130
*Taishō Daizōkyō,* 175
Taizong, Emperor, 128, 129, 169, 170, 179, 180–81; Pl. 35
*tamo* copying method, 118
Tan Wuchen, 175
Tang Yin, 148
Tang-dynasty calligraphy, 128–130, 179–184; Figs. 47–51; Pls. 35–47
Tanko Kashiwagi, 181
Tao Hongjing, 174
"Tao Sheng Album," Cai Xiang, 133
Tao Zongyi, 145
*tashu* copying method, 169
technique of no-technique, 133, 189, 199
theories and theoretical writings on calligraphy: *Brush and Ink Treatise,* 191; *Colophons of Shangu,* 188; *Critique of Calligraphy,* 129; of Dong Qichang, 203; *History of Calligraphy,* 134; of Kang Youwei, 211; *Later Works of Calligraphy,* 129; *Pinluo Hermitage Discussion of Calligraphy,* 209; of stele school, 156; *Treatise on Calligraphy,* 130, 183; *Yan Ji,* 145; of Zhang Zhao, 207
"Thirteen Postscripts to the Orchid Pavilion," Zhao Mengfu, 14, 142
"Thousand-Character Essay," Huizong, Fig. 59
"Thousand-Character Essay in Block and Cursive Scripts," Zhiyong, 14, 127, 142, 176–77; Pl. 31
"Three Gates Record," Zhao Mengfu, 14, 142
"Three Semi-cursive Albums," Mi Fu, 14
"Three Treasures Hall Copybook," 152
Three-Stage Teaching, 180
"Tingyun Hall Album," Wen Zhengming, 202
"Title Inscription for the Banruo Terrace," Li Yangbing, 130
"Title Inscription of Buddhist Image Constructed by Duke Shiping," 172, Pl. 23
Tōdai-ji, 168, 169, 177
*Tōdai-ji Kembutsu Chō,* 13
Tōfuku-ji Storehouse, Kyoto, 172, 196; Wuzhun Shifan
Tō-ji, 182
Tokyo National Museum, 180, 181, 185, 187, 189, 190, 192, 199, 201–3, 206–11; Pls. 9, 38, 39, 51, 56, 58, 70, 75, 77, 78, 85, 86, 88, 90, 91, 93–95
Tokyo University Research Center for the Humanities, 161; Pl. 1
"Tomb Monument of Dong Wuhou Wang," 121; Fig. 32
"Tomb Stele of Cao Zhi," 128
"Tomb Stele of Confucius," 15
"Tomb Stele of Confucius by Chen Shuyi," 128
"Tomb Steles of the Western Peaks of Mt. Hua," 15, 113; Fig. 13
tortoiseshell inscriptions, 161–62; Fig. 1
*Tōshō hon,* 13
"*Treatise on Calligraphy,*" Sun Guoting, 130, 183; Pl. 43
*Treatise on the Northern and Southern Schools of Calligraphy,* Ruan Yuan, 156
*Treatise on the Northern Steles and the Southern Albums,* Ruan Yuan, 156
Turfan, 175
"Twelve Verses from Tao Yuanming's Drinking Poem," Wen Zhengming, 201–202; Pl. 76
"Two Poems in Seven Stanzas by Lu You," Liang Tongshu, 208; Pl. 90
Two Wangs. *See* Wang Xianzhi; Wang Xizhi; Wang-style calligraphy

Ueno, Jun'ichi, 182

variant characters, 163, 166, 171, 177
*Verses on the Six Patriarchs,* Yishan Yining, Fig. 68
"Vinaya Preface, Volume One," Zhengfa Wujincang, 125, 175; Pl. 28
"Vision of the God of Fortune," Zhao Mengfu, Fig. 72
*Volume of Jin Stone Inscriptions,* 154
"Volume of Proclamations Granted to Liang Rujia," Gaozong, 192; Pl. 58

"Wandering Hermits Poem in Twelve Scrolls," Fu Shan, 206; Pl. 83
Wang Anshi, 193
Wang Ao, 200
Wang Bo, 181
Wang Chong, 154; 170; Fig. 82
Wang Duo, 149, 150–51, 205; Pl. 82
Wang Meng, 143
Wang Sheng, 135
Wang Shouren, 202; Pl. 77
Wang Shu, 151; Fig. 84
Wang Tingyun, 195; Pl. 63
Wang Wenzhi, 152, 153, 208; Pl. 88
Wang Xianzhi, 11, 14, 170; Figs. 28, 29; Pl. 20. *See also* Wang Xizhi, Wang-style calligraphy
"Wang Xingzhi Epitaph," 122; Fig. 35
Wang Xizhi, 11, 114–15, 116–18, 168–70, 177, 179–80; contemporary calligraphers, 168; cursive script, 183; influence on northern calligraphers, 122; on Mi Fu, 190; on steles, 174; in Tang, 129; on Wang Wenzhi, 152; on Zhao Mengfu, 142; works in Japan, 13–15; Figs. 22–27; Pls. 16–19
Wang Yangming, 146, 149, 203
Wang Zhu, 113, 134
Wang-family calligraphy, 118. *See also* Zhiyong
Wang-style calligraphy, 125, 133, 141, 156, 186, 205; and Buddhist manuscripts, 178; in Northern Wei, 126; in Song, 132, 135; in Tang, 128, 130. *See also* Wang Xianzhi; Wang Xizhi; Wang-family calligraphy
*Wansuitongtain Era Album,* 118
Wei Xiwu, 15
Wei Zheng, 128
Wei Zhongxian, 204
Wei-dynasty steles, 119–122, 170–73; Figs. 30, 32–34; Pls. 21–24
Wen family, 148
Wen Jia, 148
Wen Peng, 148; Fig. 81
"Wen Yanbo Stele," Ouyang Xun, 129, 198
Wen Zhengming, 146, 148, 149, 170, 201–2; Fig. 80; Pl. 76
Wenzong, Emperor, 143, 144
Weng Fanggang, 142, 152, 153, 180, 188; Fig. 86
wild cursive script, 130, 146, 184–85, 200, 203; Pls. 47, 78
"Writings of Li Bo," 17. *See also* "Draft of a Letter," 168; Pl. 14
Wu, Empress, 129, 181, 184
*Wu Annals,* 168; Pl. 15
Wu Chanshi, 156, 157; Fig. 98
Wu Dacheng, 156
Wu Ji, 195
Wu Jie, 135
Wu Qiuyan, 144
Wu Rongguan, 142, 170
Wu Shou, 14, 135
Wu Xizai, 156, 157; Fig. 97
Wu Xuan, 146; Fig. 78
Wu Yingguang, 152; Fig. 85
"Wu You Album," Mi Fu, 190
Wuwei tablets, 165

Wuan Puning, example of work, Fig. 62
Wu-Cai style, 195
Wuxue Zuyuan, example of work, Fig. 66
Wuzhun Shifan, 196; Pl. 65

Xi Gang, 153
Xiang Yuanbian, 148
"Xiangshan Poem," Wang Duo, 205; Pl. 82
Xianyu Shu, 143, 144, 197; Fig. 73; Pl. 66
Xiaopenglai Archives, 181
Xie An, 134
"Xie An Album," 168
Xing Peng, 154
Xing Tong, 149
"Xiping Stone Classic," 113; Fig. 15
Xu Hao, 130, 133
Xu Sangeng, 156; Fig. 94
"Xuanbi Pagoda Stele," Liu Gongquan, 130
"Xuanshi Memorial," Zhong Yao, 114–15; Fig. 21
Xuanwen Archives, 143, 144
Xuanzhang, 179
*Xue Gu Bian,* Wu Qiuyan, 144
Xue Ji, 15, 129, 174
"Xuexi Hall Album," Wang Tingyun, 195
Xutang Zhiyu, example of work, Fig. 63

*Yan Ji* (The Ultimate), Zheng Yu, 145
"Yan Pagoda Prefaces to the Buddhist Canon," Chu Suiliang, 129, 180–81; Pl. 38
Yan Zhenqing, 130, 184, 187; and Huaisu, 185; and Huang Tingjian, 188; and Mi Fu, 189; influence during Qing dynasty, 151, 152, 157; and Su Shi, 133, 186; and Zhao Mengfu, 141; Fig. 49; Pl. 46
Yang Guang, 177–78; Pl. 33
Yang Jiong, 181
Yang Ningshi, 131, 133, 184, 186, 188; Fig. 52
Yang Shoujing, 13, 156, 167, 181, 207, 208, 211; Pl. 95
Yang Wanli, 135
Yang Wei, 14
Yang Weizhen, 143, 144, 199; Pl. 71
Yang Xian, 156
Yang Yisun, 156
Yang Zai, 141
Yangzhou, as cultural center, 153
Yao Nai, 152
Yi Bingshou, 154, 155; Fig. 92
"Yi He Inscription," 173–74; Pl. 25
"Yi Ying Stele," 113, 166; Fig. 11
Yinqiaoshan, 110
*yipin,* 130
"Yique Buddhist Image-niche Stele," Chu Suiliang, 129; Fig. 48
Yishan Yining, example of work, Fig. 68
Yong, Chan Master, 180
Yongtai, Princess, 183–84; Pl. 45
Yongzhong, Emperor, 151
"You Xuan Epistle," 169
*Youjun Catalogue of Calligraphy,* Chu Suiliang, 169
Yu Chuo, 127
Yu Ji, 142, 143, 144; Fig. 75
Yu Shinan, 15, 128, 178, 188
Yu Yunwen, 135
Yuan-clan epitaphs, 121–22; Fig. 34
Yuan-clan tombs, 172
Yuan-dynasty calligraphy, 14, 141–145, 197–99; Figs. 64, 67–77; Pls. 66–71

Yuanwu Keqin, 140, 190–91; Pl. 56
"Yue Yi Treatise," Wang Xizhi, 117, 128, 193; Fig. 22
Yuejiang Zhengyin, example of work, Fig. 69
*yun,* 133
"Yunqing Hall Album," 143

Zhang Bi, 146, 187, 200; Pl. 72
Zhang Duo, 188
Zhang Huaiguan, 129
"Zhang Jing Stele," 113; Fig. 18
Zhang Jizhi, 135, 136, 194; Pl. 61
"Zhang Meng Long Stele," 121, 125; Fig. 33
"Zhang Qian Stele," 113, 166–67
Zhang Ruitu, 149, 204; Pl. 79
Zhang Sicheng, 144
Zhang Wentao, 152
Zhang Xianchang, 176
Zhang Xiaoxiang, 135
Zhang Xu, 130, 183, 188, 190
Zhang Yanyuan, 170
Zhang Yu, 135, 143, 144
Zhang Zhao, 152, 206–7; Pl. 85
Zhang Zhi, 11, 114
Zhao Bingwen, 195
Zhao Feng, 195
Zhao Mengfu, 135, 141–45, 197, 198; and copybook school, 150, 151; works in Japan, 14; Figs. 71, 72; Pls. 67, 68
Zhao Mengxian, 135
Zhao Ziqian, 156, 157, 210–11; Pl. 93
*zaohe* brush, 188
*zetian* characters, 181

Zhejiang, as cultural center, 147
Zheng Daozhao, 120, 173; Fig. 30; Pl. 24
Zheng Fu, 154; Fig. 89
"Zheng Xi Stele," Zheng Daozhao, 120; Fig. 30
Zheng Xie, 153, 207; Fig. 87; Pl. 86
Zheng Yun, 145
Zhengfa Wujincang, 175; Pl. 28
"Zhengxin Hall Album," 131
Zhengxin Hall paper, 131
Zhiguo, 127, 169
Zhiyong, 118, 127, 176–77; influence on Buddhist manuscripts, 178; on Gaozong, 191; on Yu Shinan, 129; on Zhao Mengfu, 141–42; works in Japan, 14; Pl. 31
Zhong Yao, 114–15; influence on Buddhist manuscripts, 126; on evolution of styles, 171; on Huang Tingjian, 188; on steles, 174; on Wang Duo, 205; on Wang Xizhi, 117; on Zhao Mengfu, 141; Fig. 21
Zhongfeng Mingben, 15, 197, 198; Fig. 64
Zhongshan bronzes, 163–64
Zhou Boqi, 144
*Zhou Divinations,* 164
Zhou Xing, 176–77
Zhou Yue, 133, 134, 188
Zhu Xi, 14, 134, 193; Pl. 60
Zhu Yizun, 154
Zhu Yunming, 146–47, 200–201; Pl. 74
*Zhufo Yaoji Jing,* 16, 168; Fig. 38
*zhuge* brush, 188
Zhuge Ying, 169
Zhuzi. *See* Zhu Xi
Zuo Qiuming, 181

The "weathermark" identifies this book as a production of John Weatherhill, Inc., publishers of fine books on Asia and the Pacific. Book design and typography: Miriam F. Yamaguchi. Layout of text illustrations: Yutaka Shimoji. Composition: Korea Textbook, Seoul. Color platemaking and printing: Dai Nippon Printing, Kyoto. Monochrome platemaking and printing: Kinmei Printing, Tokyo. Binding: Okamoto Binderies, Tokyo. The typeface used is Monotype Bembo.